BERL

DISCO

SINGAI

Edited and Designed by
D & N Publishing,
Lambourn, Berkshire.

Cartography by
Hardlines, Charlbury, Oxfordshire.

Photographic Acknowledgements

Front cover: skyline of the financial district by Rex A. Butcher; reproduced courtesy of Tony Stone Worldwide.

Back cover: dressed up for the parade! Reproduced courtesy of the Singapore Tourist Promotion Board.

All other photographs copyright © Andrew Bonser and Barbara Fuller 1993 except: The Raffles Hotel, page 132; the Singapore Tourist Promotion Board, pages 250, 259, 260 and 263.

Although we have made every effort to ensure the accuracy of all the information in this book, changes occur incessantly. We cannot therefore take responsibility for facts, addresses and circumstances in general that are constantly subject to alteration.

Phototypeset by Wyvern Typesetting Ltd., Bristol.

Printed by C.S. Graphics, Singapore.

Acknowledgements

I would like to thank the many people who have helped me with this book: Connie Austen-Smith and Rosie Booton who got the project started, and Guy Croton and D & N Publishing who helped it reach publication; Lorrain Chong, Pearl Seguera and Rosie Lim from the STPB; Jennifer Wee-Almodiel of the Raffles Hotel; Cecilia Loh from The Westin Stamford Hotel; The Westin Stamford Hotel for their help with the photograph on page 6; the Singapore MRT for permission to reproduce the map of the MRT on page 19; Mr Sie of MITA; all those Singaporean friends and friends in Singapore who have pointed me towards interesting places, sights, venues and events, in particular the excellent food consultant Low Soon Teck; Deb Irwin; Shova Loh and all at Times Editions; David Brazil; KJ, Christina, Agnes, Irene and Khim at Freshfields, Singapore; Freshfields for sending us to Singapore in the first place; Alison Honey and Keith McGuire; and finally a big "thank you" for constant support throughout to Andrew Bonser, my co-photographer, husband, critic, camera expert, and great friend, with whom I have shared so many enjoyable Singaporean experiences.

If you have any new information, suggestions or corrections to contribute to this guide, we would like to hear from you. Please write to Berlitz Publishing at the above address.

 The Berlitz tick is used to indicate places or events of particular interest.

BERLITZ®

DISCOVER
SINGAPORE

Barbara Fuller

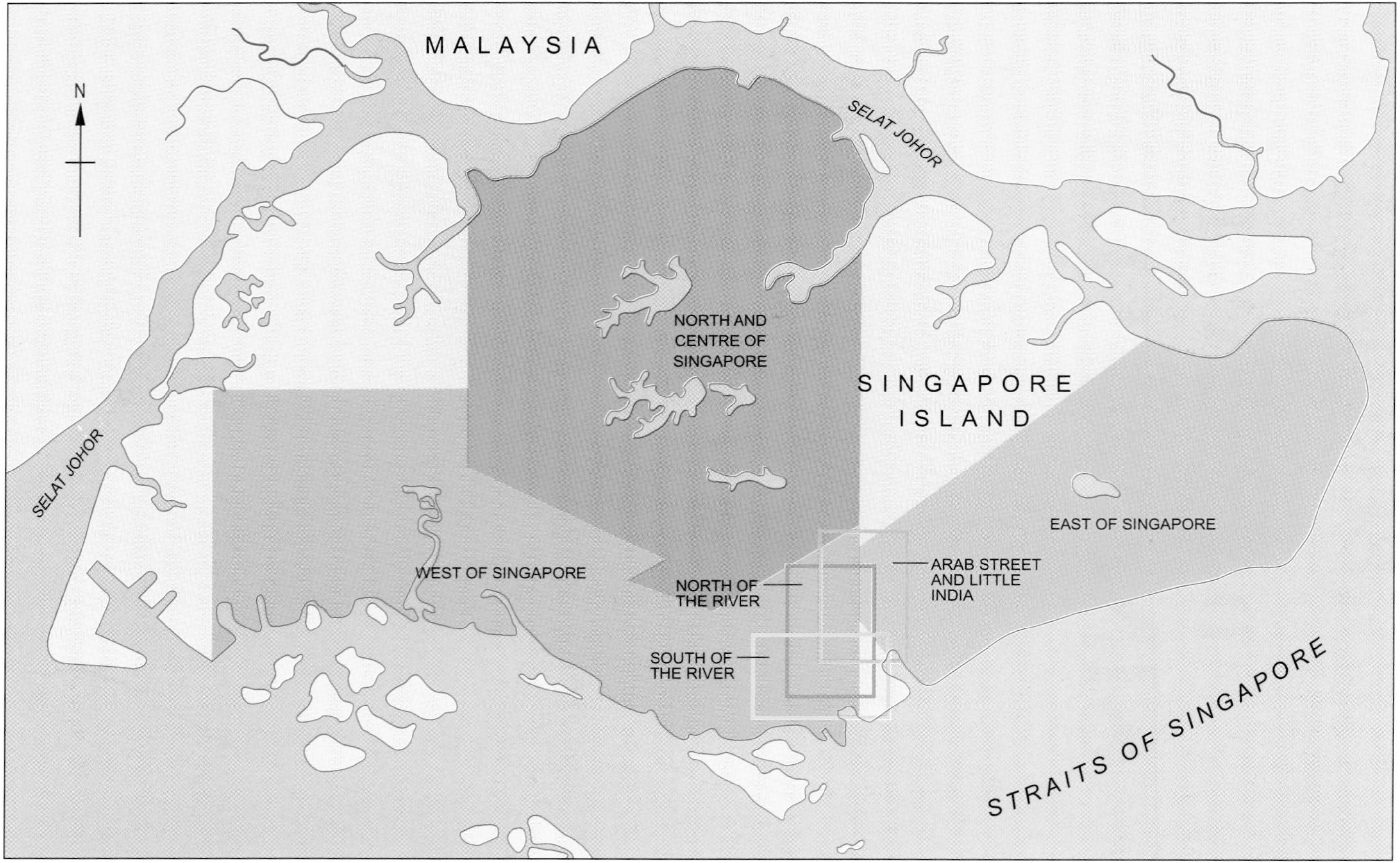

MALAYSIA

SELAT JOHOR

SELAT JOHOR

SINGAPORE ISLAND

NORTH AND
CENTRE OF
SINGAPORE

WEST OF SINGAPORE

EAST OF SINGAPORE

ARAB STREET
AND LITTLE
INDIA

NORTH OF
THE RIVER

SOUTH OF
THE RIVER

STRAITS OF SINGAPORE

N

Contents

Information to Help You Have a Good Trip

Singapore's rich history, diverse races, colourful festivals and booming economy make for a vibrant culture. Tourists may stumble on a street-side Chinese opera (*wayang*), performers wearing elaborate face make-up and delicate garments and singing in an eerie tone; or they may watch the blood-curdling Hindu Thaipusam procession, when devotees carry steel structures pierced into their skin in a state of virtual trance. While shopping, you may see a Chinese girl in a micro skirt and teeshirt next to a Malay girl wearing the traditional sarong and *kebaya*, complete with headscarf so that only her face and hands are showing. Contrasts are everywhere.

Introduction

Singapore is an island of extreme and intriguing contrasts: contrasts between old and new, east and west, countryside and cityscape, religious and secular. Here is a tropical climate, with average temperatures in the high 20°s C (80°s or 90°s F) interspersed by the occasional drenching monsoon downpour; here too are the exotic spices, chillies and potions which the Chinese,

A bird's-eye view of Singapore's striking modern architecture, seen from the Compass Rose Restaurant at the top of The Westin Stamford Hotel.

Malay and Indian Singaporeans use to create mouth-wateringly tasty dishes to delight your palate; and yet you can enjoy it all to the full since most people speak English, all street signs are in English, air-conditioning and a constant electricity supply, as well as state-of-the-art communications, medical facilities and electronics are taken for granted, you can drink the tap water and all food is prepared under strictly enforced sanitary conditions.

The city district boasts high-rise examples of the world's leading modern architects such as I. M. Pei and Kenzo Tange, yet just streets away you find Chinese shophouses with fading paintwork containing motor parts shops, medical halls, dried fish and spices, fruits, groceries, all displayed to

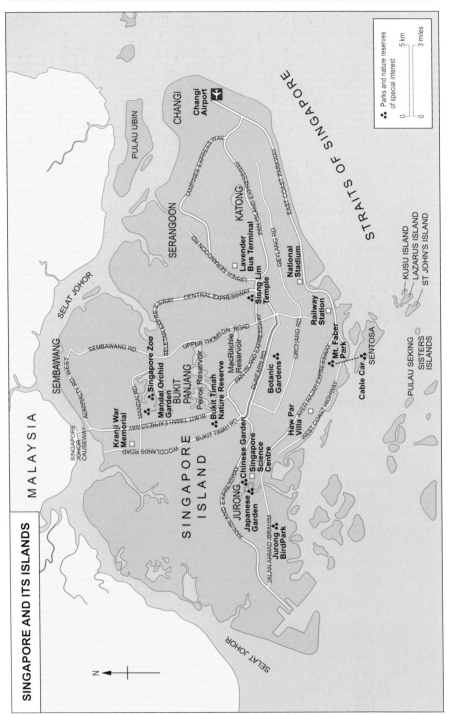

SINGAPORE AND ITS ISLANDS

MALAYSIA

SELAT JOHOR

STRAITS OF SINGAPORE

CHANGI

Changi Airport

PULAU UBIN

SERANGOON

KATONG

Lavender Bus Terminal

Siong Lim Temple

National Stadium

Railway Station

Mt. Faber Park

Cable Car

SENTOSA

SEMBAWANG

Singapore Zoo

Mandai Orchid Garden

BUKIT PANJANG

Peirce Reservoir

MacRitchie Reservoir

Botanic Gardens

Bukit Timah Nature Reserve

Haw Par Villa

Kranji War Memorial

Chinese Garden

Singapore Science Centre

SINGAPORE ISLAND

JURONG

Japanese Garden

Jurong BirdPark

SINGAPORE JOHOR CAUSEWAY

SELAT JOHOR

KUSU ISLAND

LAZARUS ISLAND

ST JOHN'S ISLAND

PULAU SEKING

SISTERS ISLANDS

TAMPINES EXPRESSWAY

PAN-ISLAND EXPRESSWAY

EAST COAST PARKWAY

GEYLANG RD.

UPPER SERANGOON RD.

CENTRAL EXPRESSWAY

SELETAR EXPRESSWAY

UPPER THOMSON ROAD

ORCHARD RD.

DUNEARN RD.

PAN-ISLAND EXPRESSWAY

WEST COAST HIGHWAY

BUKIT TIMAH EXPRESSWAY

MANDAI RD.

SEMBAWANG RD.

ADMIRALTY RD. WEST

WOODLANDS ROAD

BUKIT TIMAH ROAD

JALAN AHMAD IBRAHIM

AYER RAJAH EXPRESSWAY

N

Parks and nature reserves of special interest

5 km
3 miles
0
0

overflowing on shelves near the pavement. An old trishaw (bicycle with a sidecar) driver will take you on a tour of Little India, but he may well have had his dinner at McDonalds, while the pedestrians you see could be wearing saris or colourful silks, or jeans and teeshirts, making a call on a portable phone or buying a freshly prepared flower garland or betel nut. Alongside even the busiest expressway are planted different palm trees, flowering bougainvilleas and other flowering shrubs, all watered and tended by gardeners in ancient straw hats. The 70-storey Westin Stamford Hotel looks northwards from the central business district towards Bukit Timah hill, the site of the island's nature reserve,

Map of Singapore and the surrounding areas.

Trishaw drivers waiting for custom in Chinatown. A trishaw ride is a novel way to see the sights of the area.

surrounded by hectares of *belukar* (secondary forest) in which are sited most of the island's own reservoirs. On the top floor of a city skyscraper carpark you will stumble across a small, well-tended shrine, while the regular call to prayer from the Sultan Mosque can be heard echoing around the surrounding streets.

From Benjamin Sheares bridge on the East Coast Parkway (ECP) you have a magnificent view of the modern city of Singapore, particularly impressive at night when office lights are on in all the towers, even more so at weekends when the colonial Empress Place, City Hall and Supreme Court buildings alongside the Padang are

*A*cross the Singapore River. Parliament House (left) and Empress Place Exhibition Hall (right) are next to the river, separated by a statue of Sir Stamford Raffles. Behind Parliament House lies the Supreme Court and then the Raffles City complex. The Victoria Memorial Hall tower rises behind Empress Place.

floodlit. Nearer the ground, Orchard Road remains a bustling hive of pedestrian activity, as the shops remain open from 10 a.m. to as late as 9.30 p.m. to catch the most eager spendthrifts, while coffee shops and fruit stalls along roads in Chinatown and Geylang stay open for business into the small hours. Turning a corner in the back streets, you may stumble upon a stage set up for a *wayang* (Chinese opera), or a hired tent and tables with floral tributes for a funeral wake; during the lunar month of the Hungry Ghosts

festival (September/October) you will see small food offerings and incense burning outside Chinese-run shops and restaurants to appease wandering spirits; at festive times you could see a team practising a dragon or lion dance, or a Hindu devotee carrying the *kavadi* structure during Thaipusam (late January).

Singapore truly is a shopper's paradise, with everything from antiques to camera equipment, computers and electronics to clothing boutiques, 24-hour tailors and dressmakers, jewellery and watches, local handicrafts and fabrics on sale to tempt you. And it is also a gourmet's paradise, with a wide range of Singapore's own Chinese, Malay, Nonya and Indian cuisines as well as examples of Vietnamese, Japanese, European and Mexican cookery, and new branches of Western fast-food chains open daily—whatever your taste, you will not be disappointed here.

A very easy and comfortable introduction to the Orient, Singapore is a popular gateway to its more exotic South-East Asian neighbours. But Singapore's own attractions are worth exploring before you rush further afield: whether the beautifully landscaped Open Zoo, which uses moats and hedges rather than cages whenever possible to divide animal enclosures, or the high-tech, hands-on exhibits in the Science Centre; the bustling backstreets off Arab Street or the scampering macaque monkeys around the central reservoirs; the curling roof decorations and burning incense sticks of Chinese temples or the ornate carvings on Hindu temple *gopurams* (gateways); the Katong coffee shop *murtabak* and *satay* or the five-star hotel French meal. Explore the different parts of the island and you will be surprised at how much there is in this small and prosperous tropical island for the tourist to enjoy.

When to Go

Situated about 140 km (85 miles) north of the Equator, Singapore enjoys year-round warmth—and consequent humidity. There are two monsoon seasons in the region: the main north-east monsoon occurs between November and February; the lesser south-west monsoon of June to September is largely blocked from Singapore by the large land mass of Sumatra to the west, though there can be torrential downpours for a couple of hours. During the main monsoon season, you can enjoy full days of sun, as well as continuous days of steady rain and dramatic thunderstorms: the weather is far from predictable, so don't forgo a trip to, or a stopover in, Singapore for fear of rain. And, of course, the temperature is cooler during the monsoon season, with refreshing breezes which make walking around pleasant. Don't presume that, if you select a time outside one of the two monsoon seasons, you will necessarily escape the rain: spectacular storms with preceding darkened clouds and increasing rumbles of thunder can and do occur throughout the year, generally lasting for an hour or so, and sometimes causing flash floods despite the massive monsoon rain drains that now criss-cross the island.

The hottest, most humid time of the year is around April to June, when you really feel you are in the tropics and the hotel swimming pool is an essential rather than a luxury. However, all indoor "sights", hotels, most public transport and shopping malls are air-conditioned: the Singaporeans do not like excessive heat and humidity either and have taken impressive steps to make their environment as relaxing as possible. Pleasant months to visit are September and October, when the temperature has dropped slightly but before the rains come; and February to March, after the rainy season but before it becomes too hot.

Plan to visit outdoor sites, whether the zoo or Botanic Gardens, and to play golf or tennis, in the early mornings, when the plants, animals—and players—are fresh and the heat is not too intense. Midday excursions will exhaust tourists from cooler climates disproportionately, and the locals themselves take care at this time, often using umbrellas as protection against the heat. Do remember that the humidity and heat will slow you down: a distance that you would easily walk in a cooler climate would not be so enjoyable here, so don't be over-ambitious in your sightseeing intentions—one outdoor visit may well be enough for one day.

Many visitors to Singapore tie in their trips with more extensive travel in the region, and Singapore is an ideal starting point for exploring much of South-East Asia. The islands of Indonesia to the south, Borneo (Brunei, the East Malaysian states of Sabah and Sarawak, and Indonesian Kalimantan) and the Philippines to the east, and Peninsular or West Malaysia and then Thailand to the north are increasingly popular, but not yet over-developed tourist attractions. Other travellers stop over *en route* to or from Australia, New Zealand, European and American destinations or travel from Hong Kong and Japan. Singapore offers a great deal to the stopover shopper, the leisurely tourist and the business traveller alike.

You could try to plan your trip to coincide with one of the myriad of festivals and holidays which take place in this multi-cultural country. The

*D*ragon dance during
the annual Chingay Procession.

Chinese New Year, which usually occurs in February with the first new moon of the year, is a very colourful and joyous display of dragon dances, street processions and night markets—yet for the public holidays themselves tourists may find several sights are closed, and accommodation harder to come by. The different Buddhist, Muslim, Hindu and Christian festivals and holidays, as well as Singapore's National Day (9 August) are described on pages 86–97, so check to see what is likely to be occurring during your projected stay. Many of these festivals are fixed by lunar rather than by calendar months, so it is not always possible to find out their exact dates too far in advance. Once in Singapore, free handouts from the Singapore Tourist Promotion Board listing each week's

events are available in all major hotels and shopping malls, and the daily listings in the English language daily *The Straits Times* will ensure that tourists do not miss out on major events.

Travel Documents and Entry Requirements

Tourists from Europe, North America, Australia and New Zealand do not need visas before arriving in Singapore, nor do ASEAN (Association of South-East Asian Nations) nationals or nationals of any country not specified below. They should have an up-to-date passport and will generally be granted a Social Visit Pass on arrival. This allows a 14-day stay, which is generally long enough for most tourists—the average stay is 3½ days—but if you do plan to stay longer, it is possible to renew this visa by visiting the Immigration Department in the Pidemco Centre, 95 North Bridge Road, II Visits and Visas Section, Singapore 0105. The maximum length of stay permitted is 2–3 months. For those using Singapore as a base or starting point for travels further afield, plan to travel on to your next South-East Asian destination within the 2 weeks: even if you return to Singapore subsequently, you will be granted another 2-week visa at whichever point of entry you use.

Entry visas are required for visitors from the following countries: Afghanistan, Cambodia, Laos, People's Republic of China, USSR, Vietnam, India, Algeria, Iraq, Lebanon, Libya, Jordan, Syria, Tunisia, Yemen and Kuwait. Holders of the Hong Kong Document of Identity and holders of refugee travel documents also require visas. Visitors should possess onward or return tickets, sufficient funds for their stay and entry facilities to their onward destination. Visa applications should be submitted to the nearest overseas mission or to the Immigration Department (*see* address on page 13).

Time was, and not so very long ago, when long-haired hippies and indeed any men with over-long hair were turned away at the airport or the Causeway, or forced to visit a Singaporean barber for a trim. This is happily no longer the case, and all tourists are now welcome to the Republic. (One exception I should mention here is drug pushers: Singapore, and indeed Malaysia and Thailand, have and exercise the death penalty for drug trafficking. In Singapore you are deemed to be trafficking if you have in your possession over 15 g (½ oz) of heroin or cocaine: this is made clear on your immigration card before you arrive and in the customs hall—so don't!) Apart from those arriving from Malaysia, incoming travellers over 18 can bring in 1 litre of spirits, 1 litre of wine (including champagne or fortified wine such as vermouth), and 1 litre of beer, but no duty-free cigarettes or tobacco. Incoming travellers can make purchases duty-free on arrival in Singapore before clearing customs.

Singapore today is extremely anxious to attract tourists, and its Tourist Promotion Board is highly efficient, producing a number of free weekly publications. Singapore's tourist facilities and tour guides have won a number of awards within the Asia-Pacific region, including an award to the Tourist Promotion Board itself. The Board also tries to identify and answer

*T*he 15-m (35-ft) tall Buddha in the Sakya Muni Buddha Gaya, the Temple of 1,000 Lights.

the differing requirements of different tourist types, and to provide tours and facilities for both the Caucasian, interested in old shophouses and festivals, and the Asian, more interested in modern buildings, hi-tech attractions and night-life. An increasing number of Taiwanese tourists, for example, have been coming to Singapore, a fact not unlinked to the government's "Speak Mandarin" campaign, which enables them to communicate with a significant proportion of the Chinese population. At the same time, a temporary fall in the numbers of Japanese tourists was experienced in early 1991, attributable to the aftermath of the Gulf War.

Health and Inoculations

Cleanliness and hygiene are watchwords in Singapore: there are frequent and well-publicized campaigns for the cleanest hawker centre or housing estate, and equally well-publicized prosecutions and closing down of unhygienic premises. Uniquely for the region, you can drink the tap water anywhere in the island, and have no need to fear ice in any cold drinks you are served.

Before you set off check with your own doctor for the latest advice on inoculations. If you are planning on travelling more widely in the region, inoculations against typhoid, cholera, tetanus and polio are recommended, together with malaria tablets if you are travelling to malarial areas. Do remember malarial tablets have to be taken for 1 week before and 4-6 weeks after your trip. If you have visited an area where there is yellow fever within 6 days of arriving in Singapore, you need to have been inoculated against the disease in order to be admitted to the country. If you are just visiting Singapore, you won't generally require these inoculations, though you are advised to have a gamma globulin inoculation against hepatitis A, commonly picked up through eating seafood—particularly cockles and raw oysters—from contaminated waters.

Do take out a reasonable insurance policy before travelling, to include health care as well as theft and loss. You can arrange this through your travel agent or tour organizer; by contacting an insurance company or broker directly; or by booking your trip using certain credit cards. You should obviously bring the policy document with you, taking care to carry it in a safe place.

A word on foodstuffs: do be careful when eating seafood, and avoid anything foul-smelling or off-colour wherever you find it. There is no need to be alarmist—about 99.9 per cent of food is perfectly safe, but one bad mouthful can put you out of action for a day or ruin your visit. Much local cuisine is hot and rich in protein—or "heaty" as the Singaporeans call it—frequently containing chilli and served with *sambal*, a fiery chilli and shrimp paste sauce. Try to mix hot and cooling dishes when ordering food, and ensure that you drink enough fluids, both with food and during the heat of the day, to replace those lost through perspiration. Details of local dishes and recommendations on what to order are given on pages 258–265; restaurant recommendations are given at the end of the book.

Chemists are found in all major shopping centres, and are generally open from 9.30 or 10.00 a.m. till 6.30 or up to 9.30 p.m. Guardian Pharmacy is the most common of the major chains, though there are individual chemists and smaller chains. Prescription drugs are generally supplied through the particular surgery you visit rather than over the counter of a chemist's shop, and although basic preparations for headaches, stomach upsets and insect bites are readily available, you won't generally find all-purpose preparations to combat, say, flu—you will have to buy several potions for the different symptoms.

As well as conventional medicine and pharmacies, there are also a number of Chinese medical halls, and also an increasing number of natural produce outlets. Many cures and analyses of diseases or ailments will include a dietary angle, in order to correct the balance of "heaty" and "cooling" foods to ensure your body's equilibrium.

Emergency Services

If you are unlucky and do fall ill or suffer an accident, Singapore's medical services are excellent and highly efficient. Take with you all the documentation you have about your insurance policy, and most hospitals should be able to process the paperwork rapidly. You may need to pay a deposit or total fee by credit card and then subsequently reclaim from your insurer—check the hospital procedure and your policy.

All major hotels will be able to arrange a doctor's visit or a hospital visit if necessary—check under room service or call the reception to arrange what you require. If you are staying in a private house or a budget hotel, you will find doctors' surgeries in all main shopping malls, or in the phone book. Again, these are grouped into chains— the Raffles Medical Group, the Shenton Medical Group, and so on. Pick a conveniently located one.

There are different types of police: the traffic police who patrol the expressways and all the island's roads, motorcyclists wearing dazzling white uniforms and shiny black boots, and drivers of white cars with dual orange stripes, who wear the more subdued dark blue uniform; the CISCO police, wearing subdued dark blue uniforms and driving white patrol cars with an interlocking lock-type symbol, generally responsible for moving valuable consignments such as cash for banks; the military police; and the PSA police, who patrol the waterways surrounding Singapore to check on imports, smuggling and immigration matters. There are few police patrolling on foot, though you may spot a policeman cycling, but there are well-spaced neighbourhood police stations where you can find the assistance you require—and you may be relieved to learn that all Singapore's police are trained in capturing snakes!

The emergency telephone number for the police is 999, and for the fire and ambulance services it is 995. Emergency vehicles in Singapore do have to obey traffic lights, and do not seem to travel as rapidly as in some other countries.

How to Get There

Most tourists arrive in Singapore at one of the two terminals of Changi International Airport. This is outstandingly efficient and easy to use, both for arrivals and departures. A phone call to the airport will give you up-to-date recorded information on arrivals and departures within seconds, while the current aim is to take no more than 12 minutes from touchdown to receiving luggage on the carousel. Inevitably bottlenecks occur in passport control at peak times, but it is a pleasant, popular and easy place to arrive.

Much of Singapore's wealth is due to its unique position on trade routes, and many major international airlines fly to Singapore. At the time of writing, Singapore is linked to 109 cities in 53 countries by 1,900 flights per week, and has the capacity for handling 24 million passengers a year. (More details, addresses and telephone numbers for flight enquiries, reconfirmations and bookings are given on pages 267–268.)

Transport from the airport to the city is highly efficient: a constant line of taxis waits by the arrivals halls, while four different regular bus services leave from the bus station beneath Terminal 2 to destinations throughout the island. In addition, many hotels have their own bus services to the airport and will meet their guests. At the time of writing there is talk of extending the MRT—the subway—to the airport, though no time schedules are yet agreed.

Travellers from West Malaysia generally enter Singapore from Johor Baru along the 1-km (0.6-mile)-long causeway linking the two countries, travelling by private car, taxi or bus. It is also possible to cross on foot. The causeway reaches the new town of Woodlands on the north of the island, a 20-minute or so drive from the city

*T*he modern and highly efficient Singapore MRT (Mass Rapid Transit system); a train passing Little Guilin at Bukit Gombak.

which is on the south side. The causeway can and does get jammed at peak times, and construction work is proceeding to improve the number of customs booths at the Johor end in an attempt to alleviate congestion. This is often exacerbated by the form-filling procedures required by customs officers of both countries. Buses and coaches have supplies of these forms for their passengers: if you are driving yourself, you can pick up forms from travel agents in advance, or you can walk along the queue to the booths to collect them for you and any passengers in your car, so that you can all fill them in while you are waiting and present them when you reach the front of the queue.

A second crossing to link the industrial west of Singapore with Gelang Patah on the adjoining section of Malaysia to the west is being discussed, and if agreed and constructed will ease the pressure considerably on the existing causeway.

It is also possible to catch one of the six daily train services between Singapore and West Malaysia, travelling from Johor Baru or from further afield in Kuala Lumpur, Penang or even Bangkok. The trains are run by the Malaysian-owned KTM (*Keretapi Tanah Melayu*), which owns the track and all the land through which the railway runs on Singapore. The station is currently at Keppel Road, in Tanjong Pagar.

Travellers from Indonesia may choose to approach via the Riau archipelago off Sumatra, as regular and fast ferry services operate between Batam and Bintan, the two nearest islands, and the Singapore Cruise Centre, which is part of the World Trade Centre. Catamaran ferries to and from Tioman Island and Johor state also use this terminal.

From Finger Pier there are taxis, buses or a 10-minute walk to the nearest MRT stations, Marina Bay and Tanjong Pagar. (There is no duty-free allowance between Singapore and Malaysia, although there are duty-free arrangements between Indonesia and Singapore and, as at Changi Airport, it is possible to buy duty-free goods on entering Singapore at the Singapore Cruise Centre.)

Budget travellers on onward journeys may choose to fly from Batam to other Indonesian destinations, or from Johor Baru to other Malaysian destinations to benefit from those countries' cheaper domestic air fares, although time taken will increase dramatically.

Cruise ships from various destinations also arrive regularly in Singapore, docking at the Singapore Cruise Centre, next to the World Trade Centre. This has two passenger berths and a reserve berth, an airport-style arrivals, reductions and departures hall, and world-class ancillary facilities, including baggage handling, aerobridges, disabled access and so on.

Travel Within Singapore

The main island of Singapore is about 42 km (26 miles) from east to west and 23 km (14 miles) from north to south, so the distance to anywhere on the island is fairly short. In addition, it has 54 smaller islands, most of which are accessible by boat.

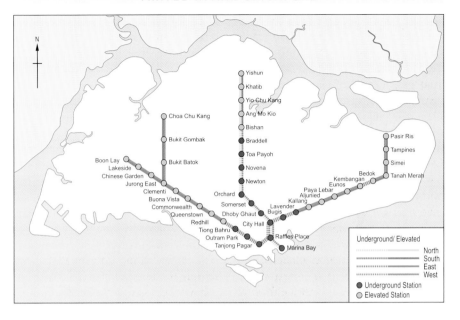

*M*ap of the MRT (Mass Rapid Transit) system.

However, with a population of 3 million people, traffic congestion in the central city district has led to restrictions on entry during the morning (7.30–10.15 a.m.) and evening (4.30–6.30 p.m.) rush hours. If you are driving at these times you need to purchase a daily or monthly area licence from a roadside booth or post office, and if you take a taxi into the restricted zone you pay a surcharge of $3; if you take a taxi out of the restricted zone you pay an additional $1.

Singapore's virulent anti-smoking policy extends to all types of public transport. You may not light up on any bus, in any MRT train or station, within the airport or in a taxi. You are unlikely to get fined for such an infringement the moment you arrive, but you will be asked to extinguish cigarettes and pipes pretty quickly by fellow passengers or official staff.

The two lines of the 67-km (42-mile)-long MRT—Mass Rapid Transit system, stretch from Yishun in the north via the main shopping area of Orchard Road to Marina Bay in the south and from Pasir Ris in the east to Boon Lay or Choa Chu Kang in the west. There are a total of 42 stations, both underground and elevated or above ground. Raffles Place and City Hall, in the centre of the city, are both interchange stations between the two lines, carefully designed so that you only have to cross a platform to continue your journey. Tickets are on sale at all stations, and consist of recyclable, magnetically coded, plastic tickets which, when passed through the automatic gates, record the distance of your trip. You can buy tickets for single trips, but stored value tickets are more convenient if you will be using the MRT more than once: buy a $10 ticket and travel until the value runs out. Machines dispense single tickets, but each station has a manned ticket booth if you have no change or would prefer a stored value ticket. An increasing number of bus routes now also accept the new transit ticket, interchangeable between bus and MRT, now available at all MRT stations.

Most Singaporeans travel about by bus, and the extensive network is quite reliable if you can fathom it out. You do need the exact fare in coins to travel by bus: no change is available, you pay the fare as advised by the driver when you enter, and he issues the ticket through the nearby machine; you should retain it for your whole journey in case an inspector arrives and checks. Tourist publications list the necessary bus numbers to various sights, and if you plan to travel this way there is an annual bus guide available at all bookshops very cheaply— though you should double-check the bus destinations as you wait at the bus stop, or by asking fellow passengers, since construction work can sometimes mean buses are re-routed.

A good way to explore is to buy a 1- or 3-day Explorer ticket from most hotels, travel agents or bus interchanges. With this ticket you can travel on any SBS (Singapore Bus Services) or TIBS (Trans Island Bus Services) bus throughout the island,

validating the ticket by a simple scratch- card system. SBS, the Explorer organizers, have identified six tour itineraries, each marked by Explorer notices at bus stops and on the nearside windscreens of the relevant buses, and this is an easy and cheap way to go sightseeing by bus. With your ticket you receive a brochure and map which shows these routes, as well as routes to the main attractions. For any further enquiries, ask your hotel or travel agent, or telephone SBS on 287 2727, or TIBS on 459 9888.

Numerous taxis ply the main shopping streets, hotel forecourts and the airport. Compared with Western countries, the fares are cheap, and it's a (relatively) hassle-free way to travel about. In addition to the metered fare, watch out for additional charges which are listed within the cab: these apply to trips to and from the airport; when entering or leaving the Central Business District during its operating hours; and to trips after midnight. You should also be aware that not all taxi drivers will know their way to out-of-the-way destinations or residential addresses, nor will they necessarily admit this until you have driven around for quite some time! All standard-sized taxis can carry four passengers; the new white London-style cabs can carry five passengers—and have an additional surcharge for the privilege.

All the main international car hire companies have Singapore outlets (*see* page 270 for further details), and you may drive for up to 1 year with a valid national licence from any Commonwealth country, the USA or Japan. An international driving licence is also acceptable. Driving is on the left, and there are numerous one-way systems which take some map-reading until you orientate yourself successfully. Faint-hearted or nervous drivers would do better to travel by taxi or other means of public transport, since the style of driving is at times quite hazardous: indicators may or may not indicate the direction a vehicle is likely to turn; lane discipline is at best lax— people overtake wherever they can, or drift between lane markings as if they do not exist; bicycles and trishaws—invariably without lights at night—often jump red lights and travel against the flow of traffic, even on one-way streets; and to compensate for the numerous one-way streets there is a system of legal U-turns which often results in slow-moving vehicles pulling into the "fast" lane just in front of you. If you do opt for self-drive, you will find multi-storey parking is expensive within the central district and fees ubiquitous throughout the day. You should also acquire a book of parking coupons, available at roadside booths, Changi airport, petrol stations and selected stationery shops, which you need for open-air parking lots and which you must validate at the time of parking.

For a taste of days gone by—and indeed they are still used by local people around areas such as Chinatown in many everyday tasks—you could take a ride on a trishaw, an archaic-looking passenger tricycle often with an equally archaic-looking driver. You'll find these at all the major hotels and tourist sights, and should agree the price before you step in; since they are now tourist attractions themselves, drivers can and do charge exorbitantly.

Tips for the Disabled Visitor

Singapore does seem to be trying to make itself more welcoming to the disabled: disabled competitors have recently taken part in its marathon for instance, and even water-skiing schemes are starting. People will generally be helpful if asked, particularly when told about the disability in advance, but you will still find public buildings (the National Library, the National Museum for example) with only stair access. The Singapore Council of Social Services (11 Penang Lane, Singapore 0923) publishes a booklet *Access Singapore*, aimed primarily at wheelchair users, which details banks, post offices, cinemas, public places, department stores, theatres, hotels and places of interest which have access ramps, toilets, etc. They do advise disabled people to telephone ahead before travelling to any site in their booklet, since information is notoriously subject to change.

A Place for Kids?

It is government policy to encourage married couples to have children, and the society is generally very "children-friendly": you see young children eating in all types of restaurant, attending all types of film (hence the censorship regulations, only relaxed slightly in July 1991), and no one seems to become agitated about the noise they make or how they behave (though local children on the whole don't, in my experience, seem to throw particularly loud tantrums!).

A boat entering the colourful dragon's mouth at Haw Par Villa *to see the* Ten Courts of Hell *tableaux inside (not for the faint of heart!).*

Pushchair and pram access to shopping facilities and the main sights is generally quite good. Changing facilities are more variable, particularly in public conveniences, which are not always ideal in terms of cleanliness. Hotel facilities, never too far away in the centre of Singapore, are a better bet.

A lot of the "general interest" sights—the BirdPark, the zoo, the nature reserve and Peirce and MacRitchie reservoirs—are ideal for picnic outings with children. Picnic sites with tables and litter bins are available at the reservoir parks, while there are also barbecue pits at East Coast Park, Changi Beach, West Coast Park, Pasir Ris Park, Sembawang Park and Tanjong Berlayar Park, which you can book at East Coast Parkway Car Park C4, telephone 448 7120. Barbecue pit bookings run from 12 noon until the following day, and pits are also available for those camping on Sentosa Island. For outdoor picnics or walks, do remember the insect repellent and insect-bite cream to minimize any discomfort: you can't hope to avoid all the mosquitoes near water and trees.

Most parks will offer a slide or a swing or two; Pasir Ris Park, on the north-west coast opposite Pulau Ubin, offers some of the best playground facilities I've seen, with three separate areas of adventure playground-type facilities for those under 4, those aged 5–9, and those from 10–15. If your hotel doesn't have a swimming pool there are several public pools—check the phone book for your nearest one, or ask at the hotel. The CN West Leisure Park on Japanese Garden Road in Jurong (*see* page 179) offers a little more than a basic swimming pool, though it's a bit sleepy and not worth a special trip out there; and the Big Splash Pool off the East Coast Parkway has an enormous water slide.

The Science Park offers kids a chance to play with video cameras, see themselves on TV and play with

Do be sure to bring adequate sun-shielding hats, clothes and lotions for young children, and take care since all children, and adults, will become rapidly dehydrated in the heat and humidity, so make sure that you take or buy sufficient cold drinks on even short excursions.

computers for as long as they want to, while Haw Par Villa's water flume and other attractions are worth taking in (though you may find the moral lessons of some of the tableaux in the Ten Courts of Hell too frightening to inflict on very young children). Sentosa Island offers a variety of attractions for all ages (see page 217 onwards). Somewhat off the beaten tourist track, at Parkway Parade on Marine Parade Road, parents can hire small bikes for toddlers and small children to play an improvised dodgems game with other children in a pedestrian area. Sports facilities, swimming pools and playgrounds can all be found, and your hotel can generally arrange for babysitting if you want an evening or other period of time away from the kids.

Accommodation

Singapore boasts hotels and guest houses to suit all budgets and tastes. There is a description of hotels from page 278 onwards, and it is advisable to book accommodation at the same time as your flight, particularly if you wish to use one of the more prestigious hotels. As always, you get what you pay for, though standards are generally high and competitive. Camping is allowed at three selected sites: at East Coast Park, where you have to book 3 months in advance through the People's Association; on Sentosa Island near the lagoon, for which you should approach the Sentosa Information Office, World Trade Centre, Telephone: 2707 888/9 at least 3 days in advance; and on Pulau Ubin, where you should register with the police on arrival. The

East Coast and Sentosa campsites have a number of facilities, including tents for hire, toilets and running water, and barbecue pits. Sentosa also has a youth hostel with competitive rates—again, contact them at World Trade Centre.

Restaurants

Eating is a major interest and source of income for a large proportion of the population. The first question you are asked is likely to be "Do you like the food? Not too hot for you, lah?"

There is a vast range of restaurants within the different hotels and shopping centres, as well as in some of the small shophouses, where you can sit in air-conditioned, smoke-free comfort and enjoy meals of every type—Cantonese, Beijing, Malay, North and South Indian, Indonesian, Japanese, Vietnamese, Thai—European cuisine is readily available, though a little expensive, since such a high proportion of the ingredients are imported from afar. Wines and alcoholic drinks are also highly priced because they are highly taxed.

Some of the best local food is served at the hawker centres, generally openair collections of different food stalls serving a common area of diners. You can order any food from any stall, and should resist over-pushy salesmen (hawkers), adept at spotting indecisive tourists. The hawker centres generally serve the cheapest food you will find, with the coffee shops—unpretentious local eating houses serving their speciality fare off plastic plates—coming a close second on price, and often surpassing them on quality. It's largely

A lorry load of professional Chinese mourners en route *to a funeral.*

a matter of recommendation and reputation: some shops will be full and others not so, though it's always worth trying somewhere if you're hungry and see an appetizing dish.

There's quite an extensive list of hawker centres, coffee shops and restaurants of the various Chinese types, as well as local Malay, Nonya and other nationalities at the back of the book. Virtually all tastes, fads and types are catered for, though I've not found any kosher restaurant or food outlet in my researches. You can find food outlets serving at all hours of the day, though do be aware that Singaporeans eat early in the evening, so you should not plan to eat after 9.30 p.m. in the evening. For those who prefer to eat familiar or Western food, all hotel coffee shops and a variety of other outlets will serve a selection of such dishes throughout the day and night.

Night-life

Swinging Singapore does have its share of discos and nightclubs, as well as drinking haunts and cocktail bars. A more detailed listing is given on pages 245–248. A number of the nightclubs have dress codes, so don't turn up wearing your favourite torn jeans, tee-shirt and trainers and expect to be let in! You will not be allowed.

Time

Singapore is 8 hours ahead of GMT, and being so close to the Equator does not change time with seasons as some other countries do. The following conversion chart may be helpful—though remember local variations of time in seasonal countries—e.g. British Summer Time.

4 a.m.	San Francisco
7 a.m.	New York
12 noon	London (GMT)
1 p.m.	Paris, Berlin
7 p.m.	Thailand, West Indonesia (Sumatra, Java)
8 p.m.	Singapore, Malaysia, Hong Kong, Central Indonesia (Bali, Lombok, Nusatenggara), Perth
9 p.m.	East Indonesia (Maluku, Irian Jaya), Philippines, Tokyo
10 p.m.	Sydney
12 a.m.	Auckland

Currency and Money Matters

You can change traveller's cheques and foreign cash easily at major hotels, banks with foreign exchange counters (though these will charge a commission), and at the many licensed money changers, who will generally give the best rates. It is best to compare two or three outlets to find the best deal, and you can try bargaining for an extra decimal point or two. Banks are open 10 a.m.–3 p.m. on weekdays, and also 9.30 a.m.–11.30 a.m. on Saturdays. Certain branches are also open in the afternoons: check with your hotel for details, or else with the Singapore Tourist Promotion Board's weekly publications. Licensed money changers are generally open 10 a.m.–6 p.m., 7 days a week. Wherever you change money, you will need a passport to cash traveller's cheques. The most commonly used traveller's cheques are the American Express and Thomas Cook ones; some money changers may not accept traveller's cheques from other major banks, though you should keep looking and other places will do.

All major credit cards are welcome in most outlets here: American Express, Diners Club, MasterCard and Visa in their various forms. You will often find your credit limit is checked however small your purchase, but should not find any surcharges for the use of credit cards (though you should make it clear if you are asking for a large discount when bargaining if you then intend to pay by plastic). If you do find any surcharges, ask your hotel or check with the STPB so you can take the matter up with the card company.

Local bank cheques are more of a problem to use, and it's more of an achievement than one would think possible to succeed in writing a cheque in payment for goods! No bank guarantee cards are in circulation here as yet, so all cheques require your passport number, address and phone number—possibly together with some other identification, and a long period of time.

Bank notes come in denominations of $1, $2, $5, $10, $20, $50, $100 and larger $1,000 and $10,000 notes: take care not to confuse the red $2 and $10 notes, though shopkeepers will generally put you right on this. New purple $2 notes have now been introduced instead. There are 1, 5, 10, 20 and 50 cent and $1 coins. Brunei currency is interchangeable with Singapore currency, so do not despair if you are given a Brunei note (though you should not accept Malaysian ringgit on the same basis, nor Indonesian rupiah).

As a rough guide there are Singapore $1.7 to US $1; Singapore $3 to UK £1; Singapore $1.3 to Australian $1; Singapore $1.5 to Canadian $1; Singapore $1 to New Zealand $1. For further currencies and exact rates, check in the daily newspapers before changing money.

Security and Safety

Singapore is a refreshingly safe city, possibly because of the draconian penalties lashed out on any offenders caught stealing, juicily reported in *The New Paper* or *The Straits Times.* Even in situations where there are large crowds—around National Day, for instance, when there is a huge street party; or during the Chingay Procession just after Chinese New Year—you are unlikely to be jostled, have your pocket picked, or be menaced in any way. It is a country where women feel quite safe to travel on public transport or walk about within the centre or their neighbourhoods, which are generally well lit, alone at night.

Even so, the usual precautions should apply: don't leave valuables lying temptingly around; do keep a separate note of numbers of traveller's cheques and credit cards; and do make

use of hotel safe-deposit boxes rather than leaving valuables in your hotel room.

If you are unlucky enough to suffer a theft or crime, call the police on 999 or ask your hotel to call the local station. If you have a consumer complaint against a shop—a camera or watch that doesn't work, or isn't the make it was made out to be for instance—there is a special fast tourist desk of the Small Claims Tribunal which deals with complaints up to a value of $2,000. An initial $10 fee is payable by the claimant, who also has to pay any transport costs, and tourist cases are generally heard and resolved within 24 hours during weekdays. The scheme was set up by CASE, The Consumers' Association of Singapore, (telephone: 270 4611) which can advise on the best procedure for particular problems. To avoid such situations in the first place, it is wise to shop at those shops displaying the red Merlion symbol, signifying that they are recognized as fair traders by the STPB (Singapore Tourist Promotion Board).

Gratuities

Tipping is not a common practice in Singapore, the thinking being that the service should be good enough in the first place without requiring extra credit. (Sadly, most visitors will not always find this to be the case, despite government courtesy campaigns and the like over recent years.) At hawker centres and coffee shops, you just pay the advertised price for what you have eaten (take care to double-check that this is what you'll pay before ordering, since it is quite common for Caucasian diners to be asked to pay the odd 50 cents or so extra by some unscrupulous stall-holders). In smarter restaurants, you will generally find a 10 per cent service charge added to your bill, as well as a 4 per cent "cess" charge, basically an entertainment tax which is used to fund such crucial organizations as the Singapore Tourist Promotion Board. (Both these charges are virtually compulsory, even if you are really unlucky and receive the most atrocious service!) You do not need to tip taxis—though you may find drivers rather slow to give you a few cents change—nor do you tip trishaw drivers, as you will have agreed a fare before you depart. Hotel porters and chambermaids may be tipped.

Post and Telecommunications

The Singapore Postal Service is very efficient and reliable, and rates compare extremely favourably with Western rates for postcards, letters and even airmail packages. The General Post Office at Fullerton Square is open from 8.30 a.m. to 5 p.m. Mondays to Fridays, and from 8.30 a.m. to 1 p.m. on Saturdays. Other local post offices have the same opening hours. Some department stores have postal counters, and main hotels will all have postal services available in their lobbies. The Specialists' Centre Post Office, opposite Centrepoint; the Telecommunications Centre on Exeter/Killiney Roads; and the Changi Airport Post Offices are all open 7 days a week, from 8 a.m. until 8 p.m.

The telephone network is reliable, and it is quite straightforward to phone IDD throughout the world. You can do this from your hotel, from public IDD phone booths (which incidentally *all* work, a fact an English person still finds remarkable!), or from a post office. The charges are quite reasonable, and lines generally quite clear. Telephone calls within Singapore island from a private phone cost 1.4 cents per minute at peak time, 1.4 cents for 2 minutes at evenings and weekends); from a public phone booth the cost is 10 cents for 3 minutes up to a maximum of 9 minutes. Several public telephones now take phonecards, which are available in various values at stationery shops, newsagents and general grocers. Credit card phone booths are now also starting. Calls from the airport to anywhere on the island are free, a particularly welcoming detail for people arriving from abroad with no small change.

Newspapers

Singapore boasts a "serious" daily English language newspaper, *The Straits Times*, as well as a more frivolous lunchtime rag, *The New Paper* which has a strong line in attention-grabbing headlines. Chinese language, Tamil and Malay newspapers are also available, as well as a range of international papers and magazines.

Shopping

Singapore is rightly proud of the range of shopping outlets it has. This international marketplace has duty-free cameras and camera equipment, video cameras, televisions, stereo equipment, computers and all kinds of electrical goods on sale at fixed-price outlets and at centres where you can bargain to reduce the amount you pay by about 10–15 per cent. If you are planning to buy any type of electrical goods in Singapore, do check the price you would pay in your own country first. You should also check your country's customs regulations before setting out: some Western countries set a strict limit on the value of new goods you can import before paying duty or tax, which may make any saving on retail price worthless by the time your goods arrive home. You should also check voltage and current compatibility on electrical goods, though many of these are made and sold solely for export to tourists. Televisions sold in Singapore, for example, are not compatible with broadcasting systems in Europe. Reputable dealers should be able to reassure you on these points, and should sell you products that work: I strongly advise you to try equipment at the store if you can, and in any event back at your hotel, so that any faults or problems can be sorted out with the retailer or, if this fails, through the CASE Small Claims Tribunal scheme (*see* page 27).

The more goods you wish to buy, the larger your potential discount with certain traders. In order to test whether a discount is likely, you can either ask "Is this your best price?/What's the actual price?" or you can make to leave the shop: if you are stopped in your tracks by frantic bargaining, you know that the profit margins and shop policy will allow you to bargain for a reasonable discount. If you intend paying by credit card, you may find more reluctance to lowering the price: clarify things by stating you will pay cash or card in the early stages of negotiation. Once you start negotiating, it generally means that you are interested in making a purchase at the right price: don't start to bargain if you have no intention of buying at whatever price, as it will confuse and could lead to irritation.

Guarantees should be checked at the time of purchase, stamped with the dealer's address and "chop"—official stamp—and may need posting to the company for registration. Some guarantees are valid only in Singapore, but many electrical goods and camera guarantees are geared towards the tourist market with international guarantees. Check first and be sure that all the paperwork is in order.

Most shopping malls have some kind of food outlet, money-changer or bank, and photo development outlet or photography film counter. On pages 272–275 there is a quick outline of what you will find in the various central shopping malls and other shopping areas, and then a quick item by item reference guide. Since Singapore changes so rapidly, it is worth picking up the STPB's free literature on shopping outlets to keep up to date, and also to check the newspapers for special promotions or sales.

As well as electrical and electronic goods, watches are widely available in Singapore. Again, if you plan to buy a designer watch, check the price range within your country and any import restrictions you may face; then compare the prices and service in a number of outlets before committing yourself. You are unlikely to get any reduction, and may cause yourself some embarrassment, if you try to bargain with the main authorized outlet of particular brands—such as Rolex. Do check their prices and guarantees against those offered in jewellers carrying a wider range of designs—you may get a better deal in the latter.

The authorities are trying to crack down on the blatant copyright infringement by "copy watch" touts, and also will be fast to act if you feel harassed by such people in shopping centres—Lucky Plaza, and Far East Shopping Centre/Plaza especially—and in tourist areas such as Chinatown,

since touting is illegal. Draconian penalties—heavy fines and up to 6 months' imprisonment—have been meted out to repeat offenders in an attempt to control the problem. Generally though it is easy to indicate you do not wish to purchase from such people, who will then disappear from view until another obvious tourist or Caucasian comes along. If you do wish to buy a fake designer watch, you should simply wander around such shopping centres and look at watch shops until you are approached by a

Spoilt for choice—some of the shopping opportunities in Arab Street.

Ladies' Clothes Sizes				
British	**American**	**Continental**	**Japanese**	**Australian**
6	4	34	5	8
8	6	36	7	10
10	8	38	9	12
12	10	40	11	14
14	12	42	13	16
16	14	44	15	18

Men's Suit Sizes		
British/American	**Continental/Australian**	**Japanese**
36	46	S
38	48	M
40	50	L
42	52	L
44	54	XL
46	56	XL

Men's Shirt Sizes	
British/American	**Japanese/Australian**
14	36
14½	37
15	38
15½	39
16	40
16½	41

tout, and you should then be prepared to be discreet about where and what he can show or sell you. Dealing with touts obviously has no safeguards—if you buy a dud you have no proof of purchase and have no legal comeback since the whole transaction is illegal in the first place (though I have managed to return and replace faulty copy watches myself). You *must* bargain with touts, and should look for at least 20–25 per cent off the first price mentioned before reaching for your wallet. Because of the increasing danger of prosecution, many copy watch touts have relocated outside Singapore: in Kukup in Malaysia, for instance, copy watches are openly displayed on sale and prices considerably lower than those in Singapore.

Thai and China silks and other fabrics are to be found at bargain prices along the stalls in Arab Street, in People's Park in Chinatown and at slightly higher prices, still way below those of the West, in the central Orchard Road shopping area. Clothing is another popular purchase: there is everything from the top Western fashion houses to various copy teeshirts at knock-down prices. It is an ideal place to buy clothes, since fabrics and labour costs are very reasonable, though bear in mind that the average Singaporean is shorter and slimmer than the average American or Australian, so if you are medium to large in your own country you may have difficulty buying items off-the-peg. Similarly the largest men's shoe size is size 10.

Ladies' Shoe Sizes

British	USA	Continental
4½	6	35
5	6½	36
5½	7	37
6	7½	38
6½	8	39
7	8½	40
7½	9	41
8	9½	42

Men's Shoe Sizes

British	USA	Continental
7½	8½	42
8½	9½	43
9½	10½	44
10½	11½	45
11	12	46
12	13	47–48

A simple and fairly reasonable alternative is to have clothes individually tailored to your requirements: suits can generally be made in 2 or 3 days; dresses and more complicated requests may take longer, though outlets will be keen to secure a sale so your travel arrangements will be carefully listened to. For lengthy orders, you can even arrange for parcels to be mailed to your home address, but be sure to have enough fitting sessions before leaving Singapore to ensure a good fit.

Clothing sizes are somewhat enigmatic—some items are marked small, medium and large, others use a European or British system, others an Australian or American system, and there are also Japanese sizes—so do try on items before purchasing them. Large, medium and small can have a whole width of meaning completely different from what you might expect. The tables on page 31 may be helpful if you can identify the manufacturer's nationality, but you are strongly advised to try on garments in the shop rather than risk a bad fit, since few Singapore stores—Metro is a notable exception—will refund readily. Large sizes of shoes and even clothes are difficult to come by in Singapore—do not expect to find ladies' shoes over size 7/8½/40 or men's shoes over size 10/11/43.

The range of clothing available is vast, from traditional office and casual wear to batik skirts, shirts and trousers; Chinese dressing gowns, scarves and jackets; to fake designer polo shirts and sportswear (again, increasing pressure is exerted on such retailers by the authorities, so copy tee-shirts may not be prominently displayed, but furtively brought from some back recess—do be careful to get yourself a good price on any such goods, as you can't complain if your product is faulty).

Antiques from all over the world and local crafts are available in the Tanglin Shopping Centre and in various other areas at much more reasonable prices than in the West. Again, you should check on import regulations in your home country if you are considering buying, say, a Persian carpet or a Korean chest.

The larger shops can generally organize shipment to your country of large or heavy items, and can arrange insurance.

Although Singapore is such a shopping centre, it is a shame that despite government courtesy campaigns you will often find surly or downright unhelpful service, often seemingly compounded by the local "Singlish" rather than English that is spoken to you.

This is particularly the case in large retail chains, when bored assistants can seem to have no interest in serving you, and is certainly not a problem unique to Singapore. The smaller, family-run outlets are generally more welcoming, even pushy, which to me is rather more conducive to making a purchase, though can be very off-putting to the more reserved Westerner.

Shopping hours are generally from 9.30 or 10 a.m. till at least 6 p.m., but often 9 or 9.30 p.m., every day. Supermarkets—Cold Storage, Jasons, Smart, NTUC Fair Price—generally open at 8 a.m. and stay open until 9.30 p.m. Newsagents are open from 8 a.m. or earlier, and generally deliver to all major hotels. Some family-run shops will shut on Sundays, as do many of the antique shops in Tanglin Shopping Centre, and Tangs, the Chinese department store, which is well worth a visit.

Saturday afternoons are particularly busy shopping times, since office hours in Singapore are generally 5½ days including Saturday morning. A quick shopping guide to items and places is given on pages 272–275.

What to Bring

Bring an assortment of light summer clothes, preferably made out of natural fabrics, so that you can stay as cool as possible. Singapore is not a particularly dressy place: men rarely wear jackets in offices, and politicians—including the now Senior Minister, Mr Lee Kuan Yew—are often seen in short-sleeved shirts with no ties. So bring a smart-casual wardrobe of shirts, teeshirts, shorts, skirts, dresses, light cotton trousers and the like. As it's so hot and humid, you do often need two or three changes of clothes a day, so you may need more than you'd think, though you could plan to buy casual clothes in Singapore. Women who are planning to travel widely in Malaysia or Indonesia should remember to bring longish skirts or lightweight trousers and long-sleeved shirts, and men should also bring trousers and long-sleeved shirts.

Bring supportive and comfortable shoes if you want to walk about sightseeing or shopping: sandals are all very well for short distances, but your enjoyment of the BirdPark or zoo, for instance, would be significantly curtailed in unsuitable footwear. Better to wear shoes which are a little too hot but supportive, even in this heat, but take care that you wear large enough shoes, since your feet may expand as they heat up.

Electricity voltage is 220–240 volts AC, and 3-pin plugs are standard. Most hotels have transformers and adapters if you wish to bring hair-dryers, shaving equipment or any other electrical goods. Alcohol is highly taxed, so you may think it's worth buying a litre of duty-free as you enter the country (*see* page 14), even if you are only staying a short while. Duty-free cigarettes are no longer allowed into the country, as part of its vigorous no-smoking policy.

If you are taking photographs, film of most kinds is readily available and film processing outlets do an adequate job on most films. Professional photographers should be advised that

Kodachrome film is not available in Singapore, nor is it possible to have it developed here—presumably because Kodak fear the native expertise in copying successful techniques at cut-price rates—so if you use this film, bring an adequate supply and take your films home for developing.

Public Behaviour: Rules and Regulations

Various activities you wouldn't think twice about elsewhere are illegal or strongly discouraged in Singapore: smoking is banned in all air-conditioned restaurants, public transport, cinemas and so on; you should only cross main roads at pedestrian crossings, bridges or underground walkways; gambling—except for the state lottery and the Bukit Timah Turf Club tote—is illegal; public demonstrations, whether technically illegal or not, just never happen (unless they show support for the government), and public speaking as at London's Speaker's Corner or Christchurch's Square is similarly absent. A recent addition to the list of prohibited activities was sitting on a parapet at the City Hall MRT (underground train) station: a regulation that aroused such consid-erable opposition and correspondence that it has been subsequently reversed. The sale and importing of all brands of chewing-gum was banned on 3 January 1992, though its actual consumption or chewing does not as yet constitute an offence. One of the things that occasions the greatest amusement amongst foreign visitors is the assortment of notices in public conveniences (themselves generally nothing to write home about even in this squeaky-clean city—always carry your own tissue supply as there's rarely paper): fines of up to $500 are threatened if you fail to flush even a urinal. Similar draconian fines are threatened for spitting, or for carrying durians—or indeed any ice-creams, drinks or fast-foods—on the MRT or into public places. Littering is seriously discouraged—fines around $500—and the result is refreshingly worth it to Western visitors: numerous litter bins mean you scarcely see a discarded drinks can or burger wrapper.

The Prime Minister, Mr Goh Chok Tong, recently asked Singaporeans to advise him of any rules they found

*S*ingapore, sometimes known as the "fine" city because there seems to be a fine for everything.

stifling in this regulation-ridden society, and a vast majority of those subsequently interviewed felt that most such rules were necessary to keep the country running smoothly. A fear that without such reminders "Singaporeans would go wild" was by no means uncommon, and only a few more peripheral suggestions for improvements were made. Part of his liberalizing tendencies may be responsible for the recent unbanning of juke boxes, banned since 1959 along with fruit machines for their association with smoky amusement rooms and secret-society operations, though private owners still need the permission of the Public Entertainment Licensing Unit before they can purchase one!

It's a very family-conscious society, and frequent articles in the local press talk of Western decadence, which is

Door panel painting at the Thian Hock Keng Temple on Telok Ayer Street.

discouraged here. This means over-zealous public displays of affection are frowned upon, and particularly "hostile" or revealing forms of dress or behaviour may arouse comment.

The different races have their own standards and etiquette rules, so that what you wear to visit a Chinese or Hindu temple may not be suitable for a mosque visit. On the more personal level, the Western "ladies first" principle is not common practice here: getting out of a lift or a bus or train, the person nearest the exit leaves first— and there's often a good deal of jostling and shoving to get out as those waiting outside start to cram in.

THE COUNTRY, ITS HISTORY AND ITS PEOPLE

From Raffles to Riches— A Vibrant and Multi-Cultural Nation

The Republic of Singapore nestles at the southern tip of the Malay Peninsular. To the south, the Indonesian Riau islands are visible on a clear day: the rest of the Indonesian archipelago stretches away to the south and east, with Sumatra lying to the north-west of Singapore.

Geography

Singapore and its 58 offshore islands comprise a total land area of 626 km^2 (242 square miles); the main Singapore island is 42 km (26 miles) from east to west and 23 km (14 miles) from north to south. It lies at latitude 1 degree and 9 seconds north of the Equator, 103 degrees and 38 seconds longitude east, and 137 km (85 miles) north of the Equator. The climate is consequently one of high humidity (85 per cent on average, sometimes over 90 per cent at

Colourful detail from the entrance of the Sri Veeramakayama Hindu temple on Serangoon Street.

night and just before dawn) and year-round warmth—on average 27°C (81°F). Its two monsoon seasons run from December to March and from June to September—the former is the wettest season, since the land mass of Sumatra to the west largely shields Singapore from the June to September south-west monsoon. Between

> **Tourist Tip**
> During the main monsoon season, it is wise to take an umbrella with you on any but the shortest trip: a fine morning when you start can rapidly change into a tropical downpour, and often with the onset of rain comes a disappearance of taxis. Queues for taxis in shopping malls are notoriously long—it is better to be able to try another means of transport such as bus or MRT if at all possible.

monsoons loud thunderstorms are common, and roads and underground car-parks can flood in minutes. Average annual rainfall is 2,369 mm (92 inches).

Singapore is made up of three distinct geological regions. In the central area is granite and other igneous rock, rising to the island's highest points. To the west sedimentary rocks—shale, sandstone and conglomerate—form folding north-west hills and rolling valleys; while the relatively flat eastern region is made of semi-hardened alluvium, as well as sand and gravel deposits and reclaimed land. It sits calmly within the Pacific Ring of Fire, as the volcanic rim runs along the tectonic plate to the west of Sumatra, Java and rises up to the Philippines well out of range.

Physically the island would be virtually unrecognizable today to the founder of modern Singapore, Sir Stamford Raffles, though he it was who began the first of the many land reclamation programmes so vital to Singapore's success. Primary jungle, which virtually covered the island during early colonial times, is now reduced to an area of the Botanic Gardens and a small patch in the Bukit Timah Nature Reserve—indeed much of the vegetation in this area is technically *belukar* (secondary forest), where nature has reclaimed old rubber plantations and the like; whilst many hills have been levelled and their topsoil turned into reclaimed land along the south-east coast. Hills remain today in the central area of the island—as well as Bukit Timah, the island's highest point at 165 m (542 feet), there are Bukit Gombak, Bukit Panjang and

> **Reclaimed From the Sea**
> The land reclamation is a staggering achievement. Raffles encouraged the early city to be built on the south side of the Singapore River, and the land of what is now Collyer Quay was reclaimed and strengthened to make the city's original waterfront. The entire Marina South Park, and the Benjamin Sheares dual carriageway bridge over Marina Bay, runs on comparatively recently reclaimed land. To the east Beach Road, where the Raffles Hotel is situated, really used to be on the beach: all development to the south of this road is on reclaimed land. Further to the east, this makes sense of numerous beach/seaside-style houses now nestling in Tanjong Katong, which would have been built originally for their sea views. Many of Singapore's beaches are man-made—those along the East Coast Park for instance—and have a sudden deep drop after the landscaped gentle sandy stretch, which can be a danger to incautious swimmers.

Bukit Mandai (*bukit* in Malay means "hill"). Early Chinese settlers planted gambier and then rubber, though the large and commercially successful estates were always across the Strait in Johor and mainland Malaya. Singapore has large reservoir areas in its central area and in the north-west, though these do not contain enough for the island's needs, and much water is imported from Johor (*see* below).

The city of Singapore is situated on the south of the island, while Jurong to the west is the main industrial area. The whole south-east coast from the city to Changi airport is lined with a public park giving easy access to the sea; the north-west coast by contrast is virtually hidden from view by large areas of military barracks and firing ranges. There remain a few rural areas, notably Ponggol Point in the north-east and Kranji dam in the north-west, though one does see constant evidence of relocation—enforced or otherwise—in rural areas.

The numerous islands, mainly to the south of Singapore, have various functions: many are oil refinery or industrial islands; explosives are stored on one and military exercises carried out on numerous others. The exact number of southern islands varies. At the time of writing, for example, there is an ambitious plan to merge seven islands (Pulau Seraya, Pulau Ayer Merbau, Pulau Sakra, Pulau Merliau, Ayer Chawan, Pesek and Pesek Kechil) into one single chemical-industry island, with three causeways and a land-filling programme. Some unspoilt islands remain—Kusu Island for example, or the Sisters Islands, and Pulau Ubin on

the north-east is pretty and unspoilt in parts, though much of the island is disused or still-operational granite quarries. One traditional Malay fishing island still remains intact, with about 20 families still living on Pulau Seking with no mains electricity, importing water and foodstuffs from nearby Pulau Bukom or the mainland. (*See* pages 217–225 for further details on islands you can visit.)

Singapore is linked to West Malaysia by a 1,056-m (1,155-yd)-long causeway to the north of the island. As well as a dual carriageway road, this also comprises a railway line and two water pipes: one for untreated water from Malaysia; the other to pump back some water treated in Singapore for Malaysian consumption. (Johor state is currently building its own new water processing and treatment plants, due for completion by 2003, when it will no longer need to buy back its own treated water from Singapore. Equally, discussions are under way with other Malaysian states, notably Pahang, as well as with Batam in Indonesia on further sources of water for Singapore's growing population.) The rail link to Johor Baru in Malaysia is owned by Malaysia, and called the KTM—*Keretapi Tanah Melayu*. You enter Malaysian territory at the Keppel Road station, and the squatter huts along the track all belong to Singapore's neighbour. Plans are afoot to move this station to Bukit Timah in

*L*ush tropical vegetation on Singapore's Pulau Ubin, one of the less-developed islands.

the centre of the island in order to free valuable land in a prime city location for redevelopment. The island is crossed by good-quality roads and expressways, and the amenities are constantly being reviewed and updated, which means that a tourist cannot fail to notice a great deal of construction.

New Towns

Singapore's PAP government has encouraged and developed a number of new satellite towns comprising large units of housing. One of the first such areas was Jurong, and the Jurong Town Council is now one of the major developers and investors in Singapore. Some other new towns, each with their own community centres, are Ang Mo Kio (literally "Red Man's Bridge"—a reference to the 19th-century government surveyor J. T. Thomson who built a bridge on this new town's site; Tampines, named after a tropical hardwood tree unfortunately cleared completely from the area in order to construct the new town—its current town council plans to plant saplings; and Yishun, named after the rubber and pineapple planter Lim Nee Soon (1879–1936) who built villages for his labourers in this area, soon to be commemorated in a 3.4-hectare (8.4-acre) park featuring replica Chinese, Malay and Indian-style houses.

The Singapore government has long-term plans for the further development of Singapore as a comfortable home for a population of up to 4 million by the year 2000. A new downtown business development at Marina Bay is scheduled to begin in that year, allowing central business concerns to expand in a central area. Jurong East, Tampines and Woodlands are identified as three potential self-contained regional commercial centres, so that economic activity will become decentralized as much as it can. By 2000 the MRT line is planned to loop from Choa Chu Kang in the west through Woodlands (near the causeway in the north) to Yishun in the north-east. Further development guide plans are under discussion, and at their most ambitious include extending the MRT line out from Serangoon Road and Ponggol to Pulau Ubin and Pulau Tekong in the north-east of the island, maximizing the urban and industrial use made of Singapore's precious land resources.

Flora and Fauna

The Nature Reserves Board manages the 2,000 hectares (4,942 acres) of the Bukit Timah Nature Reserve, comprising mainly forest. It also oversees the other remaining mangrove forest and swamp areas, where some of Singapore's native flora and fauna can still be found. There are over 320 local species of bird, of which 170 are common—these include the ubiquitous Myna, the Black-naped Oriole, the Brahminy Kite and different types of heron. Butterflies are also numerous, and sometimes extremely large. Long-tailed macaques are often seen, also the occasional civet cat or tree shrew, while the island's reptiles include 40 types of snake (of which only six are poisonous), monitor lizards, the occasional crocodile and household geckos.

In conjunction with the Botanic Gardens, and the Parks and Recreations Department, Singapore is now planted out as a tropical garden city. Every expressway and major road is lined with shady trees, pedestrian bridges are bedecked with vibrantly coloured bougainvilleas, and parks are kept beautifully clean and well maintained, as if to capitalize on the land's natural fertility.

History

First discovered by a Sumatran prince in the 13th century, Singapore only really attained a world position during the 19th century after its rediscovery by Sir Stamford Raffles. Since then its success has continued through its different phases as trading post, Straits Settlement, Crown Colony and independent republic.

Early History
The island of Singapore was originally known as Temasek—sea town—and comprised a small fishing island and vast areas of jungle. It first appeared in historical records in 1299, when a prince from Palembang in Sumatra was touring the nearby Riau islands and spotted Temasek from Bintan island. Intrigued, he explored the island, catching a fleeting glimpse of a wild animal he insisted was a lion (most probably a tiger), and renaming the island Singapura—lion city.

This prince, Sang Nila Utama, settled on what is now Fort Canning Hill until his death in 1347, and was succeeded by four further kings— Paduka Sri Pikrama Wira, Sri Rana Wikerma, Dam Raja, and Iskandar Shah—in a small but successful trading kingdom. However, the island became embroiled in the long-running conflict between Siam (now Thailand) and the Majapahit Empire of Java. A first Javanese attack was repulsed during the 1350s, but a second attack in 1392 proved more successful, forcing the last Sultan Iskandar Shah to flee to Malacca, and laying waste to Singapore. (It was while he was in Malacca that Iskandar Shah was converted to Islam.) Excavations on Fort Canning Hill, now displayed in the National Museum, show some artefacts from the 14th-century kingdom, and the shrine (*kramat*) half-way up Fort Canning Hill is believed by some to be the grave of that last sultan, and revered and tended to this day by Muslims.

After the departure of Iskandar Shah, Singapore reverted to an unimportant backwater for several centuries. During the late 18th and early 19th centuries, European traders travelled to the Malay peninsular and Indonesian archipelago, setting up trading centres when the opportunities arose. The British East India Company, based in Calcutta, obtained bases in Penang just off the Malay Peninsular and in Bencoolen in Sumatra, and British traders seized Malacca—then a Dutch colony—during the Napoleonic Wars in the early 19th century.

The "Founding" of Singapore
Singapore by the early 19th century was under the loose control of the Sultan of Johor-Riau, whose *temenggong* (chief minister) arrived on the island in 1811 with about 150 Malay settlers.

*W*axworks models in Sentosa Island's Pioneers of Singapore and Surrender Chambers. From the left: Tengku Ali, Sultan Hussein Shah's eldest son; Sultan Hussein Shah of Johor Baru; Sir Stamford Raffles; Temenggong Abdul Rahman, de facto ruler of Singapore and Johor; Major William Farquhar, First Resident of Singapore.

The British Lieutenant-Governor of Bencoolen on Sumatra, Sir Stamford Raffles, arrived to survey Singapore as a potential trading station for the East India Company in January 1819, and made an agreement with Abdul Rahman, the sultan recognized by the Dutch (then at war with the British in Europe), and ratified this agreement with Rahman's elder brother Hussein on 6 February 1819, paying him 5,000 Spanish dollars and his *temenggong* a further 3,000 annually. Hussein and his *temenggong* (also, confusingly, called Abdul Rahman) settled in style in Singapore. The war with the Dutch was ended in the Treaty of London of 1824, whereupon the Sultan of Johor-Riau renounced all claims to own Singapore, and Britain ceded its territories in Sumatra and Java to the Dutch in return for Malacca and Singapore.

Sultan Hussein became a dreadful spendthrift and his wife took on an adviser which led to scandals, so they fled to Malacca, to be replaced by his son Ali. In 1855 Ali signed a treaty with the *temenggong*, so that the latter became ruler of Johor, though Ali kept the title sultan until his death in 1885. In 1866 the *temenggong* Abu Bakar moved his headquarters to a new site in Johor and named the city Johor Baru (new Johor). He finally gained the title sultan in 1885; his great-grandson is the present Sultan of Johor.

> **Raffles**
> An able administrator and official of the East India Company, Sir Stamford Raffles was also a keen botanist. He founded Singapore's first Botanic Gardens, located on Fort Canning Hill just below his residence, in 1822, and the world's largest flower, *Rafflesia arnoldia*, was named after him and the botanist Dr Joseph Arnold after they discovered it in Sumatra. The great man was also responsible, while Governor General of Java, for the discovery of the temple complex of Borobodur.

A period of intense economic growth followed Raffles' arrival in Singapore, as the island was declared a free port and the first of the many land reclamation schemes that have made the island so prosperous was launched. He installed William Farquhar as the island's first Resident (administrator), and encouraged a stream of Chinese immigrants (men only—emigration was technically illegal from China in the first half of the 19th century), supplemented by Indian convict and indentured labourers to form the basic racial mix with the native Malays that still lasts today. The Chinese became half the population by 1827, and 65 per cent by 1860. Singapore became a centre for the East India Company's lucrative opium trade (somewhat ironic in view of today's harsh drug laws), and in 1826, along with Malacca and Penang, became one of the Company's Straits Settlements, very loosely controlled by the East India Company's headquarters in Calcutta. It soon outpaced its sister settlements in terms of growth, and the government of the Straits Settlements was located to Singapore in 1832 to reflect this.

The Straits Settlements, with their tariff-free status, proved a drain on the East India Company's resources, only becoming financially viable with the introduction in 1863 of a Stamp Act. The Company still did not object when the Straits Settlements were transferred to the British colonial administration in 1867 after merchants requested a further degree of control over the Malay hinterland, more costly and onerous than that provided by the Company. In nearby Malaya a system of administration by residents evolved, with British residents in protected states to keep an eye on trade matters while the local sultans continued to rule. British influence gradually extended to all the Malay states out of the Siamese sphere by 1895 and in 1895 a federation treaty linked Selangor, Pahang, Perak and Negri Sembilan under a British resident-general in Kuala Lumpur.

The Early 20th Century

Singapore continued to develop into an established colony and a governmental centre for the whole of Malaya, with the colonial government ruling over the three ethnic groups. In the 1900s Singapore became a centre of opposition to the imperial Manchu system in mainland China, opposed by a significant number of the colony's Chinese immigrants. Dr Sun Yat-Sen visited the island regularly on fundraising and consciousness-raising trips, as did Kway Yu-Wei. The local branch of the Kuomintang was founded in 1912 with Lim Boon Keng at its head, and funds from Singapore were spent on three abortive uprisings during the 1910s, before the successful uprising in 1912. (For further information on Dr Sun Yat-Sen and his villa, *see* page 198.)

Singapore remained a rich colony, scarcely affected by the First World War, except for a brief mutiny in 1915 by Indian sepoys, rapidly put down by a mixture of French, Japanese and Russian naval personnel then in the Singapore port, helped by a land force under the Sultan of Johor. The mutiny left 40 English dead, and numerous mutineers were subsequently executed, but scarcely affected the Chinese or Malay population of the island.

First World War Booty
The First World War led to the confiscation of the Teutonia Club by the British Custodian of Enemy Property: after the war the club was sold and subsequently became the Goodwood Park Hotel.

Between the wars Singapore largely escaped the ravages of the Great Depression, though rubber prices fell sharply during the 1930s. An almost artificial, charmed existence was led by the colonial administrators and traders in this period, pampered by servants and amusing themselves in the exclusively European clubs, and the rather giddy amusement parks, all described in the many novels written about this time.

The Second World War

The Second World War seemed in its early stages likely to be also remote to Singapore: indeed the port and the whole of Malaya profited from a staggering increase in demand for rubber.

Japanese troops under General Yamashita landed at 8 a.m. local time on 8 December 1941 at Kota Baru on the north-east coast of Malaya, and at two further beachheads further north in Thailand, Singora and Patani. (These landings were simultaneous with the attack on Pearl Harbour, the other side of the dateline.) The invasion force was spotted by intelligence reconnaissance planes on 6 December, and the British commander Sir Robert Brooke-Popham even had a plan—"Matador"—specifically designed to pre-empt such landings by reinforcing troop defences and airbase defences, a plan which was not implemented largely due to his indecision in those crucial hours of 6 and 7 December. Despite a valiant attempt at defending Kota Baru by the Indian garrison there, inflicting losses of one-third on the invaders with the help of British and Australian air bombing of their ships, Kota Baru was taken on 9 December and its nearby airbases shortly afterwards. Further north, General Yamashita rapidly concluded a safe passage agreement through Thailand and a three-pronged advance south through peninsular Malaya by a well-trained, well-equipped and highly motivated invasion force was rapidly under way.

By contrast, the troops defending Malaya and Singapore were an eclectic mixture of races, with limited training and uncertain chains of command. The different branches of the armed forces tussled together for power, with the air force in the pre-war build-up locating airbases with no prior discussion of their defence positions with the army; the navy depleted despite its new base on Singapore; and a string of commanders who leave a legacy of indecision and inadequacy for the tasks that faced them.

Bombs fell on Singapore that first night, 8 December, when the street lights remained on for the 2-hour duration of the attack. Two naval vessels, the battle cruiser *Repulse* and the battleship *Prince of Wales*, which arrived in Singapore on 4 December, set off along the east coast of Johor with no air cover, and were sighted and sunk on 10 December.

The Japanese advance through Malaya was rapid and efficient. Alor Star airbase on the north-west of the peninsular was abandoned by the British, leaving fuel and bombs which the advancing Japanese were to use against them that same day. Communications difficulties by the defending forces, led to continuing withdrawals southwards despite some successful ambushes and stands. Penang Island was evacuated on 16 December, and taken by the Japanese the following day; the battle of Slim River was won by the Japanese on 7 January 1942, and little more was to stop the Japanese advance into Johor, Singapore's final defence.

Sir Winston Churchill in London had a firm belief in the concept of "Fortress Singapore"—this in reality was a fallacy. What guns and defences there were in Singapore were to the south, since an attack by sea was feared. Furthermore, attempts by defence planners to build even elementary northern defences were dismissed by General Percival, GOC (General in Overall Command of the Allied forces), as "bad for morale". In the bunker at Fort Canning, the war cabinet pondered the likely location of

a Japanese landing, and allocated different troops to defend different parts of the island. The Allies crossed and then blew up the causeway linking Singapore and Johor on 31 January 1941; by 7 February Japanese troops were landing on the north-west coast of Singapore island, with a feint attack on Pulau Ubin to the north-east to confuse the defenders.

Valiant attempts were made by the mainly Australian defence forces to the west of the island to contain the Japanese, but again retreat became inevitable with inadequate communications. Fighting raged around Bukit Timah village, and on 14 February MacRitchie Reservoir, the last water source, was captured by the Japanese. Food reserves were already low, both for the defenders and for the Japanese, when on 15 February 1942 General Percival led the British delegation to the Ford Factory on Bukit Timah road and accepted the Japanese commander Yamashita's demand for an unconditional surrender.

All the British who had not managed to board the last ships before the surrender were rounded up and put in jail, many of the POWs subsequently being used on the notorious Burma Railway in Thailand. For the resident Chinese the Japanese occupation was in many ways worse: all were asked to assemble, their identity cards were checked, and many thousands simply disappeared, presumed murdered, because they may have been sympathizers with the 1936 Manchurian opposition to the Japanese advance. During the rest of the war the island was renamed Syonan, light of the south.

Lee Kuan Yew and the People's Action Party (PAP)

Singapore's success story is to a large extent due to the efforts of two great men: Sir Stamford Raffles in the 19th century, and Lee Kuan Yew, prime minister for the first 25 years of independence in the 20th.

Lee Kuan Yew was born in 1923, the eldest son of Lee Chin Koon, a Shell Company employee who subsequently ran a watch and jewellery shop, and Chua Jim Neo, a famed cookery author and teacher. Educated at a small Chinese kindergarten, the Telok Kurau English School and then the Raffles Institution, "Harry", as he was then called, was due to go to Cambridge University when war broke out in 1939. He studied economics, mathematics and English Literature at Singapore's Raffles College instead, learning Japanese and translating for the official news agency at the same time as working as a medical orderly. The wartime occupation of Singapore brought nationalism to many in Singapore, including Lee, who recounted on one occasion how narrowly he missed being herded into one of the lorries of Chinese who simply disappeared during the Operation Sook Ching in 1942.

In September 1946 Lee Kuan Yew travelled to London on the troopship *Britannia*, where he studied for one term at the London School of Economics, before moving to Cambridge University, where his sweetheart, Kwa Geok Choo,who has been his wife since 1950, had been awarded a scholarship. Both students gained double firsts in law, setting up the law firm Lee & Lee shortly after their return to Singapore in 1950, whence the young Lee made his reputation as a trade union lawyer. The

Lees have three children: Lee Hsien Loong, born in 1952; Lee Wei Ling, born 1955; and Lee Hsien Yang, born 1957. Brigadier-General (Res) Lee Hsien Loong is now the Deputy Prime Minister and Minister for Industry, a prominent figure within Goh Chok Tong's cabinet.

While in England, Lee Kuan Yew, along with Goh Keng Swee and Toh Chin Chye, joined the Malayan Forum, a grouping striving to gain independence from colonial rule for Singapore and Malaya. Back in Singapore, the first tentative steps towards independence were being made, with six of the 22 seats on the Legislative Council being directly elected in 1948 and then, under the Rendel Constitution of 1959, 25 of the 32 members of the Legislative Assembly, being directly elected.

These first steps towards independence led to the formation of several political parties: the Malayan Democratic Union was founded in December 1945, collaborating with the existing Malayan Communist Party (MCP) until its armed revolt began in 1948; the Singapore Progressive Party was founded in August 1947, a multi-racial party with support from Britain opposing the immediate union of Singapore and Malaya; the Labour Party was founded in September 1948; the Progressive Party merged with the Democratic Party, a small party founded by wealthy Chinese individuals, to become the Liberal Socialist Party; then this in turn merged with the Labour Front to become the Singapore People's Alliance. On 21 November 1954 the People's Action Party was founded by the young lawyer Lee Kuan Yew, the LSE economist and civil servant Goh Keng Swee, academic Dr Toh Chin Chye and journalist S. Rajaratnam. Its manifesto called for union with Malaya and an end to colonial rule, and much of its appeal was to organized labour and to Chinese students, a heavily left-wing and communist-leaning body of opinion.

After the election in 1955, when the PAP took three seats, David Marshall, leader of the Labour Front, became the Chief Minister, though he resigned following his lack of success in London to negotiate further steps towards independence. He was replaced by Lim Yew Hock, also from the Labour Front, who led a second delegation from Singapore to London during 1957. Lee Kuan Yew was part of both negotiating teams and gained a reputation for forceful speaking and a wide platform on which to air his views on these missions. In 1957 Singapore was allowed a fully elected assembly of 51 members, though one with no authority over external matters or internal security.

During 1955 the Hock Lee bus strike was exacerbated by alleged communist infiltrators; the following year the Chinese High School students' lockout was similarly influenced; and during 1957 left-wing extremists within the PAP

seemed to be gaining control of the party, until Lim Yew Hock's government conveniently arrested several leaders in August. The year 1957 has since been recognized as one of the riskiest times for the survival of the PAP and hence, in a sense, a turning point for Singapore's development.

The PAP won a landslide victory on 5 June 1959, with 43 out of 51 seats in Parliament and 51 per cent of the vote. Thirteen parties had contested the election, and the PAP's victory was largely due to the extreme left-wing elements within it calling for an end to colonialism. At the age of 35 Lee Kuan Yew became the first Prime Minister of Singapore, insisting on the release of eight colleagues of his detained in 1957 before he agreed to take office, but depriving them of any real power within his PAP once they were released. In 1960 came a split with a former colleague and former colleague and

PAP party faithfuls forming the PAP logo at the National Day rally.

Minister for National Development, Ong Eng Guan, who criticized Lee Kuan Yew's progress towards full independence and was promptly fired. Representing the newly formed United People's Party, Ong Eng Guan gained a landslide victory over the PAP candidate in the Hong Lim constituency in a by-election in 1961. David Marshall, then of the Workers Party, was elected in another by election at Anson at the same time. Also in 1961, in July the Barisan Socialis Party was founded by Lee Siew Choh and Lim Chin Siong, the latter one of the eight detainees released in 1959: in one step this party took approximately 70 per cent of the rank and file away from the PAP, and its formation as a separate organization from the PAP clarified its overtly communist stance.

Analysts such as T.J.S. George suggest that Lee used and exaggerated the very real threat of Singapore falling communist and becoming a mini Cuba at the foot of Malaya as a tool with which to negotiate Singapore's union with Malaya, and certainly the

Election campaign posters for the PAP in a contested single-member constituency in 1991. The Singapore flags are displayed on the balconies behind as part of the locality's National Day celebrations.

menace of the island falling under extremist influence was a factor in both Britain's and Malaya's attitudes to decolonization. A referendum held on 1 September 1962 on the type of merger with Malaya was won convincingly with 71 per cent by the PAP: a total defeat for the Barisan Socialis. The 1963 elections were a victory for the non-communist, pro-union with Malaya PAP, who won 47 per cent of the vote with 37 seats; the Barisan Socialis won 13 seats and 32.1 per cent, the United People's Party one seat and 8.3 per cent (both the latter parties did not favour merger with Malaya).

With the Indonesian *Konfrontasi* campaign came a sweep-up operation known as Operation Cold Store in late 1963: 15 Barisan Socialis members were arrested, including Lim Chin

Siong, who was imprisoned in Changi Prison for 7 years, and Said Zahari, only released on to Pulau Ubin in 1978 and fully released in 1979.

Along with the arrest of prominent pro-communist Barisan Socialis members, 1961–63 also saw the taming of the unions, changing from the violent strikes of the late 1950s to a system of docile labour relations. The Singapore Association of Trades Unions, thought by the PAP to be infiltrated by communists, was gradually pulled under the controlling umbrella of the, National Trades Union Congress (NTUC), whose secretary Devan Nair worked at rooting out such infiltration. In August 1963 seven unions whose funds were believed to be used for political activites were deregulated, effectively removing one further communist platform in Singapore.

Singapore's union with Malaya in 1963 and the subsequent separation two years later are covered on page 51). In the fully independent republic, the PAP won all 58 seats in the 1968 election and all 65 seats in the 1970 election. Barisan Socialis started to boycott Parliament in 1966 after separation from Malaysia, effectively depriving itself of a voice. From then on, indeed from Singapore's separation from Malaysia, the country's history has been closely tied to that of the PAP and its leader, Lee Kuan Yew: only twice, in 1957 and in 1961, was there a danger of the country following a different course.

And what of Singapore's, and indeed the world's, longest-serving Prime Minister and the qualities which guided him and the PAP through the difficult formative years to today's economic miracle? According to his former Press Aide and semi-official biographer, Alex Josey, Lee totally abhors the cult of personality, although in many ways he is venerated and respected as an almost god-like figure, with modern Singapore's economic achievements seen by many as almost solely due to the PAP and its leader. His family life remains private and important to him, his house hidden along Oxley Rise which is now a residents-only street, closed to through traffic. In his private life he keeps fit, plays good golf, drinks and eats in moderation. Lee is highly intelligent, unable to suffer fools, and prepared to push himself hard to achieve his goals and expecting the same doggedness from others. Speaking Cantonese, as well as English and Malay as a child, in 1954 Lee Kuan Yew (literally "The light that shines far and wide") taught himself Mandarin in order to communicate with his electorate; in 1961 he also learned Hokkien for the same reason. He places a high emphasis on education and its values, a Chinese trait, which is noticeable in the Singapore press today.

Self-confident and convinced of his own long-term vision for Singapore, his ambition has at times seemed almost ruthless, certainly pragmatic as when he used the dangerous forces of Communism in order to achieve independence and was then able to imprison and tame communist leaders. His attitude to power is Confucian: one should respect and obey it, rather than question its validity. Critics such as T. S. Selvan write of a climate of fear, not so much of the Internal Security Act as of potential hindrance to career paths, inability to obtain necessary licences for opponents of the PAP. Whatever your opinion of some of the methods, it remains extremely doubtful whether anyone else could have achieved so much, turning a small rejected island with no economic hinterland and a tiny domestic market into the world's busiest port and a South-East Asian success story.

The Post-War Period

With the peace of August 1945 came increasing demands for independence Far from an almighty force, the British colonial masters had been seen to be defeated, and also had been seen to save their own people—principally women and children evacuated on the last ships—while doing little to help the Asian population. At the forefront of these demands was Lee Kuan Yew, an able English-educated lawyer building up a small but significant practice working with union and labour claims (*see* pages 46–48). Singapore was made a separate Crown Colony in 1946, separated for the first time from Penang and Malacca, both of which were to become part of the Federation of Malaya in 1948. Singapore had its own Governor, though elections were allowed in the Legislative Council. Certain levels of autonomy were allowed, and the British Government became increasingly encouraging on this front.

However, during this period, those communists who had fought the Japanese in the Malayan jungles alongside the British and the secret Force 136 launched a campaign known as "the Emergency" in the jungles, using the British ammunition against their colonial "oppressors" once the war had ended in order to gain control of the country. Within Singapore and the main towns of Malaya, the communists were believed to have infiltrated trades unions, religious organizations, and educational organizations in order to spread their message. The "Emergency" lasted for 12 years, 1948–1960, years of guerrilla campaigning, with brutality meted out by the guerillas to non-collaborators, and a concentration-camp treatment of local villagers conducted by the British forces. The bulk of the communist leaders were Chinese, indeed their inspiration came from mainland China, which was possibly a major reason for Communism's failure in Malaya, where the bulk of the population was Malay, keen to end British colonial rule but not at the cost of Chinese communist rule.

> **A Play on Words**
> This period of insurrection and guerrilla activity was known throughout as "the Emergency" in order to circumvent insurers' attempts to avoid compensating those Malayan planters who lost property during this time. Had the period been acknowledged as an "insurrection" or even a "civil war" or "period of civil unrest", insurance companies could have pleaded *force majeure*.

The Emergency was still continuing in 1955, when the Rendel Constitution presented Singapore with a first step towards independence with an opportunity to elect a Legislative Assembly headed by a Council of Nine Ministers, under a Chief Minister and responsible for all except defence, internal security and external affairs. New political parties and alliances flourished—the People's Action Party being founded in November 1954—and the election was won by David Marshall's Labour Front. The Marshall Government lasted a year, a time of increasing riots, the growth of communist sympathy, and frustratingly slow talks in London on full self-government. Marshall was succeeded by his deputy, Lim Yew Hock, who presided over further riots and communist propaganda campaigns, as well as seeing through a Constitutional Agreement signed in London in 1958.

Under this agreement, Singapore gained internal self-government, and in the subsequent general election Lee Kuan Yew's PAP won a large majority in the 1959 Legislative Assembly. Unlike David Marshall, Lee Kuan Yew's statecraft led him to ally first with the communist element in politics in the first thrust of anti-colonialism, though he was to turn and stab them fiercely in the back during a round-up operation in February 1963.

The independence envisaged by Lee Kuan Yew and most other politicians at that time entailed union with what is now Malaysia, then Malaya. The then leader of Malaya, Tunku (literally "your highness") Abdul Rahman, was amenable to this, wanting a share in Singapore's wealth and to avoid a left-wing Singapore sitting like a mini Cuba between Mainland West Malaysia and its Borneo territories, then planned to include Brunei, as well as Sarawak and Sabah. Lee Kuan Yew benefited from the Tunku's fear of Communism—indeed, according to T. J. S. George he largely manufactured the communist threat—in order to ensure that Singapore could take its place within Malaysia. Talks began in 1961 between Lee Kuan Yew and Tunku Abdul Rahman, reaching broad agreement in September and ratified by a referendum in Singapore in September 1962. As a first step, Malaysia was inaugurated in September 1963, though without Brunei, and causing Indonesia to adopt a policy of Konfrontasi, terrorist acts in Malaysia,

including Singapore, in opposition to the new Malaysian dominance in the region. The Konfrontasi campaign lasted until June 1966.

After Malaysian independence, differences between the PAP and the Malay leadership became increasingly obvious. Two years further on, and Singaporeans saw their leader, Lee Kuan Yew, reduced to tears after long talks with the Tunku, and a tiny nation launched itself alone on the hard road to independence. The split with Malaysia had, largely, been on racial grounds: Malaysia then as now was largely run by members of the United Malay National Organization, UMNO, who saw the advancement of Malay bumiputra—literally, sons of the soil, i.e. ethnic Malay race people—as a goal of government. Singapore's success had largely been built on the efforts of the industrious Chinese races, mainly Hokkien, with no special favours granted to any race (other than to the British colonials). To share its hard-earned wealth with less industrious people was seen in Singapore as penalizing the successful, and against this background race riots quickly whipped through Singapore in 1964.

The new independent nation that was to emerge and survive this cataclysmic birth process presided over a rapid period of industrialization, a massive rehousing programme, encouraged multinational companies to set up and work from Singapore, and built up a defence force from scratch in place of the British force which was withdrawn in the late 1960s. The economic miracle is outlined on page 56, and the political scene today on pages

59–61. Nowadays Singapore still shows the influence of its dramatic rise to independence: even despite the disbanding of the Communist Party of Malaya in 1989 with its avowed intent of reuniting Singapore and Malaysia, and the Communist leader of pre-independence days, Fang Chuang Pi (known as the "Plen" by Lee Kuan Yew) now living in exile in Thailand and openly renouncing any idea of challenging Singapore's sovereignty, Communism remains a feared and severely punishable belief system; while the continuous stress on Singapore's multi-cultural society, coupled with the many regulations to prevent proselytizing religions, offensive films and such like, stem largely from a fear of upsetting sensitive racial groups. In 1990 the nation celebrated its first 25 years of independence with gusto, and the man who had led the way stepped down to make way for his successor, Mr Goh Chok Tong.

*T*he statue of Sir Stamford Raffles, at the spot along the Singapore River where he is believed to have landed.

Economy

Singapore's great potential as a natural crossroads on trade routes through the Straits of Malacca on to China and Hong Kong was recognized by Sir Stamford Raffles in the early 19th century. His analysis holds good for today's shipping and airline trade and the island remains a highly profitable midway station.

19th-Century Trade

The small settlement of 150 families Sir Stamford Raffles found in 1819 were mainly employed in fishing and associated small agricultural pursuits. Some of the 30 or so Chinese were also involved in small pepper and gambier plantations, using the gambier in dyeing and tanning processes, and its nutritious waste to fertilize the demanding pepper crop.

The island's potential, then as now, was largely due to its strategic position at the bottom of the Straits of Malacca, a staging post on the highly profitable trade routes with China and the Moluccas or Spice Islands (now Maluku). With Raffles' declaration that Singapore be a free port, existing trade which had previously paid high impositions and tariffs to the Riau islands swiftly relocated to Singapore.

Trade routes in the early 1800s, indeed until the invention of the steamship, were largely seasonal, depending on the directions of the fierce monsoon winds for their passage. Thus Bugis traders in their small *prahus* (narrow flat bottomed boats, 10–15 m (33–49 ft) long with two pairs of oars as well as rectangular sails) from what was then Macassar in the Celebes (now Sulawesi) would arrive from south of the Equator in September or October on the south-east monsoon winds, returning with the onset of the north-west monsoon in November. Conversely junks from China and Siam (Thailand) would use the north-west monsoon winds to bring them to Singapore between December and February, returning on the south-east monsoon winds from April to May. Between May and November small boats—*prahus* or *sampans* (smaller flat-bottomed boats 6–10 m (20–33 ft) long, generally with a pair of eyes painted on the front)—would arrive with cargoes from Borneo, Java and Sumatra, while the larger Indiamen or square-rigged ships of European design would ply the route between Calcutta and Singapore year round.

Early entrepreneurs and merchants seized trading opportunities along the Singapore river: the Hokkien Tan Tock Seng traded along Boat Quay, while Seah Eu Chin, the Teochew "gambier king" also diversified into trade along the river, as did the Cantonese businessman Hoo Ah Kay, known as Whampoa. British agencies and individuals such as Alexander Guthrie and William Paterson arrived and established trading networks and business empires further upstream, and

Arab traders were encouraged to stop in Singapore with their wares, materials and luxury goods.

The infrastructure to cope with the increasing trade was developed as needed. Warehouses or *godowns* sprang up along the Singapore River where so many boats brought their wares. The first Singapore Chamber of Commerce was founded in 1837 to combat a threat by the East India

Early Traded Goods

The cargoes and commodities were an exotic but profitable bunch. From Sulawesi came *sarongs*, gold dust, beeswax, edible birds' nests, agar-agar, ebony, camphor, ivory, coffee, rice, tortoiseshell, mother-of-pearl, rattan, sandalwood, benjamin, gutta-percha, birds of paradise and parrots. These were exchanged for cargoes of opium, salt, tobacco, firearms, ironware, manufactured goods and Manchester cotton. Boats stopping at Sarawak brought antimony and sago, while those from Java, Sumatra and the rest of Borneo brought pepper, nutmeg, cloves, rhinoceros horn, cinnamon, coriander, rattan, batik and camphor. Return trade was again firearms and British manufactured goods, as well as Indian textiles and raw silk. From China came immigrants, tea, piece goods, nankins, sugar candy, china, copperware, gold and silver threads, which were traded for opium, tin, betel nuts, pepper, birds' nests, British cotton fabrics and emigrants' letters and remittances.

Linking the South-East Asian leg of the East India Company's empire with its base in Calcutta, large Indiamen ships like the Cutty Sark would bring silk, cotton, opium, saltpetre and piece goods from India, returning from Singapore with sago, gold dust and gambier.

Company's head office in Calcutta to impose duties on Singapore trade, and groups of Chinese merchants clubbed together to purchase four armed ships to fight the ever-present piracy threat, shaming the Company into funding a further two armed ships. The first reliable banks were operating by the 1860s. Trade expanded to employ 43 merchant houses in Singapore by 1846—20 British companies, 6 Jewish, 5 Chinese, 5 Arab, 2 Armenian, 2 German, 1 Portuguese, 1 American and 1 Parsee. By 1867 there were over 60 European trading companies, with trade four times that of 1823–4, amounting to $58,944,141.

Singapore was fortunate to survive the 1840s and 50s, when rival companies could have opened up other ports in the region to offer similar free-trade benefits. Hong Kong, ceded to the British after the first Opium War (1839–42) was a very real potential rival in this respect, though in the event Singapore benefited and profited from being Britain's forward base in the war. She similarly profited from the Australian Gold Rush of the 1850s.

The invention of the steamship in 1845 revolutionized shipping times and lessened the dependence on monsoon winds of much of Singapore's trade as the *prahus* and junks were replaced by steamships. A new port was built to accommodate these larger ships, with work starting in 1855 and the Tanjong Pagar Dock Company being founded in 1864. By the time Singapore became a Crown Colony in 1867 it was the East India Company's second busiest port after Calcutta. The opening of the Suez Canal in 1869 turned the Straits of Malacca into an even more important world waterway. A complicated land reclamation scheme of the Telok Ayer basin was launched in the 1880s to improve the route between the harbour and town.

19th-Century Agriculture

Agriculture was considerably less successful for Singapore than its flourishing trade, entailing expensive and dangerous jungle clearance—tigers remained a menace to planters throughout the 19th century—and then the chances of crop, weather and world prices. Gambier plantations did meet with some success, though by 1848 the number of plantations had increased to 600, causing prices to fall and profits to slump. After the mid-1850s gambier planting was relocated to Johor, the soil on most estates having become exhausted. Nutmeg was popular during the 1850s, partly as a result of Raffles' wish to turn Singapore into an orchard of spices and fruits—plantations stretched along the east side of today's Orchard Road, as well as within the Tanjong Pagar district—though a blight in the 1860s destroyed many of these. Sugar and cotton plantations in Singapore proved financially disastrous, and even coffee was no particular success in Singapore, though more so in peninsular Malaya.

Rubber was a major breakthrough in the late 1880s, when a crash in

> **Plantations to Plazas**
> Today's main shopping street, Orchard Road, is so called because there used to be nutmeg plantations to its east and orange groves in what is now Orange Grove Road. Other plantations of sugar cane proved less successful.

world coffee prices threatened the livelihoods of many Malayan planters. Henry Ridley, director of the Botanic Gardens, developed a technique for tapping rubber or latex from rubber trees and sold seeds to doubtful planters in the 1890s. Rubber took off as a crop with the invention of the rubber tyre in the 1900s, and demand for it grew with both world wars.

Other cash crops encouraged initially by Henry Ridley were oil palm—for soap and cooking—and cocoa. Gutta-percha, used for moulding knife and dagger (*kris*) handles for Malays, as well as for riding whips, goloshes, golf balls, and even insulating electric wires, proved another popular crop. Indian labourers and immigrants introduced cattle- and buffalo-rearing to

A small-scale farm on the island of Pulau Ubin. Very few small-scale agricultural enterprises remain in Singapore today.

the Serangoon Road area in the 1880s, and smallholdings in rural areas set up chicken and pig farms to cater for local demand. Fishing remained an important source of food.

19th-Century Mining
Tin, mined in Singapore at Bukit Timah (literally "tin ore hill"), and further in peninsular Malaya, became an important commodity after the 1860s when the food canning process was developed. The Straits Trading Company's first tin smelting plant was founded in Perak in 1885, the first in Singapore in 1890.

The Early 20th Century
The demand for both tin and rubber continued to expand in the 20th century, with the first motor cars, which reached Singapore in 1896, increasing home demand for inflatable tyres. In 1905, 432 tons of rubber were exported and 8,792 tons in 1911, with many of the *godowns* along the Singapore River full of rubber awaiting shipment. The

Borneo Wharf of the grocery chain Cold Storage opened in 1905, the railway station opened in 1906, and the Singapore Harbour Board was formed in 1912 to oversee continually expanding port activity.

The First World War in Europe served merely to increase demand for Singapore's tin and rubber, so the colony experienced something of a boom during those years and this continued until a fall in rubber prices in the early 1930s. The causeway linking Singapore with Johor was built in 1923, another infrastructure link to speed up the transport of goods. With the build-up towards the Second World War, Britain completed its naval base on Singapore in 1938; with the outbreak of hostilities, rubber and tin were once more in demand and the economy flourished until the Japanese Occupation in 1942.

Post-War Economic Growth

Singapore's post-war economic expansion and success is closely tied into the People's Action Party's planning and investment.

In 1965 the prime minister of the newly independent state embarked on a deliberate policy of plugging the nation into the global economy, encouraging foreign investment, skills and technology transfers to increase markets, jobs and industrial management skills. He also continued the free-trade policy started by Raffles in 1819 to ensure competitive prices. In the 1960s and 70s he encouraged multinational companies to benefit from the republic's cheap and responsible labour. Labour relations have rarely been a problem in independent Singapore,

since the NTUC—National Trades Union Congress—is effectively a branch of government, and workers and government join together at May Day rallies to aim for higher productivity in order to generate more wealth.

An ambitious housing programme was launched in 1960 with the formation of the Housing and Development Board (*see* page 214), which constructed 51,000 housing units in its first five-year plan. The fledgling country survived the potential bombshell of the British withdrawal of all their forces from Singapore in 1967—which had accounted for 15 per cent of the postwar economy and generated about 40,000 jobs—by a consequent period of national military service. The Jurong Town Corporation was founded in 1968, the Development Bank of Singapore in the same year, and the swampy area of Jurong to the west of the island was turned into the main industrial base. Manufacturing industry was encouraged and introduced to reduce the island's dependence on international trade.

The 1985 recession affected Singapore, which lost some of its competitiveness to local rivals. Now that other countries in the region can offer lower labour costs, Singapore concentrates on middle-management skills and training, in order to be able to offer foreign investors reliability and a safe return on investment.

Singapore's Economy in the 1990s

Today's economy shows high rates of growth, well outpacing many Western economies. A buoyant investment in infrastructure by the government, combined with harnessing the Chinese work ethic to a national goal, led in 1989 to a growth rate of 9.2 per cent.

Industrial production in Singapore today consists of electronics, computers, appliances, fabricated metal products, transport equipment (including ship-building and overhaul facilities), telecommunications equipment, machinery, petroleum products, industrial chemicals, gas, paints, pharmaceutical, and other chemical industries. Research continues into the latest manufacturing methods and computerization, as Singapore strives to maintain its leading position in South-East Asia.

Singapore is the third largest oil refining centre in the world, despite being a 100 per cent importer of crude oil. Offshore oil refining accounts for a high proportion of export earnings: oil exports in the first quarter of 1991 grew by 31 per cent, to total $5.24 billion. Chemical plants are already sited on the southern islands, and a nylon products facility is currently being researched to further diversification. Everywhere you can see evidence of the construction industry's 11 per cent growth in the first quarter of 1991, from roads and infrastructure to Singapore's apparently insatiable demand for shopping centres, food outlets and luxury condominium developments.

Tourism is a growth industry that Singapore is keen to encourage, with trade missions regularly visiting new tourist markets such as Korea and Scandinavia in order to promote the country's myriad attractions. Not least among these are the endless shopping opportunities for photographic and computer equipment, clothing, and other duty-free items.

Singapore's Port is now thought to be the biggest in the world in terms of cargo tonnage: the Tanjong Pagar container terminal, recently recognized as the world's number one in terms of tonnage was moving 5.22 million containers or TEUs (twenty-foot equivalent units) in 1990 and plans to move 6 million by 1992. Jurong Port handled 25.8 million freight tonnes in 1990, a 12 per cent increase over the previous year. At any time there are over 600 ships in port, with 700 different lines servicing 80 countries using the 24-hour facilities. About 38,900 ships call at the Port of Singapore every year, so that on average a ship arrives or departs every 7 minutes.

Property prices in the central city district are now over $86,000 per square metre. As ever, the government is determined not to rest on its laurels, but is already planning for future growth of port and trade facilities, with a new container port newly opened up on Pulau Brani in early 1992 and plans for a total of five main and four feeder berths, able to handle 3.8 TEUs.

Changi Airport, with its recently opened Terminal 2, already has plans for Terminal 3, again in order to keep ahead of rival Bangkok as the main regional gateway; its efficiency and comparatively low departure and servicing taxes are designed to attract stopovers from worldwide destinations. Changi today handles more than 1,900 flights from 53 airlines to and from 109 cities in 55 countries each week, and aims to improve the turn around time for passengers from landing to walking out after baggage reclaim to an average of 12 minutes. It currently handles 12 million passengers a year, and hopes to increase this to 26 million by 1995.

Singapore's financial earnings, through banking, investment, and stock exchange activities, continue to flourish. Financial and business services overtook manufacturing as the leading sector of the economy in 1989. Singapore has 377,000 share investors, of which two-thirds are Singaporean individuals.

On the agricultural front, Singapore is, as ever, hi-tech. Today hydroponic farming—growing lettuces and the like without soil, with careful layering and fertilizing—is being expanded and encouraged, using less land area than traditional farming methods. Orchid farming, likewise, is encouraged for both export and local markets. Most of the old pig farms, located in the villages to the north and north-west of the island, have now been closed down for hygiene reasons, while former plantations have either reverted to *belukar*—secondary forest—or have been developed into new housing and industrial areas. Traditional fishing continues, with large wet markets at Ponggol and at Jurong, and *kelongs* (fish traps on stilts over the sea) still dotted along the north and west coasts. Tropical fish breeding is also increasing. There is thorough regulation of standards in fishing and in agriculture, and all imports are checked for hygiene and freshness before entering the country. The 1990 census showed only 4,400 citizens engaged in the farming and fishing industries.

Crucial to the whole success story is Singapore's major resource—its workforce. Around 1.26 million people work in the Republic, with an average monthly wage of $764 in 1990, with 65 per cent having an income level below $1,000 per week. Its people generally work a 5½ day week, and are forced to save one-third of earnings in the Central Provident Fund for pensions, education, healthcare and housing, so that Singapore has so far escaped inflationary calamities. Roughly 50 per cent of women work, helped by government schemes and encouragement of childcare centres, and by the cheap availability of foreign maids to care for children. Unions are in effect government-backed organizations, and strive to increase productivity as well as to organize leisure outings, sports facilities and even holiday resorts for workers—their role is not that of increasing workers' rights or pay deals. Productivity grew on average 4.6 per cent a year during the 1980s. Output per worker in the manufacturing sector has increased from $25,000 in 1980 to $41,000 in 1990; in the business and finance sector the increase is from $68,000 per worker in 1980 to $127,000 in 1990. A gradual upgrading of the workforce is taking place, with roughly one in four workers currently holding a professional, technical, administrative or managerial job.

Singapore's aim is to be a developed economy by the end of the 1990s, from being a developing country in 1965 and a newly industrializing economy in 1989. Its government-backed infrastructure and economic planning, worker productivity and social stability are thought to be the key to a sympathetic business environment where initiative thrives, and where it is hoped there will be future economic growth and success.

Politics and Government

Much of Singapore's political and legal structure is based on the system of its former colonial power, Britain, though this works in subtly different ways and has been adapted over the years to Singapore's needs as an independent republic. Politics as such is not a major topic of interest: different points of view are not analysed and probed in the way this happens in Western countries. Instead the same party has held a strong majority since independence in 1965, with the change over of power from Prime Minister Lee Kuan Yew taking place in November 1990.

The Legislature and Machinery of Government

With a legislative structure based on the pre-existing British one, Singapore has a unicameral Parliament, which is elected at least every 5 years from the date of its first sitting, by every citizen over 21 years of age. The prime minister decides when to call an election, and then he dissolves Parliament. In 1991 an election was called on 14 August to be held on 31 August, just over the bare minimum of 14 days' notice. Voting in general elections is compulsory. Like the United Kingdom, on which model much of the machinery of government is based, the electoral system is run on a first-past-the-post basis. There are 81 seats, representing 36 electoral divisions, 21 of which are single-member constituencies, and the remaining 15 group-representation constituencies (GRCs), each electing four MPs, one of whom must by law

The view across the causeway which links Singapore to Johor Baru in Malaysia.

An integral part of future economic growth plans is the Economic Growth Triangle between Singapore and its neighbours Johor (in Malaysia) and Batam (in Indonesia). An integrated economic expansion programme to include tourist facilities and light and heavy industry is planned, with Singapore's financial and managerial skills combined with its hinterland's land and cheap labour resources, an ambitious plan intended to bring growth to all three participants.

represent a minority—Malay, Indian or Eurasian. For these GRCs each party fields a whole ticket of four candidates: constituents may not vote for individuals from different parties.

In the event of no opposition members being elected, a mechanism called the non-constituency MP (NCMP) may come into effect, whereby the opposition member who gained the highest number of votes without winning a constituency is returned to Parliament. The number of NCMPs was to be increased to four, as a means for the opposition parties to gain access to Parliament, though the whole mechanism is currently under review since the opposition parties gained more seats than expected at the 1991 election.

Parliament sits sporadically when debate is needed, with no scheduled dates, and is open to the public. Debate is conducted in any of the four national languages—English, Mandarin, Tamil and Malay—with simultaneous translation provided to MPs. A Speaker is elected by Parliament, along with two Deputy Speakers, to conduct the debates.

The Prime Minister, who is appointed by the President, selects his Cabinet of Ministers who administer the country and provide Parliament with policy decisions to debate. Singapore's first Prime Minister, from independence in 1965 until November 1990, was Mr Lee Kuan Yew. He remains as Senior Minister in the current Prime Minister, Mr Goh Chok Tong's Cabinet. The President has until now been elected every 4 years by Parliament; a change of legislation now allows for an Elected President, with a wider franchise of Singaporeans allowed to vote, though the exact electorate has not, at the time of writing, been clarified. The Elected President cannot belong to any political party, must be of integrity and good character, and holds office for 6 years. Singapore's past Presidents have been Yusof bin Ishak, Dr Benjamin Henry Sheares, Mr Chengara Veetil Devan Nair and the current President Mr Wee Kim Wee.

The Opposition

The People's Action Party (PAP) has won every election since 1965; it won the most recent (1991) with 61 per cent of the vote. At the time of writing (1991), there are four opposition MPs. Mr Chiam See Tong, MP for Potong Pasir, is chairman of the Singapore Democratic Party; the SDP also has MPs for Bukit Batok and Nee Soon constituencies; while the Workers Party has an MP in Hougang. In 1981 there was another, indeed the first opposition MP to be elected for 15 years: Mr J. B. Jeyeratnam, an eloquent lawyer and the leader of the Workers Party, won the Anson by-election and took his seat in Parliament. However, Mr Jeyeratnam was subsequently investigated for tax irregularities, struck off the Singapore legal roll and concurrently a Constitutional Amendment was passed requiring MPs to lose their seats if jailed for a year or more or fined $2,000 or more. J. B., as he is known, lost his case in Singapore, but took it to the then ultimate appeal court (*see* page 61) the Judicial Committee of the Privy Council of the United Kingdom, who found him not guilty—but then another Constitutional Amendment held the Privy

Council to have no jurisdiction over the Law Society of Singapore or over Internal Security Act provisions—so he wasn't able to resume his seat. He has subsequently been virtually bankrupted through losing a libel action on a totally unconnected matter against Lee Kuan Yew, and was banned from standing for election until 10 November 1991.

Under that selfsame Internal Security Act, a relic of colonial British times when the Communist Emergency was in operation, Singapore's best-known detainee Chia Thye Poh was held in prison from October 1966 until May 1989. He is now "released" on Sentosa Island, but has to have permission to visit the mainland and cannot sleep there. Mr Chia was never tried—it is not required under the Act—but the government has consistently stated that if he admits he was a communist and renounces the armed struggle he will be freed. Mr Chia does not admit he ever was a communist, so sees no reason to do so. Not surprisingly, Western human rights groups such as Asia Watch point to such a case in their condemnation of Singapore.

The Judiciary and Legal System

Singapore's legal system is based on that of Great Britain—not perhaps all that surprisingly, with the country's main spokesman an English-trained lawyer. There is a Supreme Court, which comprises a High Court, a Court of Appeal and a Court of Criminal Appeal, and then Subordinate Courts. The President appoints the Chief Justice and other judges on the advice of the Prime Minister. The final appellate court is the Privy Council in London. There is the death penalty for drug trafficking and serious criminal convictions, and corporal punishment is also used.

Nation Building

Singapore as a nation has been in existence for a short but highly successful 25 years, and it is the government's aim to ensure it continues to flourish. The compulsory 2 years' national service for all males over 18 is part of this process, as well as a necessary deterrent from external threat.

As part of this process, the government has tried to develop a national ideology of five shared values for Singaporeans: the nation before community, and society above self; the family as the basic unit of society; community support and respect for the individual; consensus not conflict; and racial and religious harmony. These were greeted with publicity when

> **Defence Matters**
>
> Singapore is fiercely proud of its independence, and of the deterrent effect of its armed forces, despite being such a small nation. National service is obligatory for all Singapore-born and permanent resident males over 18, for an initial period of 2 years, followed by regular reservist training throughout working life. Military installations line the west and north coasts (those coasts where the Japanese invasion took place in 1941); it is quite normal to see air-force planes on training missions throughout the island; and several of the large expressways are designed so that they could, in an emergency, become additional air-force runways.

Colourful Campaigns

The government runs a number of campaigns to increase awareness of its citizens. In the past these have included courtesy campaigns, campaigns to stop spitting, stop smoking, prevent litter, decrease family size, increase family size if you can afford it, and, more recently, as elsewhere in the world, anti-Aids campaigns.

announced in 1991—it is unclear quite how they will be implemented.

There are more obvious government campaigns periodically—on courtesy, not littering, speaking Mandarin rather than dialect Chinese, not smoking, toilet hygiene (i.e. flushing) and on ideal family size. The fledgling Singapore embarked on a strict policy of birth control, but today's republic is keen to increase its labour force to keep its winning economic edge. It is particularly keen for graduates to marry and produce more than two children if they can afford it, hoping that the collective gene pool of two graduates will ensure brain power for future generations. As part of this process, the government-sponsored Social Development Unit (SDU) currently has over 10,000 single members, each of whom is allowed up to 90 "tries" over 5 years, at a series of social functions, business lunches and other meeting opportunities.

Within the debate on nationhood, suggestions have recently been raised about dual nationality for Singaporeans who marry foreigners. National institutions have been built to survive and serve the country, but the slightly controversial Minister for the Arts, BG (Res) George Yeo, a sort of unofficial government spokesman closely involved in the government's forward strategic planning, has recently spoken out against allowing government institutions too much control, since this will quash any attempts to develop smaller-scale civic society. Much publicity has surrounded recent town council changes, allowing the people more say in their own affairs—though it is not clear how ready people are to take on the running of these themselves. BG Yeo also recently stated "We must separate commitment to Singapore from commitment to the PAP".

Goh Chok Tong's style of government is consultative, based on consensus. He seeks to persuade, and will listen, indeed he encourages people to speak out against restrictions and controls over their daily lives that they find repressive and to suggest improvements to civil service departments through the Service Quality Improvement Unit. Over 1,000 individuals are credited in the government's manifesto for the next election and the next decade—*The Next Lap*. He takes frequent walkabouts and constituency meetings, as well as attending a wide spectrum of religious and community gatherings and celebrations. But don't forget, it was Goh Chok Tong who ordered the arrest of 22 church workers in 1987 on suspicion of their being Marxist conspirators, and it was he who took on the foreign press and gazetted (restricted the circulation of) the *Far East Economic Review* and the *Asian Wall Street Journal* for interfering with domestic affairs.

He has been accused of being a seat warmer for Lee Kuan Yew's son, BG

(Res) Lee Hsien Loong, who entered Parliament in 1984, became a Cabinet Minister in 1987 and is now Deputy Prime Minister and Minister for Industry. BG Lee's foreign trips do get a lot of media coverage in Singapore— but so do any Singaporean political figure's trips abroad.

People also ask about Lee Kuan Yew's own role within Goh Chok Tong's Cabinet. Lee Kuan Yew himself justified his current position: "Goh Chok Tong said he wants me as a gurkha guard". He also claimed that older Singaporeans and foreign investors in Singapore felt happier to see him around, keeping the continuity going. And as Senior Minister, he intends to see that what he's built in Singapore grows, as well as helping the government to present its policies most effectively in order to maximize its number of votes at future elections. And will he, as some speculate, run as Elected President? Again, who knows!

International Relations

South-East Asia is at the forefront of Singapore's foreign policy, and it is a keen member of ASEAN (Association for South-East Asian Nations), a grouping of non-communist nations aimed at closer economic co-operation, understanding, technology transfer and mutually beneficial investment. Singapore is also a member of the United Nations and the British Commonwealth, and has close ties with the USA. Economic links with Japan are strong, and those with the states of the CIS are growing.

People

"One People, One Nation, One Singapore". So ran the slogan for the republic's 25th birthday in August 1990, a slogan which highlights the search and desire for unity between the different races who make up Singaporeans.

Singapore today is a multi-cultural society that flourishes on its diversity. Of the three million population, 76 per cent are Chinese, just over 15 per cent are Malays, 6.5 per cent are Indian and the remaining 2.5 per cent are other races, including Eurasians. The country has four official languages— English, Chinese (Mandarin), Malay and Tamil.

Immigration to Singapore started swiftly after Raffles' arrival in 1819. When he arrived there were 150 people, including 30 Chinese gambier and pepper planters. Some of the first immigrants were Malays and Chinese from Malacca, then inhabitants of the Indonesian islands including Javanese, Bugis and Balinese traders. By January 1824 the population had risen to over 10,000, of whom 60 per cent were Malay (or Indonesian), 31 per cent Chinese and 7 per cent Indian.

The Chinese

Immigration from China started in the 1820s, with the first ship from Amoy (Xiamen) arriving in February 1821, and increased rapidly with the growing opportunities for trade and employment which Singapore offered at a time of widespread famine in mainland China. With it came concurrent problems of secret societies and corruption, as single men often arrived severely in debt. The first Chinese women only arrived in the 1870s, previous male immigrants having either returned to the mainland, or married local women to create Peranakan, or Nonya families. These Straits-born Chinese families developed their own culture, customs and cuisine, a mixture of Chinese and Malay. Today's Tanjong Katong and East Coast Road is a traditional Peranakan area, and you can visit a Peranakan interior in the National Museum.

A census of 1860 showed a population of over 80,000, with the Chinese constituting 65 per cent of the population by 1867. Certain hangovers from former times are still very occasionally seen in today's Singapore: the *samsui* women who worked as building labourers, unmarried, in black or blue *samfoos* (trouser suits) with brilliant red folded hats; and the black and white *amahs*, housekeepers and childminders who used to wear white blouses and black trousers, with a long black pigtail.

The different Chinese dialect groups congregated in different areas of Singapore, specialized in different trades and formed different clan associations. In later years they also built their own schools. The Hokkiens, often sailors and then businessmen, settled in the Telok Ayer and Hokkien Street area, where they built the Thian Hock Keng Temple, modelled on temples in their native Xiamen. Until recently there was also an exclusively Hokkien village of the Phua clan, who used to work as farmers, off Upper Thomson Road, but all residents have now been resettled in the nearby new towns of Ang Mo Kio and Yishun. By the end of the 19th century the Teochews moved inland for gambier and pepper plantations, and also settled along the upper reaches of the Singapore River and Boat Quay. In 1820 the Cantonese founded Tua Pek Kong Temple on Telok Ayer Street; while the Hakkas built Wang Hai Fu De Si Temple at Tanjong Pagar and congregated along Kallang Road near the unloading point for imported tin (they were traditionally blacksmiths). The Hainanese congregated along Middle Road, as well as in Changi village. The Chinese

A Chinese sailor at Clifford Pier. The Chinese first started arriving in Singapore in the 1820s.

A colourful street scene in Chinatown.

Chamber of Commerce was founded in 1906, dominated by the Teochew and Hokkien races, which enjoyed strong financial status. Amongst members were several rich *towkays*, though the clan associations generally found their time spent in schemes to help the poor and working class, by far the majority of the Chinese population.

The different races are still apparent in today's Singapore: Lee Kuan Yew is a Hakka, a race that has traditionally travelled and relied on hard work and initiative to succeed. Because of the great diversity of dialects, today's government has been encouraging all Chinese to learn and speak Mandarin—though this obviously causes problems within families when elderly relatives can no longer communicate directly with the youngest generation. Uniting threads for the different Chinese races include a common bond of ancestor veneration, a Confucian-based respect for and unquestioning obedience to authority, and the pursuit of prosperity and wealth as desirable goals in life. Some even go so far as to show the phenomenon known as *ki-asu*—originally a fear of losing, which generally manifests itself as a kind of one-upmanship.

Family life is incredibly important to the Chinese, and the procreation of children vital to those who hold ancestor worship sacred—without children, who will venerate your tombstone? Matchmakers are rarely used nowadays to find marriage partners—except for the government SDU (Social Development Unit) that is—but young people generally mix and date through school and college friends. Weddings—generally in the auspicious

fifth lunar month, or else during the eighth—take different forms, depending on the different religions, but uniformly include the registry office signing and the Chinese tea ceremony—when the newlyweds offer tea to the elders of both their families as a mark of respect, receiving in return *hong baos*, red parcels of money. A reception is generally held, with a large banquet the central feature, and the whole celebration takes place during the meal—once the food is finished the party is over. Wedding photographs are often taken at outdoor scenic locations—the Botanic Gardens, or the steps of City Hall are the most popular.

Various taboos surround the birth of children, who are considered one year old at birth (in the same way that the ground storey of a building is called the first floor). The first-born traditionally used to have a first-month celebration party, when the baby's hair was ritually cut off and put in a jar for safe keeping. When the child subsequently quarrelled with its siblings, the hair was reputedly boiled up with water and the child made to drink the water to prevent further quarrelling.

Funerals are elaborate and colourful affairs: you may well pass a large marquee erected outside a housing estate, with burning joss sticks and large floral arrangements. You may also see professional mourners on their way to attend such a funeral. A wake will generally last for at least 3 days, generally for 7, during which time everyone who knows the surviving family members, whether as a colleague or a school friend, will visit to pay their respects, and will partake of food and soft

四泰武

三宝聖誕

含境平安

望聖宝三

添油箱

三宝聖誕

戍檔泉出組
7530600·7559106

It is very common to see tents and joss sticks such as this during the Hungry Ghosts Festival.

drinks. Christians may have short services each evening, and the immediate family will attend all these. Indeed, when the body is in a marquee, the family keeps constant vigil until the funeral—a custom stemming from the belief that if a pregnant cat or rat jumps over the body it will be turned into a zombie. Many Singaporeans nowadays use the funeral parlours instead of the full-blown marquee outside their homes; but all will hold a traditional wake.

The Chinese have few food taboos—they, particularly the Cantonese, are reputed to eat everything that moves. When eating a fish, there is an old belief that by turning it over you turn over a boat on the South China Sea—so try to scoop out the flesh from beneath the spine without turning the fish over. The Chinese prepare local and imported seafood in intriguing ways, as well as the local favourite dishes (*see* pages 258–265). Chopsticks are generally held with the first three fingers of the right hand (if you are right-handed), pivoting the upper stick and using the lower one as an anchor; soup spoons are generally served with soup and liquid dishes such as *laksa* or claypot dishes, when you should lift up the noodles from the bowl and then deposit them on the spoon to eat them. Slurping soup is quite acceptable.

The main Chinese festival is Chinese New Year, when the whole island virtually closes down for the two days' public holiday. In addition, Chinese Buddhists celebrate Buddha's birthday and ascent to nirvana on Vesak Day; Qing Ming, the period of tending ancestors' graves; the Mooncake Festival is popular with children; and the Birthday of the Monkey God, The Pilgrimage to Kusu Island, The Festival of the Nine Emperor Gods, and Hungry Ghosts Month are all Chinese events, as is the Dragon Boat and Dumpling Festival. All the different festivals are described on pages 86–97.

A Cultural Mix

At the National Day parade, and at the Chingay Procession at Chinese New Year, the different races show the finest dance, music and performances in a relaxed setting, in an attempt to define the special mixture of cultures that makes Singapore.

The Malays

The Malays are the second largest racial group in Singapore and Malay is the language of the national anthem. For this deeply religious people (99 per cent are Muslim), achievements in terms of job success, monetary gain and measurable prosperity are of limited value compared to the quality of their lives. The family is all-important in the Malay community, as it is to the different Chinese dialect groups, but to the Malays the time to enjoy life and one's family is more important than the pursuit of worldly goods. Indeed, one of the major Muslim festivals, Hari Raya Haji, shows the Muslim willingness to sacrifice worldly wealth as a witness to Allah or God, and to distribute it among the needy. With such a difference in approach, it is not surprising that the Malays have seemed to lag behind the all-achieving Chinese in terms of education and

A Malay boy dressed in celebratory finery for the annual Chingay parade.

employment prospects, a fact the cultural organization Mendaki—aimed at promoting their participation in national events—is designed to correct. That is not to say that there isn't a growing and flourishing Malay middle class—in Kembangan, for instance, mock Tudor bungalows house those prosperous enough, who value education as a ticket to a better life.

Courtesy and kindness are watchwords within the Malay community, which has a fairly rigid etiquette pervaded throughout by the Islamic religion. Women and men do not sit together in the mosque, and do not touch—indeed, many Muslim women cover their heads and wear long trousers or *sarongs*, never revealing flesh on the legs or arms.

Marriage customs have changed in recent times, and have grown simpler since the days when the new couple could need 12 changes of clothes for the entire ceremony. Nowadays a young couple will generally know each other rather than meet through an arranged marriage. There are large banquets to celebrate the engagement—often a couple of years before the marriage—and the wedding itself.

For two nights before the wedding, and for one night after, the bride's fingers are dabbed with henna—*berinai*—which signifies the married status. The wedding ceremony itself—the *akad nikah*—takes place on a Saturday evening, when both bride and groom separately sign the marriage certificate. The groom then pays a marriage fee to the bride and greets her by salaaming. The following day the *bersanding* is held, the climax of the ceremony. Guests are invited to a reception

between 11 a.m. and 5 p.m. After passing through several obstacles, the groom meets the bride and sits enthroned amidst much revelry and music, and it is after this occasion that the couple leave together to begin married life.

Various beliefs surround birth in the Malay community—women do not sew when pregnant for fear of damaging the baby, nor are they cruel to any living creature for fear of hurting the baby. Women adhere to a special diet during their confinement—generally about 40 days. The father is closely involved in many of the traditional birth rituals, which form a close bond between father and child from birth. Children are habitually named 7 days after they are born. Little scolding or punishment is meted out to Malay children, who are reared in a loving environment. Old-fashioned customs, such as piercing girls' ears, or washing a child's hair with gold or silver to bring good luck before it is first cut, have largely died out in urban Singapore.

Infant girls are circumcised, young boys also generally before they reach puberty—both are religious requirements. A high standard of hygiene and healthcare is involved today, and these ceremonies take place either in hospital or at a particular mosque.

Muslims must be buried within 12 hours of their deaths, ideally sooner. The head of the body is placed to face Mecca, and the Imam from the mosque comes to the home and will ritually cleanse the body. Prayers are offered both at home and at the graveyard. Again, it is polite to offer respects if you know the family.

The religious restrictions on food are discussed in the section on religion (page 84). Malays will be careful not to eat off the same crockery or cutlery as non-Muslims, and you should take care not to mix Muslim utensils with other foodstuffs which are not *halal*.

The Indians

Indian immigration to Singapore started with Raffles' first trip to Singapore. On board with him was an Indian trader from Penang, Naraina Pillay, whom he encouraged to stay in Singapore and to develop the growing trading station. Stay he did, first as a government clerk and subsequently as a building contractor running a brick kiln in Tanjong Pagar. With other Indian immigrants from Sri Lanka and mainland India the Indian community grew rapidly. The British solved the nascent problem of labour shortages by declaring Singapore a penal zone in 1823, so Indian convict labourers worked in the booming construction industry, building the first of the three Sri Mariamman Temples, the *Istana* (Government House) and the mock Gothic St Andrew's Cathedral. Indentured Indian labourers subsequently joined their convict co-nationals in the construction trade.

Racially, Tamils comprise two-thirds of the Indian community, followed by the Malayalees and Punjabis, the Hindis, Gujeratis and the Sindhis. The Tamils originate from South India and are Hindu. They settled at first in the Tanjong Pagar area, today's Little India being initially a European and Eurasian area. Another 50,000 are Muslim or Buddhist, their ancestors originally coming from Sri Lanka and other areas of the Indian subcontinent. The Indian Muslims bridge the Indian and Malay communities, with their religious interests largely catered for through Malay organizations at present, although this may change. The Hindi language is now allowed for school N, O- and A-level examinations (*see* page 102–103), and there is one temple in Singapore where preaching is done in Hindi, at the Shree Lashminaryan Temple on Chander Road.

During the 1870s cattle trading flourished along Serangoon Road, and the area took on the bustling Indian charm you can see today: men in *dhotis*, women in *saris*, the occasional *kacang putih* (nuts and titbits) hawker, flower garland stalls, jewellers.

Women with red dots on their foreheads are married—North Indian women have a red streak on the parting of their hair. Unmarried women sometimes wear a black dot on the forehead, to counter the evil eye.

Some Indians celebrate their daughters' reaching puberty, or else celebrate this just before their weddings. Many symbolic objects are carried around the girl three times by three married female attendants during this private ceremony, after which the girl is taken to be bathed and her sari is given away. There is no parallel celebration for boys' puberty.

Marriages are generally arranged by parents with their children's consent, although they can also choose their own partners in these more modern times, providing caste and class are the same. There is increasing awareness of the risks of an arranged marriage these days, and many temples now arrange informal social gatherings for eligible men and women to meet. An engagement, rather like a small wedding celebration, takes place a few months before the wedding. The groom's family visits the girl's home for the exchange of rings, while a priest chooses an auspicious day for the wedding.

The wedding itself can last for several hours and can include a tree planting ceremony, symbolizing new life. The couple then change clothes, the bride wearing a new outfit given her by her groom to symbolize that she is his responsibility. The couple walk around the holy fire to purify themselves before the husband ties a *thali*—necklace—around his wife's neck and drums are beaten loudly to drown the noise of any bad omens. The couple usually spends their first married night in the groom's home.

Births within the Indian community have their own set of rituals and beliefs. A mother stays at home in confinement for 28 days after the birth, and the baby is only called by name after that time. Babies are given special baths for their first 6 months.

For funerals oil lamps are left burning day and night in the home out of respect for the dead person's spirit, believed to leave the house only after 16 days from the death, on its way to reincarnation (*see* page 74). Funerals are usually held in the home, the body remaining in the home for a maximum of 12 hours. Adults are usually cremated.

Most Indians are Hindu and therefore do not eat beef, since the cow is sacred because people consume its milk, rather like a human mother giving milk. Some are vegetarian, and many more do not eat meat on

A group of Indian women waiting at the Sri Mariamman Temple to watch the Thimithi ceremony.

Fridays. Alcohol is not taken by strict Hindus.

The Indian community now has its own organization—Singapore Indian Development Association or Sinda—which aims to promote the equality of the Indian race within Singapore's rat race, rather as Mendaki does for the Malay community. An Action Committee aims to increase Indian examination passes, university and polytechnic entrance and VITB (*see* page 103) entrance numbers in order to improve the number of Indian highflyers.

The Eurasians

The offspring of European men and local women, whether Chinese or Malay, have their own special identity and history in Singapore, where they are known as Eurasians or *serani*. Many have surnames with recognizably Portuguese origins—Pereira, D'Oliveira, Rodrigues for instance—and originate from Malacca. Singapore's first President, Benjamin Henry Sheares, was one of the more prominent members of the Eurasian community.

Most Eurasian families were originally Roman Catholic, and the community evolved a whole set of its own church customs and celebrations. Babies are baptized before they are 2 weeks old; a child makes his or her first communion at the age of 8; and the confirmation ceremony is at the age of 10 or 11. Birthdays are always celebrated with cakes and candles, and weddings are grand affairs involving lengthy preparations and large numbers of guests—or at least used to be in the heydays of the 1930s.

The close community of matriarchal families is linked by intermarriage, so that many Eurasians will discuss relatives as soon as they meet one another in order to establish a common link. Community feeling is further fostered through clubs and organizations: the Eurasian Association is the main group today, but in the past the Singapore Recreation Club, facing the Singapore Cricket Club across the Padang, was originally a Eurasian club, since only Europeans were admitted to the Cricket Club itself. Sport is an extremely popular Eurasian pastime: Eurasian women formed the Girls' Sports Club in the 1930s, which was also responsible for organizing the annual New Year's Eve dances at the Victoria Memorial Hall in days gone by.

Eurasian cuisine is, as one might expect, a successful fusion of South-East Asian and European styles, with no food taboos so there is wide variety. *Sambal* is added to ham or cheese sandwiches, cloves and cinnamon added to stews and casseroles. A favourite is Curry Devil, made of leftover meats and fiery chillies. A time-consuming cake called *bluder* is made from fermented coconut sap, flour, butter, eggs, sugar, spices and brandy. Alcohol consumption is also a part of the Eurasian heritage, with Anchor beer a particular favourite.

During the Japanese Occupation, the Eurasians were particularly singled out for maltreatment, since they were seen to have defiled the pure Asian race. Many had fought against the Japanese in the Volunteer Corps and were interned in the Eurasian camp in Bahau, Negri Sembilan in Malaya.

Foreign Workers and Expatriates

The 1990 Census showed a total of 300,000 foreign workers living in Singapore on Census Day, a fairly high proportion. They vary from the Western personnel of multinational corporations based in Singapore for their regional operations, to those involved in technology transfer and skills training, and to those mainly Thai and Sri Lankan labourers and construction workers and Filipino maids at the bottom of the employment ladder.

Some foreigners, married to Singaporeans, or with work that is likely to keep them in Singapore for some considerable time, are able to apply for Permanent Resident status. The majority are on employment passes, entitling them to avoid the time-consuming visa form filling that tourists do on entry, and paying Singapore taxes on the income earned in the country.

Religion

Singapore is a multi-religious state, one where any religion is tolerated, though proselytizing and over-zealous conversion procedures are illegal, since such actions could upset the delicate balance of different beliefs and races.

The Senior Minister, Mr Lee Kuan Yew, is officially agnostic, though he, like many Chinese, has sympathy with the tenets and outlook of Buddhism, and many of his philosophical remarks are Confucian in outlook. His successor, the Prime Minister Mr Goh Chok Tong, takes extreme care to celebrate the major religious festivals of all Singapore's religions equally, attending the Hindu Thaipusam festival, the Buddhist Vesak Day celebrations and various different Hari Raya Puasa (end of Ramadan) festivities (*see* pages 86–97). Newspapers likewise portray the current President Wee Kim Wee celebrating and meeting religious and community leaders on the different religious occasions. Employers wish their employees of different religions the appropriate greetings on the various occasions. All religions practised in Singapore do stress family values and loyalty, as well as inculcating respect for one's elders and those in authority, all of which find deep echoes in the different races' history. In their own ways, the religions practised serve to bolster the government's social policy and status quo.

Hinduism

A large proportion of Singapore's Indian population is Hindu, originating from the Tamil states of Tamil Nadu in South India. During two spectacular festivals Thimithi and Thaipusam (*see* pages 96 and 87) the public can witness the level of devotion demanded by this religion.

Hinduism, possibly one of the oldest of living religions, did not arise from any one founding individual or prophet. Rather it developed almost spontaneously as a varying collection of beliefs and practices, inspired in part by a number of ancient religious texts. These include the *Vedas*—"roots of knowledge", the *Upanishads*—discourses between the guru and his pupil "to sit and imbibe" the *Puranas*, the *Dharma Sutras*, the *Dharma Sastras*, the *Ramayana,* the *Mahabharata* and the *Bhogavadgita*. The *Bhagwad Gita* is the fundamental scripture, a type of guidebook for each individual to interpret according to circumstances. Different groups have believed in different texts and various sects have developed to cater for this.

Hinduism is a way of life, a philosophy of man from conception to cremation, when we return to the ashes and dust, or the *Panchbhoot*, the five elements of which we are made—fire, water, air, earth and ether. Each individual has a spark of supreme divinity, which can be realized by merging with the divine spirit.

The Hindu pantheon contains 33 different gods, and is confusing to the outsider because some gods have different names and then there are the different incarnations of the same god, which add further confusion. A central belief in one God or the Universal Spirit, Brahma, the Absolute and Universal Soul, who is *Nirguna*—without shape or form, beginning or end—is a fundamental part of mainstream Hindu belief. Brahma is portrayed with four heads facing all directions, since he has created the universe. He often sits on a lotus: as this flower sits on muddy water, so men too are born into temptation, but can achieve beauty by merging with God. The feminine aspect and consort of Brahma is Saraswati, who sometimes also sits on a lotus; sometimes on a peacock— symbol of man's pride or ego which should be suppressed; and sometimes on a swan—to show that true knowledge is man's aim in life. In the Hindu Trinity, Brahma personifies God's creative aspect; Vishnu his preservative aspect; and Shiva his destructive side.

All gods and their incarnations which represent evil are also worshipped for their good, so Shiva the destroyer is widely worshipped as the god of regeneration and kindness.

Shiva is portrayed in various different ways in temples: sometimes as a long-haired warrior, with a garland of human skulls around his neck and a tiger skin at his waist; sometimes as the dancing god with four arms; and sometimes with a female breast as well as a male penis to signify his sexual ambiguity. He has two sons, Ganesh and Skanda (also called Vinayagar and Murugan or Subramaniam). Ganesh is easily recognized with an elephant's head. Vishnu has various incarnations, which include Krishna, Buddha, Rama (originally a mortal king but subsequently elevated to this status), and, still to come, Kaikin. The most important female goddess is Devi, the mother earth goddess. Parvati is Shiva's wife, while a strong incest belief surrounds Prajapati.

Hindus believe in an unending cycle of death and rebirth within one of the four castes of the *varna dharma*. There are three ways to escape this perpetual cycle, realize God and attain salvation. The first is the way of knowledge (*jnana marga*); the second is the way of action (*karma_marga*); and the third the way of worship and prayer (*bhakti marga*). Man himself is essentially spiritual, with an immortal soul on a par with the gods, though his egotistical actions (*karmas*) cause suffering and let him down. By freeing himself from these *karmas* he can gain life eternal, or *Moksha*.

From this brief outline it becomes clear that Hinduism is not, contrary to popular belief, necessarily a polytheistic religion. Rather it is a complicated synthesis of polytheism, monotheism, monism and atheism.

To Hindus the cow is sacred as the giver of life and milk, as women are: Hindus do not eat beef. At certain times of the year, and before the major festivals of Thimithi and Thaipusam, devout Hindus become vegetarian, out of respect for life and as a cleansing process.

Hindu temples generally comprise an entrance courtyard leading to the main shrine, with other, lesser shrines in the surrounding area. Often accommodation areas—in the Sri Mariamman temple for example—are located within the grounds. A feature is the *gopuram*, or gateway, which is generally decorated with numerous statues of gods, sacred cows and scenes from Hindu myths. Brightly coloured, almost gaudy, with vivacious facial expressions and details, Hindu architecture can come as a shock to Western tourists used to more restrained religious depictions. Visitors are welcome to enter all Hindu temples, even during prayers and festivals, though they may not be admitted to some of the holiest shrines. Notices generally advise you to remove your shoes—you should do this even without such notices, since it is discourteous to bring outside dust into the inner temples. No particular dress restrictions apply to Hindu temples, though a modicum of decorum is desirable. Photography is generally allowed, though do take care not to intrude on worshippers. Collection boxes are placed near the entrances, and a small donation towards the upkeep is appreciated.

Ordinary Hindu believers have a family altar in their homes, where incense is burned daily and prayers are offered at dawn. On Fridays prayers are offered at the temple, with different offerings of bananas and coconuts blessed by the priest and then taken by the devotees home to eat or to place on the family altar.

Chinese Temples and Religions

With their pointed roofs, coloured ceramic tiles, dragon decorations and assorted gods, the Chinese temples of Singapore are mysterious and colourful places. The earliest temples were designed and built by craftsmen from mainland China, with materials often shipped from that country to ensure authenticity. The temples themselves are generally constructed on platforms, to signify their importance, and coloured in auspicious colours: red, the colour of fire, for joy which also symbolizes the sun and the *yang* principle (*see* page 79); red and gold ceiling decorations which represent power and glory; green, the colour of wood for longevity. Floor tiles emphasize longevity and prosperity, while the whole structure depends on a cantilevered beam frame structure which leaves internal walls free from weight. A general pattern is to have a central courtyard, with two or three prayer halls separated by further courtyards; a bell and drum tower on each side of the main courtyard; and monks' quarters somewhere within the compound.

Long dragons are often seen dancing on temple roofs, symbolizing justice, strength and authority, as well as acting as guardians to each temple's treasure. Other common images

Daily worship and incense burning at the Tua Peh Kong Temple on Balestier Road.

Confucianism

Confucius, to use his Latin name, or Kong Qiu, was born in 551 BC. An expert on ancient religious practices, he developed a philosophy of love for man and respect for authority, which was to guide people through virtue and propriety. He taught *ren*—humanity, benevolence, and perfect virtue—and *shu*—tolerance and reciprocity, and advocated the five virtues—courtesy, magnanimity, good faith, diligence and kindness.

A statue to Confucius stands in many Chinese temples (as well as in the Chinese Garden in Jurong, *see* page 178 and in Marina City Park, *see* page 153): a bearded scholar, he wears a head-dress and scholar's gown. Devotees bow, but do not burn joss sticks or incense to him.

include phoenixes—symbolizing sincerity, uprightness, and fidelity—and *chilins*, mixtures of unicorns and chimeras. On internal walls bamboos and plum blossom representations are often seen; on external walls monkeys, bats (called *fu* in Chinese, which sounds like the word for luck), and tortoises—which are the base of the beginning of things. Geomantic symbols such as the *yin yang* symbol, the *taiji*—two fish swimming head to tail—and the Eight *Trigrams* (*see* page 78) shown on walls, where they are believed to work against evil influences. A pair of stone lions, the male with a ball under his paw, the female with a cub, generally stand guard outside the temple and symbolize uprightness and justice.

Various taboos and beliefs surround temple architecture and etiquette when visiting. Geomancy or *feng shui* principles (*see* pages 79–80) are used to determine the precise time to install the main roof ridge, for example, and only odd numbers of steps—often three—are built, while the numbers one, five and nine are favourable for installing roof tiles. It is unlucky to stand on the door lintel of a temple, or to use a spirit way (a ramp decorated with dragons leading to the entrance), since the spirits have a separate entrance from the people. Temple doors are left open at night for spirits to enter and leave at will. There are no particular clothing taboos in Chinese temples, nor do visitors need to remove shoes. Photography is generally allowed, and visitors can usually explore the whole compound: just be careful not to disturb those praying, waving an even number of joss sticks to reinforce their prayers at the four corners of the prayer hall, or burning offering papers in the drum towers. Several temples have ancestral tablets and altars in subsidiary prayer halls, where relatives will often leave food and flower offerings as well as burning red candles or joss sticks.

The religion practised in Chinese temples varies within Singapore and South-East Asia, and it is not always easy to identify immediately. Often a mixture of different strands is believed and practised in particular temples and families.

The early Chinese believed in hundreds of deities which looked after the different aspects of life, as well as gods of the sky, wind and thunder. Some of these remain important—Guan Yin, the goddess of Mercy, for example, continues to be popular. During the Han period (206 BC–AD 220), Confucianism attacked many of these primitive beliefs, and became widespread in their place. At the end of the Han dynasty, Buddhism arrived in China, and joined with the strands of Confucianism, Taoism and ancestor worship to form the complicated pattern of beliefs held today. Many Chinese temples in Singapore are what is known as Syncretic—they embrace Buddhism and Taoism, communicating with the gods through prayers and signs. Such temples are the Thian Hock Keng Temple on Telok Ayer Street, or the Hong San Si Temple on Mohammed Sultan Road.

Brief outlines of the different beliefs follow, but for a more detailed description you should read Evelyn Lip's excellent book *Chinese Temples and Deities*.

Taoism

Taoism was founded by Lao Zi in the 5th century BC, becoming an organized religion by AD 430. It is a search for earthly happiness and longevity, and a belief in many gods each of whom grants a certain favour. The way to eternal life is by understanding and living in harmony with nature, and through the balance of *yin* and *yang* (*see* page 79).

Taoists believe in 10 heavenly paradises, 36 subsidiary paradises and 72 blessed places, and practise their beliefs through fortune-telling, geomancy and magic charms. Their symbols include *fu*—papers with magic powers to ward off evil spirits, and the *Eight Trigrams*, an eight-sided figure, to ward off evil spirits.

A statue of the Taoist Supreme Deity *Yu Huang*, the Jade Emperor, is found in all Taoist temples. He wears a crown with hanging beads, a gown patterned with dragons and clouds, and he sits on a throne in front of a screen painted with dragons and clouds. Devotees pray to him for good health, well-being, and all they wish for in life. Tian Hou, the queen of heaven and the goddess of seafarers, wears a gown with glass embroidery work and a crown with beads. Taoists also believe in the Eight Immortals (also known as xian) and the Nine Emperor Gods. An example of a purely Taoist temple in Singapore is the Yue Hai Qing Miao or Wak Hai Cheng Bio Temple on Phillip Street.

Sixty-eight per cent of Chinese Singaporeans today are Buddhists or Taoists. The Singapore Taoist Federation, keen to make religion more applicable to everyday life, points out parallels between the hierarchy of the gods and the modern management structure engendering a team spirit in business! *Taiji* is practised as a health exercise as much as a philosophical one.

Ancestor Worship

The doctrine of filial piety, that children should provide for their parents while they are alive and pray and look after their graves when they are deceased, is widespread amongst the Chinese population, both in Singapore and South-East Asia, and in mainland China. Many temples have prayer halls for ancestral tablets which are regularly visited by relatives bearing offerings of food and other items.

Geomancy surrounds the location of Chinese burial sites: all are on sloping hills, with running water nearby, both of which are considered crucial to ease the spirits' time in purgatory.

Geomancy, or Feng Shui

Not a religion as such, geomancy is more a complex set of beliefs and astrological predictions and analyses that some might even term superstitions, practised to a greater or lesser extent by large numbers of the Chinese over the past 2,000 years. The science of wind and water (*feng shui*) is used to ensure harmony with nature, so the geomancer is called to ensure that a new house, bridge or wall is correctly situated, with particular regard to the earth's surface—*di-li*—and to the *yin* and *yang* principles.

Yin, the female principle, is associated with the earth, the north and the cold, shade. *Yang*, the male principle, is related to heaven, the south, the dragon and all odd numbers. They both are believed to have come from the Primeval One (*Tai-ji*), and from *yin* and *yang* come the five elements or states of being: wood, east, blue; fire, south, red; metal, west, white; water, north, black; and earth, centre, yellow.

Geomancy principles broadly dictate that all houses in a village should be the same size; none should obscure another. Particular areas would be seen as lucky or unlucky shapes—for example, the Hill Street Police Station is said to have very bad *feng shui*, since it changes the previous shape of the area, thought by geomancers to resemble a fish—*yue*—a propitious symbol. Geomancers have been consulted about a number of Singapore's buildings, and auspicious opening dates have been chosen: the OUB Centre in Raffles Place, for example, was opened on 8 August 1988, since the number 8—*ba*—is very significant, despite being an even (*yin*) number. Similarly the Hyatt

The former Hill Street police station, now the Archives and Oral History section of the National Library. This building was believed to have bad feng shui, *since it destroyed the previous shape of the area.*

79

Hotel on Scotts Road now has glass zig-zag doors, since in the original plans the architect had placed these square on to the main thoroughfare, and they were parallel to the cashiers' desks so, by the rules of geomancy, the wealth would have flowed away. Flowing water is another lucky geomancy characteristic, and the Shangri-La Hotel has a spectacular waterfall. Burial sites have to be south-facing, on a gentle slope, with protective walls or structures to keep away east and west winds, and often a nearby stream is considered auspicious.

In bookshops in Singapore you can find numerous titles on geomancy. Probably only comparatively few people believe in all its principles, but a high percentage of Chinese do make use of its everyday applications, and in choosing numbers of apartments, racing horses and the like, very few will choose the unlucky four; copious numbers will choose eight. And several will consult the Chinese Almanac, basically a diary or calendar, which has geomancy advice for each day.

The central courtyard of the Thian Hock Keng Temple on Telok Ayer Street. As with many temples, geomancy principles were used to calculate its proportions and overall construction, as well as choosing the correct time to install its roof.

The tai-ji *symbol, an empty circle divided into light* (yang) *and dark* (yin).

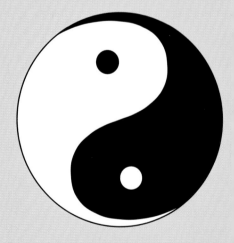

Buddhism

Initially an offshoot of Hinduism (*see* page 74), though it does not acknowledge any of the Hindu gods, Buddhism was founded by Prince Siddhartha, the son of an Indian chieftain near Nepal, who was born in 642 BC and died in 560 BC He gave up the wealth of court life to search for knowledge to relieve the suffering and poverty of the world, and found this knowledge—or enlightenment, *nirvana*—after 6 years while sitting under a Bodhi tree. He believed that ignorance was the cause of all suffering, an over-attachment to the world. He became known as the Gotama or Sakyamuni Buddha.

A humanistic, non-theistic religion in its original form, Buddhism includes the law of *karma* and rebirth as in Hinduism, as well as advocating the avoidance of extremes and of violence. It has four noble truths and eightfold discipline demands. There are two main sects of Buddhism today: Mahayana Buddhism, which is the most widely practised form in Singapore, originating from Tibet, China and Japan, which can include other gods, even worshipping Buddha as a god; and Theravada Buddhism, as practised in Sri Lanka, Burma and Thailand, a more ascetic and atheistic form with a doctrine of respect for elders and anti-materialism, and vows of poverty and alms-giving. Singapore Buddhism is non-sectarian: a Theravada Buddhist can teach in a Mahayana temple, and vice versa. The high point of the Buddhist calendar is Vesak Day, the day when Buddha is believed to have died, attained nirvana and also his birthday.

Buddhist participants in the Vesak Day three-steps-one-bow procession at Kong Meng San Phor Kark See Temple, Bright Hill Drive.

In a (Mahayana) Buddhist temple, the main altar is to the Sakyamuni Buddha, with subsidiary altars to Guan Yin (the Chinese Goddess of Mercy) and other *bodhisattvas*— those god-like beings who have attained nirvana but have elected to delay their ascent to nirvana so they can help man on earth attain nirvana. *Guan Yin*, a real person during the Zhou dynasty (1000 BC), about whom there are various legends, is sometimes portrayed riding a dragon/lion creature; sometimes holding a rosary and gold bottle, wearing a white gown and sitting on a lotus plant; sometimes with many hands and a gold crown; or else in white with a child in her arms. Devotees pray to her for children, wealth, and health. Other statues may include the Kshitigarbhe Buddha, the guardian of earth who presides over the Ten Courts of Hell, carries a staff and rides a chimera; the pot-bellied and laughing Maitreya Buddha, giver of happiness; and Cheng Huang, the god of the city, to whom devotees pray for peace, prosperity and good health.

Just over 28 per cent of today's Singaporeans are Buddhist. Devout Buddhists are vegetarian, with a strong dislike of taking life of any kind. Examples of purely Buddhist temples in Singapore are the Kong Meng San Phor Kark See Temple in Bright Hill Drive, the Shiong Lim Si Temple on Jalan Toa Payoh (founded in 1884), and the Long Shan Si Temple on Race Course Road.

Sikhism

The Sikh religion was founded by Nanak, a great poet of the Sant tradition, who was Hindu by birth but influenced by Islam. He was the first *Guru*, since when there have been a further nine.

Sikhism is a monotheistic religion, a belief in the oneness of God the creator, sustainer and destroyer. Man is believed to have a divine element in him, and can escape the eternal chain of birth, death and rebirth by purging self-contentedness and purifying himself. The *Guru* is a spiritual guide to help man attain salvation through inner purity of mind.

External rituals are denounced, though the repetition of God's name —*Nama Simaran*—is very important, as is meditation and the singing of devotional songs. Cold-water baths, daily prayers and a kind of baptism ceremony for boys and girls are practised. Sikhs have long, uncut hair, traditionally worn in a wound turban, wear an iron bracelet, and carry comb and sword. In every Sikh temple is a copy of their canonical scripture, the *Adi Granth*. The main Sikh Temple in Singapore is on Serangoon Road.

Ramakrishna Mission

This mission is one of religious harmony, with links with Islamic, Christian and Buddhist organizations as well as Hindu ones. It is one of a total of 129 missions worldwide, but mainly in India, inspired by Sri Ramakrishna (1836–1886), and his main disciple Swami Vivekanada (1883–1902). The Singapore mission was founded in 1928, and the current building on Bartley Road reopened after restoration in 1952. It houses Indian boys from broken homes, as well as organizing educational programmes.

Religions of the Book

The three religions of the book, Judaism, Christianity and Islam, are all practised in Singapore to varying extents. All three draw on a common repertory of the Christian Old Testament stories and believe in the one God, differing only in their interpretation and approach.

Judaism

Singapore has always had a small but significant Jewish community. Among famous Jewish families are the Meyer family: Sir Reuben Manasseh Meyer founded the rather charming Chesel-El Synagogue on Oxley Rise in 1905. This is one of Singapore's only two synagogues; the other is on Waterloo Street. The community remains small and Israeli visitors or Jewish immigrants are not encouraged, largely out of deference to the much larger Muslim community in the country. At the time of writing I could not trace any kosher food outlets in the country.

Christianity

A fairly large and increasing number of the Singaporean Chinese community are Christian, whether Methodist, Anglican, Presbyterian or Roman Catholic. It is therefore quite common to find Christian names as well as Chinese names, though some families give their children Western names just for the social and international cachet, so you can't assume a Chinese person with a Christian name is in fact a Christian.

Those who are Christian take their religion very seriously. Lent is fairly well observed, with regular church attendance and prayer, though little actual fasting—however, fish is often preferred to meat at this time, not just by Catholics. At Christmas, Christmas Eve is the main family occasion, with a family meal and often an evening church service as well as a morning service on Christmas Day itself. Christmas in Singapore has now become a kind of shopping festival for everyone of whatever religion, and presents have become common at the workplace.

Etiquette on entering churches in Singapore is much as elsewhere: the dress code is not important, though do take care not to wear anything too revealing or outrageous.

In the past, the Singapore government was very wary of Christian groups of all kinds, largely because some Christian youth movements were exposed as communist fronts in the 1970s. This virtual hostility, with numbers of participants in various activities listed and monitored by secret services, was largely sponsored by the now Senior Minister, Lee Kuan Yew; his successor Goh Chok Tong has, so far, taken a much more relaxed view of the religion.

The tenets of the different Christian sects are broadly as practised elsewhere in the world.

Islam

Virtually all the Malay population is Muslim, as are a significant number of Indians (about one in four according to the 1990 census), and a very few Chinese. The Prophet Mohammed was born in Arabia in AD 570, and died in AD 632 He preached monotheism and decried the idolatry he saw about him—to this day, Islam forbids making images of the human form, and you will see no statues or figurative paintings of any kind in mosques. When Mohammed was 40 years old the Angel Gabriel called on him, and related the word of God to him: this is related verbatim in the *Koran*, and all Muslims learn Arabic script in order to read the word of God.

Muslims believe in one God, and see Mohammed as the last of the prophets. They believe in the sacredness of the scriptures—including the *Torah* and the *Gospels*—though the *Koran* is particularly sacred to them. They see Christians as having gone astray by worshipping Jesus rather than God, and venerate him as a prophet only. They believe in life after death, heaven and hell, and the absolute submission of man to God's will as a duty of believers. The *Koran* lays out many ethical virtues, and the five pillars of Islam: the repetition of faith in the absolute oneness of Allah; daily prayer; alms-giving or *zakat*; fasting during Ramadan; and going on the *Haj* (*see* below, page 85). In addition, believers may be asked to go on a holy war—*jihad*. There are two main sects of Islam: the Shias, who are followers of Ali, Mohammed's son; and the more moderate Sunnis, who take a different approach on the caliphate succession after Mohammed, and practise a more moderate form of the religion. Muslims of South-East Asia are almost all Sunni Muslims.

Of all Singapore's religions, Islam imposes the most on its adherents' every-day lives: Muslim women obey a strict dress code, revealing little flesh and often covering their hair, if not their faces, with colourful headscarves. All food eaten by Muslims has to be *halal*—to have been correctly slaughtered by a Muslim, who says the words *"Allah Akbar"*—God is great—as he cuts the jugular vein. The eating of pork is forbidden (*haram*) and eating crustaceous seafood—such as crab or lobster—is not encouraged (*makruh*). It is forbidden for men and women to touch—men should avoid brushing accidentally against a Malay lady in her long *kebaya* even in a crowded bus, as it will cause her great offence.

The daily prayer times are marked by the now recorded *muezzin* calls from mosque minarets, and men will generally attend the mosque at one of these sessions. At these times, you may come across a devotee saying his prayers anywhere—in a car-park or changing room for instance—with his prayer mat facing Mecca, and you should avoid walking in front of a praying person at all costs. Friday is the Muslim holy day, and Muslim employees will often take an extended break over lunch to attend the mosque (if they are male). In Singapore, and a great deal of South-East Asia, much of women's religion is practised in the home rather than in the mosque, almost a male preserve.

All Muslims observe the month of fasting, Ramadan, and from dawn until dusk no food, liquid, spittle, or even dust should pass the lips. Meals are taken before first light, and then after the evening prayer call. During Ramadan mosques serve food to devotees after the evening prayers, and a festive light-up and night markets thrive along the bustling streets of Geylang (*see* page 91). The only exceptions to the fasting rule are soldiers in battle, women during menstruation, and travellers. The last ten days of Ramadan, the *Lay Latul Qadr*, is when Muslims believe the Koran was revealed to the Prophet Mohammed. This is a time of *taqwa*—literally God-consciousness—when the faithful bear witness to their spiritual strength. It is a time for self-evaluation, compassion for those less fortunate—as shown with the giving of the *fitrah*, the religious tithe equivalent to 2–3 kg (5–6 lb) of rice—and a feeling of brotherhood. Each night during Ramadan a Muslim repeats his or her formal intention in a solemn oath to Allah: "Oh Allah, I intend to fast tomorrow as a compulsory act of worshipping you". The fast is broken with *iftar*—dates or fresh fruit, before attending evening prayers—*maghrib*. Hari Raya Puasa, the end of Ramadan, is also a time to remember loved ones who have passed away. Tombstones are cleaned, and verses recited at them at this time.

The pilgrimage to Mecca, Mohammed's birthplace, known as the *Haj* is a crucial step in each Muslim's life, and each adherent attempts to make one in his or her life. It involves months or even years of spiritual preparation, and generally the journey takes up a lifetime's savings—but after the pilgrimage a person will take the title Haji in front of his or her name.

The Arabic word for mosque, *masjid*, literally means a place of prostration. All mosques face the *qibla*, Mecca, and have a main prayer hall—*musalla*—divided into two separate areas for men and women, both fully carpeted; a *mihrab*, a highly decorated directional device to show the centre of the *qibla* wall; and a *mimbar*, a three-

*T*he Malabar Muslim Jama-Ath Mosque on Victoria Street.

tier platform, also highly decorated, from where the leader of the congregation, the *imam*, delivers his sermons on Fridays.

When visiting mosques, it is crucial to dress respectfully: no shorts, short skirts or short sleeves. Shoes should be removed before entering the carpeted hall. Women should keep to the public areas and be careful not to enter the male prayer hall; they should not enter a mosque while menstruating. Visitors of either sex should only look in, and not enter, the central prayer hall where men are praying, but you can always visit the peaceful external courtyards.

Festivals

There are many different festivals in Singapore, reflecting the different faiths and origins of its multi-racial people. Some, but not all, of the festivals are public holidays; when they are, they are generally celebrated on the exact day they fall, rather than attached to the nearest weekend (as is the case in the UK for example).

Muslim, Hindu and Chinese calendars are fixed by reference to lunar months, so that it is misleading and indeed impossible to fix these accurately within the Western calendar. The STPB (Singapore Tourist Promotion Board) in your home country should be able to advise on any festivals likely to occur a couple of months or so before your visit, and provides excellent publicity material at the airport and in hotels and shopping centres during particular festivals. *The Straits Times* runs regular features on how festivals and particular beliefs are practised within the different racial and religious groups, as a means of promoting cultural diversity and understanding, and these are well worth reading.

New Year's Day (1 January)

A public holiday to help those celebrants recover from the night before.

Thai Ponggal (Festival of Harvest)

A Tamil and Hindu harvest festival on the first day of the lucky month of Thai, early in the calendar year, marks the end of the monsoon season and the start of spring. Thai is the month when most Hindu weddings take place.

Ponggal was believed to be the first day the sun left the Tropic of Capricorn and entered the zodiacal house called *Makaru*. The day before Thai Ponggal, *Bhogi Pandigai*, it is customary to pay homage to Lord Indra, controller of the clouds. According to legend, some cowherds incurred the wrath of Indra by worshipping Krishna instead of Indra, whereupon Indra sent a thunderstorm to punish them. Lord Krishna protected the cowherds by raising a mountain to stop the storm from hurting them, and asked the people to worship Lord Indra on this day.

On the eve of Thai Ponggal (Ponggal means "boiling over" in Tamil), families clean their houses, and often burn their old clothes and cooking pots; then on the day itself they rise early, take a bath, dress in new clothes and cook newly harvested rice with milk, ghee, raisins, cashew nuts, lentils and sugar, with shoots of turmeric and sugar plants around the rims of new cooking pots. This food is blessed in such temples as the Sri Perumal Temple on Serangoon Road, which is decked out in colourful flower garlands for the occasion, and which tourists can visit to see the public side of this family festival. Prayers are offered at home, along with offerings of milk, sweet rice and fruits at the family altar. Home entrances are sprinkled with decorations made of *kolan*—rice flour with water.

The *Panchangam*, the ancient Tamil almanac based on astrology and mathematics, is read in all Hindu temples on Ponggal, through which people can make predictions on the price of gold and petrol, the likely rainfall and such like. The day after Thai Ponggal cattle are given a special wash and fed the boiled rice.

The Sinhalese also celebrate this festival, known as *Aluth Avuruddhe*, attending churches, Buddhist temples and visiting friends bearing festive cookies.

Thaipusam

This spectacular, if stomach-turning, festival takes place when there is a full moon in the month of Thai, the tenth month in the Hindu calendar, which is generally in January. It celebrates the victory of Lord Subramaniam, otherwise known as Lord Murugan, the son of Shiva, over evil, and devotees carry the *kavadi* to thank the god or to ask him for special favours on this day of atonement and purification. According to one Hindu legend, Iduban, a devotee of Lord Subramaniam, received a message to go to a hilltop shrine and pay homage. He did so, taking two pots of milk as an offering, tied on a pole, and sang hymns to Lord Subramaniam as he climbed the hill. Another legend has it that Saint Agastya needed two hills, and asked Iduban to get them for him. Lord Subramaniam sat on one so he couldn't lift it, but once Ibuman did penance he relented and helped him.

On the eve of Thaipusam there is a procession of the image of Lord Subramaniam from the Sri Thandayutha-pani Temple on Tank Road to the Vinayagar Temple on Keong Saik Road. The image is carried in a 90-year-old silver chariot and symbolizes Lord Subramaniam paying homage to his brother Vinayagar (Ganesh) to seek his blessings before receiving offers himself from worshippers. The image remains in the Vinayagar Temple for one day and is then returned to Tank Road, where *palkuddams*—pots of milk which are hung on *kavadis* (see below) are offered at his feet.

Banned

The Hindu festival of Thaipusam has been banned in India for several years because of its gruesome nature and its potential for violence in a violent country. The custom is practised in only three countries at the time of writing: Singapore, Malaysia and Sri Lanka.

A Hindu devotee carrying the kavadi *during the Thaipusam festival.*

For between 3 days and 1 month beforehand, devotees will have fasted and prepared themselves mentally for the forthcoming ordeal, often sleeping on the floor with no pillow and abstaining from all worldly pleasures and social activities. Male and female, lower and higher castes are all seen as equal as they participate in this rite, though because the women do not bare their flesh, it is not pierced in the same way as male practitioners'. Then, from early in the morning until well after dark, several thousand individuals (5,800 in 1991) will walk to the Sri Perumal Temple on Serangoon Road and don the blessed *kavadi*, a metal structure weighing about 45 kg (100 lb) decorated with flowers, pots of milk, peacock feathers and the images of deities before undertaking the 3-km (2-mile) walk, barefoot, through the centre of town to the Tank Road Sri Thandayuthapani Temple. *Kavadi* literally means sacrifice at every step. In addition, the cheeks and tongue are often pierced with a metal *vel*, an arrow-like structure with a heart-shaped head to symbolize purity and a shaft to symbolize closeness to God. According to Hindu mythology, the *vel* was given to Lord Subramaniam's mother, Sathki Devi. Each devotee is surrounded by his own band of followers who encourage him to continue with regular drum beating and invigorating chanting.

At the start of the procession, the Srinivasa Perumal Temple on Serangoon Road, devotees leave banana leaves containing bananas, milk, fruits, flowers, honey and incense to ask for God's blessings and to pray that the procession proceeds smoothly.

Coconuts are smashed at the start and the end of the procession to symbolize the smashing of the ego. Lemons and limes are cut at every road junction and placed around the *kavadi* carriers to remove all evil forces (and, it being Singapore, all swiftly cleared up at the end of the procession). At the destination, the Chettiar Temple on Tank Road, the *kavadi* bearers are divested of their burdens, which generally leave no scars on the trance-like pilgrims despite their weight and the visible way they pull the flesh. The *kavadi* carrying part of this festival has now been banned in India, where it is seen to be too masochistic and potentially dangerous: it continues in Singapore and Malaysia, where medical help is on hand but rarely called upon.

A smaller-scale echo of Thaipusam is observed by some Hindus in Singapore, the *Panguni Uthiram* Festival, to celebrate the marriage of Lord Shiva and Shakti. The procession, again a 3-km (2-mile) walk carrying the *kavadi*, and occurs in March or April.

Chinese New Year

Chinese legend has it that a monster appeared on New Year's Eve, terrorizing villagers and destroying harvests, but it was afraid of noise, light, and the colour red. Thus New Year is a bright and noisy festival.

This festival always falls within the month of February, and is heralded by the new moon. The full festival lasts for 15 days: Singapore has two consecutive public holidays, and most businesses return to work shortly after these, though very traditional Chinese firms will close for the whole festival. For a week before the festival, stalls and night markets go up along the Singapore River and in Chinatown, and they sell festive fare and trinkets to all and sundry. In recent years a noisy firework display from a barge in the river has opened the festivities, along with a nightly light up along the Singapore River, spectacular floats of gods and legendary figures in the River, and performances of lion and dragon dances, Chinese "pop" music and the nightly performances of Chinese opera or *wayang*. Lucky red lanterns are suspended throughout Chinatown, and night markets selling festive goodies do a rapid trade during the evening hours.

The actual New Year itself is largely a family affair, and on the evening of the festival families will traditionally gather together for a reunion meal— *Tuan Nian*—generally a steamboat (*see* page 264). Candles will burn throughout the night on New Year's Eve, and after the family reunion dinner, the family will pay homage at the family altar at 11 p.m. The children of the family will then serve the elders tea in a traditional custom. At midnight a great deal of noise is made to ward off evil spirits (when they were legal, fire crackers were mainly used), and all doors and windows are opened to welcome in the benevolent spirits of the New Year.

Chinese New Year is the time for those red packets or *hong baos*, which are small packets of money given by married people to unmarried relatives and children. All gifts are given in pairs and even numbers, which are lucky, and visits are made to relatives and friends on the first, second and fourth days of the festival, but families tend to stay at home on the third, an unlucky day for visiting. All the foodstuffs served at this time are chosen because of a double meaning in their names: thus mandarin oranges are given out of respect, since the Cantonese word for these (*kam*) sounds like the word for gold, while the alternative word (*kat*) sounds like luck or prosperity; raw fish (*yue sheng*) is traditionally tossed for luck and served at this time, since the word also sounds like prosperity. Other dishes served are likely to wish you longevity or fertility—dates (*tsao tzu*) for example should enable you to have children at the earliest opportunity; while melon seeds are another symbol of progeny. Another charming New Year dish is the love letter (*koay-ka-pek* or *koay-be-landa*), a triangular-shaped folded home-made biscuit eaten in honour of family ancestors.

Chinese New Year

The literal meaning of Chun Jie (Chinese New Year) is a spring festival, signifying a fresh start and new hopes for prosperity and happiness. For a month before the New Year, Chinese families embark on a thorough spring cleaning of their homes, since it is considered extremely unlucky to sweep during the start of the New Year and this time is one of numerous visits and visitors.

To Taoists in particular, the 23rd day of this 12th month (7 days before New Year's Eve) is significant, since on that day the Kitchen God returns to heaven to report to the Jade Emperor on their household's conduct—so special food is prepared for him to encourage a good report, and honey is smeared on the mouth of his picture on the family altar.

Chingay Procession

The Chingay Procession of floats, dancers, acrobats and assorted colourful displays wends its way down Orchard Road on the Saturday following the start of the new Chinese lunar year. Chingay means "the art of masquerading", and in traditional Chinese style consisted of decorated floats depicting historical scenes carried on men's shoulders. Originally a purely Chinese, religious, celebration of the new lunar year, the parade now encompasses all branches of the community who join in with relish. It has recently been changed from a morning to an evening spectacle, and is a vibrant and exciting one to watch—though as several thousand spectators attend, it is a good idea to arrive early in order to ensure a roadside viewpoint.

A variety of commercial concerns and community groups sponsor the different floats, and use the occasion to push their particular product or idea: in previous years these have included the Social Development Unit (SDU), the government-sponsored graduate matchmaking unit, with dewy-eyed brides and grooms following a valentine-type float! This is an opportunity too to watch traditional Chinese dragon and lion dancers, pole balancers, Malay drummers and a host of other acts, processing in a long chain the length of Orchard Road at 2- or 3-minute intervals for over an hour. If you arrive early, you can watch the different floats and acts preparing to start, and catch impromptu smiles and excitement before the activity proper begins. The different floats—exhibits almost—range from the extremely

A *participant wearing a colourful fan-like structure on one of the many floats in the annual Chingay Procession.*

tacky and highly commercialized to traditional forms of cultural expression from the different communities. Pole balancers finish the spectacular 2-km (1¼-mile) parade from the junction of Orchard Road and Scotts Road down to Dhoby Ghaut.

All Soul's Day—Qing Ming Jie

One month after Chinese New Year comes Qing Ming, a family celebration for the Chinese. This is the time for visiting ancestral graves and ancestral tablets in temples, and graves are swept and well tended during this period. Many ancestors' ashes are in columbariums, and family members visit to dust the urns. Qing Ming is also the time for *chunji*—spring prayers offered by clan associations to more distant ancestors of the same surname. On the eve of Qing Ming it is traditional to have a cold meal with the family. A private, family celebration, there is little for the tourist to watch.

A Chinese Legend

A legend associated with Qing Ming is that of the faithful servant Jie Zi Dui, who saved his starving master's life by cutting off and serving up his own leg to eat. He subsequently retired to a mountain retreat, refusing to leave when bidden by his master, who ungratefully had him burned to death as punishment.

Hari Raya Puasa

The Muslim celebration of the end of Ramadan's month of fasting is a time of prayer and family visits, but also a time of lively street markets and festive foods. For the month of Ramadan, mosques arrange for evening meals for nearby fasters after dark, while along Geylang Road and the adjoining Joo Chiat Road are numerous *pasar*

*T*he festive light-up along Geylang Road, the historic Malay/Muslim quarter, during Ramadan.

malam stalls—night markets, stalls selling all types of Malay delicacies, batiks, clothes and household goods, and a festival light-up. It's worth a visit in the evening, when it is extremely busy and friendly: as well as invitations to buy wares, you'll see smiles everywhere. At the National Museum in 1991 there was a highly successful Hari Raya festival of food stalls, songs, choral singing and dancing, which is likely to be repeated in future years.

During the month of Ramadan preceding this festival, the fasting times are published daily in *The Straits Times*. During this time no Muslim should take any food, drink (including water) or smoke a cigarette, unless excepted for reasons of health (including women's menstruation periods), travel or warfare. Muslim housewives rise extremely early in the morning in order to prepare their families' food for them to consume before the fast begins at daybreak each day. The evenings, once darkness falls, are relaxed times when *halal* food can be and is eaten with great enjoyment. Malay families make or buy new clothes, curtains and upholstery, or repaint their homes to give a new start at Hari Raya Puasa.

Labour Day (1 May)

An occasion for self-congratulation—this time a huge union rally is organized by the NTUC (National Trades Union Council), and speeches on mutual prosperity and improved productivity reflect the clever pact between the PAP (People's Action Party) and the unions forged so many years ago by Lee Kuan Yew. Vital matters such as choosing Mr and Miss Union are

decided on this day! And don't you forget it, this is a socialist state in some senses—hence the national celebration of workers' day.

Vesak Day

Vesak Day is the 15th day of the fourth lunar month, the day of Buddha's birth, enlightenment and ascent to nirvana, according to both Theravada and Mahayana Buddhist belief. Incense and candles are lit in a number of temples on this holy day, and items of man's four basic needs—food, clothes, shelter and medicine—are placed on altars. All types of Buddhist (*see* page 81) will strive to attend their local temple to pray on this day. Well before dawn on Vesak Day itself, as well as the previous evening around dusk, a long procession of devotees wends its way along a 2-km (1¼-mile) devotional path along the Phor Kark See Temple, each devotee taking three steps—one for the Buddha, one for his teachings, and one for the monks—during the ritual chant and then prostrating him or herself. It is a spectacular and moving sight, which visitors are welcome to watch—and photograph. Similar celebrations are held at the Temple of a Thousand Lights on Race Course Road. Within individual families, celebrations are private affairs, a time for prayer and family reunion.

Some devotees will bathe the statue of the baby Prince Siddhartha in a basin of perfumed water in the evening, scooping water over the statue to symbolize purification. Captive animals, such as turtles and birds, are released on Vesak Day to recall Buddha's universal compassion. Vegetarian food is often provided at temples, linked to the Buddhist respect for life and the teaching not to take life. Buddhists take home packets of holy water and flowers from the temples, and visit charity homes to give food and gifts on this day.

Dragon Boat and Dumpling Festival—Duan Wu Jie

This colourful weekend festival, on the fifth day of the fifth lunar month—generally in June—originates from a Chinese legend dating back over 24 centuries. A capable cleric, poet and minister, Qu Yuan, was exiled from the court of the kingdom of Chu in China after antagonizing the officials there by alleging political corruption. His honesty won him popularity among the people, but the enmity of his colleagues, who plotted to expel him. Exiled, he wandered a great deal in China, writing poems denouncing the political corruption and intrigue, and finally he committed suicide in the Mi Luo River in Hunan province. Fishermen set off to look for him, beating gongs and cymbals to frighten the fish from eating his body, and throwing rice into the river both as food for him and to appease the gods, but his body was never found. *Zongzi* or *bak chang*—triangular rice dumplings wrapped in reed leaves with minced pork fillings and garnished with mushrooms, chestnuts or dried prawns—are traditionally sold and eaten during this time in memory of the legend.

Today's manifestation of the legend is a world international invitation boat race, held in Singapore since 1978 and promoted by the STPB. Some 71 local crews and 13 foreign teams competed in 1991. Each boat has 22 paddlers, plus drummer and helmsperson. The teams participate in a furious round of heats and races along a 700-m (766-yd) stretch of Marina Bay, with winning times of just below 3 minutes. You can see the local boat crews practising along the Singapore River for several weeks in advance of the event if you can't see the race itself.

Hari Raya Haji

This public holiday is on the tenth day of the month of *Zulhijah*, the 12th month of the Islamic calendar. It is held during the *Haj*, the journey to Mecca every Muslim should attempt once during his or her life. It also commemorates the faith of Ibrahim (Abraham), who was prepared to sacrifice his son Isaac to God, who seeing this devotion substituted a lamb for the sacrifice. Thousands of lambs and goats are sacrificed for this festival, the slaughtering being known as the *Korban*, with one-third of the meat kept for the person who offered the sacrifice; one-third for friends and neighbours; and one-third to be distributed to the needy. In 1991 4,500 sheep were imported for this purpose. The *Korban* signifies Muslim willingness to sacrifice wealth willingly and give to the poor, fostering a strong community spirit.

The Festival of the Hungry Ghosts—Zhong Yuan Jie

On the 15th day of the seventh lunar month, generally August, is the Festival of the Hungry Ghosts. Throughout this month you will see small food offerings and burning joss sticks outside shops, restaurants, small offices and

workshops, even in car-park lobbies. Originally a harvest festival, it is celebrated by Buddhists and by Taoists alike—and of course by those who are in effect a mixture of both these. The Buddhists celebrate the legend of Mu Lian, who found her dead mother in Hades but could not feed her because of the other hungry ghosts until Buddha helpfully interceded. Taoists leave out food offerings since they believe that on the seventh day of the lunar month the gates of Hell are opened so that unborn souls wander the earth, and they are particularly careful to leave sufficient offerings and joss sticks on the 15th day.

Celebrations during this time could include Chinese street operas (*wayang*), performed to honour and entertain the dead and the wandering ghosts. The Chinese are unlikely to get married in this month, traditionally unlucky and reserved for ancestor worship.

National Day celebrations and patriotism at the National Stadium.

National Day (9 August)

A time of pageantry, military display, self-congratulation and pomp—much the same as a national day anywhere. National Day Parades take place generally in the national stadium, and comprise flip-chart block displays, military bands, fly-pasts and a civilian element, generally emphasizing the oneness of the nation. The 25th anniversary national day (1990) was the last one presided over by Mr Lee Kuan Yew, now the Senior Minister, and as always an occasion for a hard-hitting, no-holds-barred speech on the hard work required to maintain Singapore's world position. Tickets for the parade and show are very hard to come by, but you can watch it all on TV, see the aerial fly-pasts from anywhere central, and join in the informal street party Swing Singapore held either on the previous evening or on a suitably close evening along Orchard Road.

Mid-Autumn (Mooncake) Festival—Zhong Qin Jie

This starts one month after the Festival of the Hungry Ghosts, on the 15th day of the eighth lunar month, and is again originally a harvest festival. Various legends relate to this rather charming festival, when streets, houses and waysides are decorated with red lanterns, and small children walk around carrying lanterns in the dusk. The Chinese Garden holds an annual display of lanterns, and the Singapore River is lit up, complete with a few night stalls.

The most widespread legend is of a dragon attacking a certain village, but being confused by the number of lanterns so not knowing which was the moon. Another legend is that the earth had ten suns, and to prevent it from becoming scorched the warrior Hou Yi shot nine of the ten when they were all shining simultaneously. Thereafter he stole the elixir of life and became more and more of a tyrant until his wife, Chang, drank the elixir and floated up to the moon.

Delicious sweet mooncakes are on sale in shopping centres, street stalls, and offices take large orders—no Chinese person would visit another's home at this time without taking some mooncakes. The recipe, dating from Manchu times, is a mixture of ground lotus seeds, sugar, peanut oil and *mai ya tang*—a sugary substance. The crust is made of eggs, water, flour and oil. Another tale is linked to these cakes, which were reputedly used to carry messages from Zhu Yuan Zhang to his fellow rebels plotting against the Yuan dynasty in the 14th century. The plotters were successful, and founded the Ming dynasty.

The Pilgrimage to Kusu Island

During the ninth lunar month, Chinese and Malay pilgrims pack the regular ferries to this "turtle" island to the south of Singapore. Chinese pilgrims take flowers and other offerings to the Chinese temple by the jetty; while Malay pilgrims ascend the steps leading to the hilltop *kramat*, Malay shrine. (For the history and legends of Kusu Island, *see* page 224; for ferry times *see* page 271. Ferries to the island during the pilgrimage season are extremely full, and more regular than those at other times of the year.)

Festival of the Nine Emperor Gods—Kau Ong Yah

This takes part during the first 9 days of the ninth lunar month. Like the Monkey God, believers in the Kau Ong Yah, the Nine Emperor Gods, believe they cure illness and confer wealth on their devotees. They also enter temple mediums during their 9-day visit to earth. Devotees profess their faith at the end of the festival by fire walking in temple compounds—those with true faith feel no pain.

The Tou Mu Kung Temple in Upper Serangoon Road is the centre of celebrations for this festival. Joss papers are burned and Chinese *wayang* is performed to entertain the deities, who arrive in a piece of burning sandalwood in an urn from the Serangoon River. The deities are sent off again late at night when the urn is placed in the river waters.

Navrathri

Taking place over the same 9 days as the Chinese festival of the Nine Emperor Gods, Navrathri celebrates the three incarnations of the goddess Devi. It is largely a cultural and musical festival, with classical South Indian dance performances and celebrations in Sri Mariamman Temple, Tank Road and Serangoon Road temples.

The Birthday of the Monkey God

Two festivals celebrate this extremely important god who cures the sick and removes sins. During these times visitors to certain temples may see mediums writhing and putting themselves in trances, as the Monkey God is believed to enter mediums. Less gruesome sights are Chinese street opera (*wayang*) performances.

Deepavali Festival

This major Hindu festival celebrates the victory of light over darkness, good over evil, and commemorates the occasion when Lord Krishna conquered the demon Narakagsura. It usually occurs during the month of September or October. For the whole month period there is a light up along Serangoon Road, together with a trade fair and even more culinary delights than usual. The festival day itself is more of a family occasion, though the celebratory aspect always the religious one: families rise early, take a holy bath in oil, put on new clothes and light oil lamps in each home. The elders are revered, parents are usually given a gift by their offspring, and the younger family members kneel and are anointed with ash. Devotees go to the temple to pray, bringing offerings from the temple to their altars at home.

Celebrations of Deepavali vary between North and South Indians. North Indian celebrations are linked to the *Ramayana*, when Rama returned to the kingdom of Ayodhya after killing Ravana, and are held one day after the national holiday of Deepavali. The festival used to be celebrated in offices, and was a day to worship Lakshmi, the Goddess of Wealth. For the South Indians, celebrations generally take the form of open house in order to fulfil social obligations and repay the hospitality shown by other races.

Mango leaves decorated with turmeric and vermilion are hung over doors, and colourful *kolam*—rice flour motifs—are hung outside houses during Deepavali.

Thimithi Festival

This Hindu festival occurs 10 days before the festival day of Deepavali. The festival is tied up with the Hindu epic the *Mahabharata*, and is to pay homage to the Goddess Draupadi who walked on fire to prove her chastity after being dishonoured. She vowed never to use oil or flowers in her hair until evil was vanquished. The figure of Draupadi has been assimilated into Shakthi, the fundamental principle of cosmic energy, as embodied in Parvati, Shiva's consort.

Devotees prepare themselves for weeks ahead with special prayers and fasting, and on the eve of the festival a chariot carrying the image of Sri Mariamman is taken from that temple to other Hindu temples. Throughout the afternoon, a barefoot procession walks along Serangoon Road to the Sri Mariamman Temple on South Bridge Road, all wearing stained yellow sarongs, and bringing gifts of milk, fruit, flowers and green leaves.

In the temple itself, each group of devotees pauses on entry to stand in front of the image of Draupadi, and each participant is whipped three or four lashes with a thick rope before running one at a time across a 3-m (9-ft) area of burning coals. The head priest of the Sri Mariamman Temple goes first, carrying on his head a *karagam*, a pot of water sealed with coconut, mango leaves and flowers. As at Thaipusam (*see* page 87), ambu-

lances and medical services stand by, but very few entranced participants need more than the traditional bathing of the feet in coconut milk, and few are pained by the experience.

Christmas Day (25 December)

The run up to Christmas is an excuse for a festive light-up of Orchard Road and an orgy of shopping. Christmas Day itself is again a quiet day, though many shops remain open. Chinese Christian families tend to celebrate with a family meal on Christmas Eve, either at home or in a restaurant (book ahead if you plan to eat out then).

> **Festive Cheer**
> Singapore's Christmas decorations are colourful, bright and often bordering on the tacky, as Father Christmas, bob-sleighs, lots of fake snow and a variety of Christmas themes, carols and cartoon characters are displayed outside and inside the different shopping malls. Fake snow is a real favourite, exerting a bizarre fascination over a nation so far from ever seeing the real stuff. A competition is generally held for the shopping plaza with the "best" decorations.

*P*articipants walking along Serangoon Road on their way to the Sri Mariamman Temple for the Thimithi fire-walking festival.

Entertainment

Films, theatres, revues, musical performances, Chinese operas—a wealth of cultural entertainment awaits you in Singapore, if you can trace something to your taste. Alternatively, sports enthusiasts will find a wealth of spectator and participatory games.

The average Singaporean would list food and shopping as the main entertainments of the country, though there are a variety of other entertainments available. Check exact details with your hotel, with *This Week Singapore* or in the back of *The Straits Times*.

Film Classification

Singapore now has a system of film classification similar to those in many Western countries. Those rated R (A)—Restricted (Artistic)—can be viewed by those over 21 years of age and may contain explicitly sexual or violent scenes in the name of "Art"; PG—Parental Guidance—may contain scenes of violence, and children under the age of 14 should have parental consent to view these.

Films

There are a number of cinemas, broadly grouped into the Cathay chain, the Shaw Brothers chain and the Eng Wah chain of Chinese cinemas. A recent innovation has been Cathay's arts cinema, The Picturehouse, which charges double the normal price and shows less mainstream, more "arty" or "alternative" movies, seemingly successfully. Shaw Brothers, not to be outdone, have now replaced one of their existing cinemas with Jade Classics, and for a similar entry fee show a similar range of internationally acclaimed movies. You will find a predominantly American range of mainstream films in the other English-language cinemas, and a colourful-sounding selection of Hong Kong-made films in the Chinese cinemas. A new chain, Golden Village Enter-

*T*ypical Chinese movie poster. All films are advertised with these printed hoardings.

tainments, is, along with the existing chains, planning to venture into multiplex cinemas within 2–3 years.

Other venues for films include the Goethe Institute, which shows films for the Singapore Film Society, and the Alliance Francaise—check the press for details during your visit. (*See* page 249 for addresses and phone numberss.)

Concerts

The Singapore Symphony Orchestra is based at the Victoria Concert Hall, and gives frequent classical concerts there, as well as occasional performances in the Palm Valley of the Botanic Gardens—an atmospheric venue even if the standard of musicianship often leaves something to be desired. I've enjoyed the smaller chamber music performances more than the large-scale orchestral works—there's somehow less to go wrong—but give it a try if there's a suitable programme. Other concerts are held periodically at the Singapore Conference Hall or on the campus of the National University of Singapore—check the press for details.

Occasionally, visiting artists perform at the Victoria Concert Hall, or at the larger capacity facilities at the Singapore Indoor Stadium or Kallang Theatre, or even outside on Sentosa Island. Such shows are more likely to be sold out in advance—recent performers have included Placido Domingo as well as Eric Clapton—so do try to book if you hear of them. One-off performances, such as a recent visit by the Japanese saxophonist Sadanao Wanatabe, held at the exclusive Alkaff Mansion, again sell out in advance, so do check what's on in advance. Nightclubs such as Top Ten and Khameleon periodically play host to worldwide stars, whose visits attract widespread newspaper coverage. On a lesser level, live jazz and blues are played at Saxophone on Cuppage Terrace every evening and at Somerset's at the Westin Plaza—you just have to sit, drink and talk while you listen. Piano players grace various other bars and up-market restaurants to create a suitable ambience. A number of local bands do cover versions of Western pop songs in the town's nightclubs and bars (*see* pages 245–251 for addresses)—or you could provide the entertainment yourself in a karaoke bar (*see* page 248), or join in the annual street party Swing Singapore along Orchard Road in August.

Theatre

There are occasional theatrical performances at the Victoria Theatre, and also at the TheatreWorks Black Box troupe's new location at the Fort Canning Centre on Fort Canning Hill, a building which it shares with the Singapore Dance Theatre's ballet studio. A local favourite is the musical writer and musician Dick Lee, whose musicals about Singapore—*Army Daze* and *Fried Rice Paradise*—using liberal amounts of local "Singlish", are virtually incomprehensible to the casual visitor, but vivacious and amusing. Open-air performances of Shakespeare and a varied theatrical arts festival have been staged outside the Fort Canning Centre, and an ambitious production of *The Trojan Women* was recently staged in a Bukit Timah slate quarry for added dramatic impact. The Drama Centre on Fort Canning Rise also has a small theatre for amateur dramatic performances, while the Substation on Armenian Street, an "alternative" arts centre, also hosts small-scale performances and workshops in its Guinness Theatre. The Substation also holds different theatrical, photography, writing and poetry courses and readings, as well as a small crafts and collectibles fair on Sunday mornings. Occasional theatrical performances by visiting troupes, generally of light comedies, are staged by the Hilton Playhouse, and the Raffles Hotel.

Art Exhibitions

Frequent art exhibitions are staged in the various dealers' galleries—check the press for details. There's often something at the mezzanine level of the Hilton and, as well as the large-scale Chinese art exhibitions, there are smaller-scale shows on the ground floor of the Empress Place Building.

Local Forms of Entertainment

"Instant Asia" shows, giving tourists a flavour of local entertainment, are staged daily at the Cockpit Hotel, and, Jubilee Hall at the Raffles Hotel at 10 and 11.00 a.m., noon, 2 and 3.00 p.m.

If you can see an individual performance, rather than the tourist targeted amalgam of cultural media, you may find it more interesting. If you have the chance, watch a Chinese opera (*wayang*) performance to see a colourful and completely different spectacle. There are local community groups who perform regularly, together with performances by the China Theatre

Circle and troupes from mainland China. During the Chinese New Year light-up along the Singapore River, you can watch different performances every evening, and familiarize yourself with the different instruments and opera characters as they enact scenes from various Chinese legends. There are four traditional roles, which you should be able to identify in the performance you see: the male *sheng* character—*wenwu sheng*, the young scholar warrior is a common manifestation; the female *shan* character—whether you see the young demure female *wenwu dan* or the *huadan*, the young vivacious lady should again be obvious; the clown character, *shou*; and the painted face *jing*. Performances can last for 2 or 3 hours, though for performances in the street particularly you can just watch the acting, listen to the extraordinary singing sound, and admire the ornate costumes and make-up even if there is no one to explain the plot to you. There are frequent Chinese opera performances during the Festival of the Nine Emperor Gods—largely performed for the gods' entertainment.

Malay Opera (*bangsawan*), like Chinese *wayang*, was originally performed in the street, and nowadays is found only in local community centres, having only recently stopped being played on SBC Radio 2. A group on Kampong Ubi continues the tradition, though with less and less appeal to the young. Colourful costumes, and vibrant stories from Singapore's past can make for good entertainment.

Malay dancing—*ronggeng*—is performed on particularly festive days—for instance at the Hari Raya Puasa festival. At this time you may also see a performance of *dikir barat*—folk songs from Kelantan in Malaysia, accompanied by co-ordinated body movements and hand claps by the chorus. Inter-school competitions of *dikir barat* are held fairly regularly.

There are local troupes of *gamelan* players, again confined almost exclusively to local community centres—one troupe in Kembangan is comprised of Singaporean Malays of Javanese descent. To experience the true performance you should travel to Kelantan in Malaysia, or to Java in Indonesia.

The Indian community hosts occasional dance troupes and theatrical performers from India, particularly during the Deepavali celebrations.

Sports

All main sporting facilities exist on Singapore—*see* pages 251–254 for details. Most hotels will have swimming pools and squash and tennis courts; there are several golf-courses on the island, some of which are open to the public or to certain hotel guests; watersports such as sailing, water-skiing and windsurfing are all available; as is the ever-popular tenpin bowling.

As well as the occasional international competition—a Dunhill International Golf Tournament, or a Formula One Powerboat Grand Prix for example—you will frequently find cricket and other sports being played on the Padang, or may catch a football match since Singapore takes part in the Malaysia League Cup. Your hotel should be able to advise you on what spectator sports are taking place, as will *This Week Singapore* and *The Straits Times*.

Education

A society which depends on talented individuals, well trained and versed in up-to-date technical skills and a degree of decision making, values schooling from the earliest age.

Education is very prominent and highly valued in Singapore, a society with a 90.1 per cent literacy rate, where 46 per cent of the population speak and understand two or more languages, and where two in five have secondary or higher educational qualifications. Families, particularly the more competitive Chinese ones, will queue throughout the night in order to place their child in the primary school of their choice. Homework and extra-curricular study are often the norm from an early age, as parents encourage children to outdo their classmates and do well in exams. Parents will even prepare special potions of chicken essence—believed by the Chinese to enhance the powers of the memory—for pupils who are taking exams. Education and self-improvement are goals in themselves—look in any bookshop and see the range of titles on getting on in employment—and without education qualifications it is increasingly hard to get on in the employment

Achievements and Rewards
Prestigious awards are given to successful scholars for a variety of academic achievements, and these are always given great press coverage. Lee Kuan Yew Scholars and President's Scholars are some of the more prestigious titles, which come with an element of reponsibility as well as reward, since great careers of public service are often expected from recipients.

market in today's Singapore, so the competition starts at an early age.

The government's current aim is to have 40 per cent of each age group qualifying for a polytechnic or university education, and to ensure that every child has at least 10 years' schooling.

Schooling

There are approximately 220 primary schools, 140 secondary schools, 14 junior colleges (JCs) and four centralized pre-university institutes. The school year is divided into two semesters, each in turn divided into two terms. The first term of the first semester starts in early January, ending in mid-March; the second term of the first semester continues after a week's holiday at the end of March until the end of May. The second semester begins at the end of June, with its first term continuing until early September; the second term of the second semester runs from mid-September until the end of November.

Primary education generally starts at the age of six, and the first 3 years concentrate on the English language, the mother tongue—Chinese (Mandarin), Tamil or Malay—and mathematics as a grounding for the later education syllabus. A 1-year preparatory course is being introduced in some primary schools for 5-year-olds, to concentrate further on language skills and mathematics; and it is also intended to increase this stage of primary education from 3 to 4 years. At present, after Primary 3, pupils are streamed into three different language ability streams at the orientation stage: Normal Bilingual, Extended Bilingual and Monolingual. It is anticipated that 80 per cent of pupils will take English as their first language during this stage of education, which concludes with the Primary School Leaving Exam (PSLE), taken usually at the age of 11, which helps decide which secondary streams children should join.

Secondary education can take 4 or 5 years, depending on a child's ability and the stream he or she is in. The Special or Express courses take 4 years to reach the Singapore–Cambridge General Certificate of Education Ordinary Level Examination (GCE O-Level); those in the Normal stream take 5 years to reach the same level. Both these streams follow a common curriculum for the first two years, then choose to be in the Arts, Science, Commerce or Technical stream by Secondary 3. A new Normal (Technical) course is being introduced in addition to the two above streams in 1994, offering computer applications as well as English and mathematics, and an N-Examination after the fourth year before taking up technical training opportunities, or progressing to O-level if appropriate. Schooling in Singapore is generally run on a double-session system: one school will have two different sessions, morning and afternoon, to cater for its intake of pupils—so you see schoolchildren at all times of the day whose own sessions may have stopped or not started for the day. It is planned to make all secondary schools single session by the mid-1990s, and certain primary schools are already moving that way.

Post-Secondary Education

Post-secondary education takes place in junior colleges, which offer 2-year

A schoolgirl waiting for a lift home in a trishaw.

courses to Singapore–Cambridge General Certificate of Education Advanced Level (GCE A-Level) examinations. Alternatively, centralized institutes or pre-university centres offer 3-year A-level courses, though it is envisaged that the Vocational Institute Training Board will take over this function.

The VITB was established in 1979 to promote and provide vocational training for school-leavers, keeping up national skills standards and training apprentices. It also runs part-time continuing education courses and training schedules for workers keen to improve their skills. Singapore has three polytechnics—Singapore Polytechnic, Ngee Ann Polytechnic and Temasek Polytechnic—which offer a wide variety of technical courses to post-secondary school-leavers. The Republic also has two universities—the National University of Singapore, established in 1980, with eight faculties, all including postgraduate studies; and the Nanyang Technological University, formerly the Nanyang Technological Institute, which offers engineering, accountancy and commerce and applied science courses. Several Singaporean students opt to study in foreign universities, a trend that is recognized if not exactly encouraged by the government as a mind-broadening exercise. An Open University scheme is currently being developed for mature students and those wishing to continue their education while in work. An Institute of Manufacturing Technologies (IMT), a post-graduate research institution to promote advanced manufacturing technology and hence increase economic growth, started operation in 1991.

This highly developed education system is largely funded by the Ministry of Education, which spends roughly $2,000 per child in a primary school, $2,500 for a child in secondary school and $3,500 for one in a junior college per year. An Edusave system, whereby each child between the ages of 6 and 16 receives a yearly grant for education, $100 or so a year, has recently been started. Parents pay for extra-curricular activities and for independent school fees, and insurance policies to cover such expenses—particulary the expense of university or technical education—are becoming quite common.

The large number of teachers involved in this educational system—almost 10,000 primary school teachers, 7,500 secondary school teachers and 1,500 junior college teachers—are largely drawn from Singapore's Institute of Education, established in 1973. This institute provides teacher training and upgrading programmes for teachers already in employment.

Just the Essentials

Many visitors to Singapore only come for a limited time; maybe as little as an afternoon, maybe a day or so. To select what to see more easily, a shortlist of major landmarks and places to visit is proposed here to help you establish your priorities.

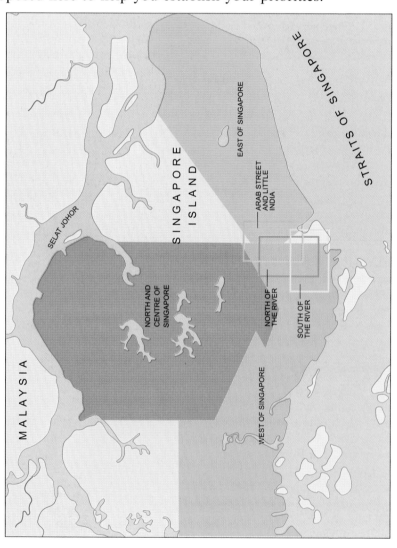

North of the Singapore River

The Singapore River: where it all began

Empress Place Exhibition Hall: good exhibitions of Chinese art and culture

The Padang: a cricket ground surrounded by colonial-style buildings

The Raffles Hotel: newly restored jewel of colonial times

The National Museum: Singapore's treasures over the ages displayed together with temporary exhibitions

Orchard Road: shopping thoroughfare

South of the Singapore River

Telok Ayer Festival Market: tempting local food and souvenirs

Telok Ayer Street: typical Chinese shophouses and important temples including Thian Hock Seng Temple

Sri Mariamman Temple: oldest Hindu temple in Singapore, site of Thimithi festival every October

Chinaman Scholar Gallery: glimpse into Cantonese family history in Chinatown

Tiong Bahru Bird Singing: quaint Chinese tradition from days gone by

Arab Street and Little India

Sultan Mosque: main Muslim mosque in Singapore

Arab Street: shophouses and fabrics

Dunlop Street: typical shophouses and Abdul Gafoor Mosque

Sri Veeramakayama Temple: colourful *gopuram* and lively religious centre

Temple of a Thousand Lights: huge Buddha image

West Towards Jurong

Haw Par Villa: Chinese mythological theme park with moral undertones

Jurong BirdPark: huge selection of birds, bird shows and attractions

Tang Dynasty City: model of old city of Xian in China

Singapore Science Centre: hands-on exhibits and Omni-Max cinema

Northern Sights

Singapore Botanic Gardens: examples of lush tropical vegetation

Mandai Orchid Garden

Singapore Zoological Gardens: animals in open enclosures whenever possible. Beautifully landscaped

Siong Lim Temple: Singapore's largest Buddhist temple complex. Currently suffering from termite damage

Eastern Parts of Singapore

Changi Prison Museum and Chapel: moving exhibition of POW life and replica chapel in prison grounds

East Coast Park: reclaimed land, sand beaches, water sports and space

Geylang: historic Malay quarter, currently best surviving examples of shophouse architecture here

Singapore's Islands

Sentosa Island

Pioneers of Singapore and Surrender Chambers

Butterfly Park and World Insectarium

Underwater World

Other Islands

Kusu Island: pilgrimage site for Malay and Chinese

Pulau Seking: last remaining rural island lifestyle

Excursions from Singapore

Johor Baru

Istana Besar: European-style palace

Sultan Abu Bakar Mosque: overlooking Straits of Johor

Kukup: charming fishing village

Malacca: former Straits Settlements town

Kuala Lumpur

Railway station: Arabian minaret-style architecture

Museum

East coast of West Malaysia: beaches, unspoilt villages, access to islands of Tioman, Rawa etc.

Indonesia:

Bintan: access to historic island Pulua Penyeget

Going Places with Somewhere Special in Mind

Although it is a small island, there are several walking or driving tours of a thematic nature which can assist the tourist with a particular interest. Central city locations are all best explored on foot; more widespread and wide-ranging themes will require a car or else the use of public transport. All bus numbers and MRT stations are given in the main entry in the sightseeing chapters.

The Colonial City: Architectural Tour

In the heart of the city, near to the Singapore River and further inland up Orchard Road, are many vestiges of Singapore's colonial days. Most of the former administrative buildings retain similar functions in today's republic.

1 EMPRESS PLACE EXHIBITION HALL
Former government offices where well-

Street scene—a Chinese shrine and lanterns, together with a trishaw parked in a sleepy 5-ft way in Rowell Road, Little India.

staged exhibitions of art and artefacts often from mainland China are held, as well as lesser exhibitions and sales of ceramics, paintings and furniture. A silk shop and a dim sum restaurant are also located here.

2 VICTORIA THEATRE AND MEMORIAL HALL
Plays, musicals, Chinese operas and pantomimes are performed in the theatre, while the concert hall is the home of the Singapore Symphony Orchestra. Visiting conductors and ensembles also perform here. The central booking office for all types of performance, whether here or in other locations, including the Kallang Theatre, is located in the foyer.

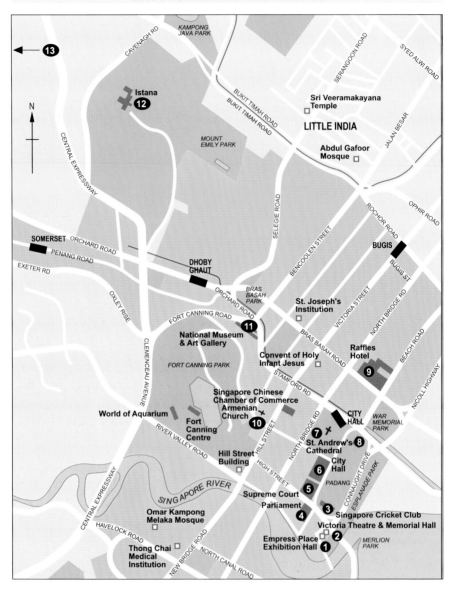

An architectural tour of the colonial city of Singapore.

3 SINGAPORE CRICKET CLUB

A classy and classic colonial-style pavilion facing across the Padang cricket ground to the Singapore Recreation Club opposite. Both clubs are open to members and their guests only, though the former racial exclusivity has, obviously, disappeared.

4 PARLIAMENT HOUSE

Designed in 1826 by the prolific colonial architect George Drumgoode Coleman as a private house for the merchant John Argyle Maxwell, the parliament building sits opposite the cricket club and behind the Victoria Theatre and Memorial Hall. The public is admitted to its sporadic sittings.

5 THE SUPREME COURT

A heavy Neoclassical pile with a green dome which mirrors London's Old Bailey.

6 CITY HALL

A popular spot for wedding photographs and other group photos, it was on these steps that Lord Louis Mountbatten accepted the Japanese surrender in 1945. The building is currently used for civic functions, as well as housing the Supreme Court's Registry.

7 ST ANDREW'S CATHEDRAL

A fine and somewhat disconcerting example of English neo-Gothic architecture, constructed in 1861 by Indian convict labour and now dwarfed by the nearby Westin Stamford Hotel.

8 SINGAPORE RECREATION CLUB

Facing the Singapore Cricket Club across the Padang, this was originally a Eurasian sporting and social club. Ambitious plans are afoot for underground expansion, to provide members with modern facilities without affecting the colonial period exterior.

9 RAFFLES HOTEL

Restored and reopened in September 1991, this jewel is an instant showpiece of days of former glory. Wander at will through the various courtyards, examine the merchandise in the extensive shopping outlets, dip into history in the third-storey museum, take tea, tiffin or a Singapore Sling in one of the restaurants or bars, and be sure to take a look inside the impressive lobby.

10 ARMENIAN CHURCH

The oldest church in Singapore is a delightful white circular building completed in 1835 by architect G. D. Coleman. A peaceful spot off the busy Hill Street thoroughfare.

11 NATIONAL MUSEUM

Formerly the Raffles Museum, this imposing Neoclassical-style building houses a permanent collection on Singapore's history and its different races as well as hosting a variety of temporary exhibitions. Adjacent and behind it is the National Art Gallery.

12 THE ISTANA

The former Government House, now the residence of the President of the Republic and the location of the Prime Minister's office, is located within spacious grounds to the east of Orchard Road. The gardens are open on 4 days a year, when one can admire the private golf-course, beautifully tended gardens, the Japanese Gun presented to Lord Louis Mountbatten after the Japanese surrender, and the imposing Classical-style building.

13 THE GOODWOOD HOTEL

On Scotts Road (off map), the Good-

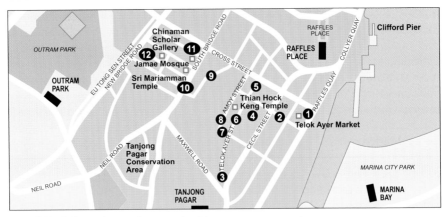

wood Park has always been a rival to the Raffles Hotel, boasting its own famous guests and amusing anecdotes as its rival. Both buildings were the work of architect R. A. J. Bidwell of Swan and Maclaren: the Goodwood with its Germanic tower is a decorated high Victorian architectural style, and its Christmas decorations are always eagerly awaited.

Chinatown Walk

An area to explore on foot, in Chinatown you can stumble on fruit stalls, grocers selling sea horses and sea cucumbers, lantern-makers, mask-makers, calligraphers—a range of traditional and modern pastimes and trades continues in this compact and changing area near to the bustle of the commercial district.

1 TELOK AYER MARKET
A Victorian cast-iron covered market, which contains a food court, restaurants, numerous souvenir stalls and steps. The market spills out on to adjacent Boon Tat street in the evenings and weekends.

A walk through Chinatown.

2 BOON TAT STREET
A typical Chinatown street of shophouses, Boon Tat Street dissects the main city thoroughfares Shenton Way, Robinson Road and Cecil Street. It is possibly named after a wealthy owner of brickworks, sawmills and rubber estates in the late 19th century, Ong Boon Tat.

3 TELOK AYER STREET
A bustling street of shophouses and temples, an ideal introduction to Chinatown, Telok Ayer Street was originally on the seafront.

4 THIAN HOK KENG TEMPLE
Singapore's oldest Hokkien Buddhist temple on Telok Ayer Street dates from the 1840s and was originally built by Hokkien sailors to give thanks to the sea goddess Ma-Zu-Po for their safe arrival in Singapore. Computerized palm-readers, snake-charmers and

trinket salesmen often wait for the coachloads of visiting tourists here.

5 HOCK TECK CH'I TEMPLE
A smaller and less-frequented temple than Thian Hok Keng on Telok Ayer Street, perhaps giving the intrepid visitor a more realistic insight into religious observance.

6 NAGORE DURGHA SHRINE
A pale blue mosque built by Indian Muslims, with two minaret-type towers and an imposing façade. Visitors are not encouraged to enter, but the building can be appreciated very well from the outside.

7 FUK TAK CH'I TEMPLE
A tiny and recently restored temple at the junction of Telok Ayer and Amoy Streets, next to the bustling Telok Ayer food centre.

8 AMOY STREET
Running parallel to Telok Ayer Street, this street has further examples of decaying and restored shophouses, though many are currently undergoing restoration work.

9 CLUB STREET
Clan houses, mask-makers and other traditional crafts are still practised along this hilly street which joins the equally charming Ann Siang Hill and Ann Siang Roads, leading to South Bridge Road.

10 SRI MARIAMMAN TEMPLE
Singapore's largest Hindu temple, venue for the Thimithi fire-walking festival in November, and a vibrant introduction to Hindu religious practice.

Remove your shoes on entering the temple.

11 JAMAE MOSQUE
An Indian Muslim mosque dating from the 1830s next to Sri Mariamman Temple. Its façade can easily be admired from South Bridge Road: visitors are not encouraged.

12 CHINAMAN SCHOLAR GALLERY
Above a Chinese grocer's shop, this small museum is well worth a visit, though do allow an hour or so as the owner is keen to explain points of Cantonese culture and history to visitors. The adjacent streets—Trengganu, Pagoda and Sago Streets—are currently undergoing extensive renovation work, so much of them is like a building site (not that that stops souvenir and trinket shops from trading, or copy watch touts from prowling!).

Arab Street

Arab traders arrived in Singapore in the 1820s and were encouraged to settle in the Kampong Glam area where they set up shophouses and built a mosque on the site of today's Sultan Mosque. The area remains a Muslim stronghold, a centre of Malay religious observance and culture.

1 NORTH BRIDGE ROAD
A colourful stretch of shophouses and Muslim eating houses, amongst which is the splendid Jubilee Cafe and Restaurant with 1930s decor and service. The road bends around the Sultan Mosque.

111

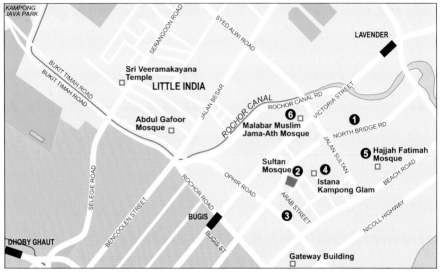

The sights of Arab Street, a Muslim stronghold.

2 SULTAN MOSQUE
Built in the 1920s, this impressive building dominates its surroundings despite the nearby HDB estates and the towers along Beach Road. Visitors are allowed, provided they are properly dressed, except during Friday prayers when the mosque is a buzz of activity.

3 ARAB STREET
Fabrics of all types, though mainly Chinese and Thai silks, Malay batiks and various synthetics and cottons, are sold in the busy shophouses on Arab Streets, along with headscarves, kits, basketware and titbits.

4 ISTANA KAMPONG GLAM
Tucked away up a small road off Beach Road, the former sultan's relatively small residence is currently rather shabby. Plans are afoot to revitalize this area, so yet more building work could shortly be seen.

5 HAJJAH FATIMAH MOSQUE
A mosque with a leaning tower dating from the 1840s, a peaceful spot set back from Beach Road surrounded by HDB blocks. Nearby jackfruit trees add a rural touch.

6 MALABAR MUSLIM JAMA-ATH MOSQUE
A shining gold dome caps this blue Indian Muslim mosque on Victoria Street.

Little India

Renovation work is currently in hand along both sides of Serangoon Road, but it is still possible to wander

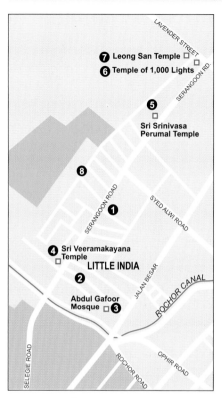

Leong San Temple

Temple of 1,000 Lights

Sri Srinivasa Perumal Temple

Sri Veeramakayana Temple

LITTLE INDIA

Abdul Gafoor Mosque

A walk through the Indian quarter of Singapore.

through the various backstreets and feel you are in a truly foreign place. Betel nuts, curry powders, drying chillies and fish, roadside coffee shops serving meals on banana leaves, men in *dhotis* and women in sarees, stunning silks and flower garlands: the Indian quarter of town continues much as it has done for decades.

1 SERANGOON ROAD
The famous Komala Vilas vegetarian restaurant has recently had a face-lift; other coffee shops retain their old-

world charm, though the north side of Serangoon Road is currently under renovation.

2 DUNLOP STREET
A typical street of colourful shophouses selling everything from fabrics to car doors.

3 ABDUL GAFOOR MOSQUE
A South Indian Muslim mosque dating from the 1920s is hidden off Dunlop Street behind a stone wall. An impressive façade, green dome and several lesser turrets grace the structure. Nearby terraced houses are home to devotees.

4 SRI VEERAMAKAYAMA TEMPLE
Very colourful figures are carved on the temple's gateway or *gopuram*; inside decorations are also colourful and there is often some activity, whether prayer offering or preparation of foods as offerings. Frequent trade fairs are held on the adjacent open space.

5 SRI SRINIVASA PERUMAL TEMPLE
The starting point for the gruesome Thaipusam festival in January, when devotees carry steel *kavardis* or frames to the Chettiar Hindu Temple on Tank Road.

6 SAKYA MUNI BUDDHA GAYA TEMPLE
The Temple of a Thousand Lights, this Buddhist temple houses a 300-tonne statue of the Buddha.

7 LEONG SAN TEMPLE
Across the road from the Sakya Muni

Buddha Gaya Temple is a smaller Chinese temple devoted to Guan Yin, the goddess of mercy.

8 RACE COURSE ROAD

The racecourse has long since been relocated to Bukit Timah, but the area is renowned for its banana-leaf restaurants, almost all of which serve fish-head curry, the Singapore speciality.

Second World War

Bombs first fell on Singapore on 8 December 1941, when the Japanese invasion of Malaya began. Their lightning progress through mainland Malaya, combined with a catalogue of misjudgements and miscalculations by the colonial British rulers and service commanders, culminated in Singapore's unconditional surrender on 15 February 1942.

1 CITY HALL

Site of the surrender of Singapore by the Japanese General Itagaki to Lord Louis Mountbatten on 12 September 1945.

2 THE PADANG

Where the European population was massed in February 1942, prior to the march to Changi prison.

3 CHOPSTICKS MEMORIAL

A memorial to the civilian victims of the Japanese occupation, unveiled in 1967. Its four columns represent the four communities of Singapore: the Chinese, Malay, Indian and Others, including the Eurasians.

4 LIM BO SENG MEMORIAL

A memorial to the wartime hero and resistance fighter Lim Bo Seng, who had raised funds for the China Relief Fund during the late 1930s and joined the British guerrilla Force 136 in the jungles of Malaya after the fall of Singapore. He was betrayed by a spy and was tortured and died without naming any of his colleagues.

5 CHANGI PRISON

The European population was interned in Changi Prison during the Japanese Occupation, with details sent out on labour projects which included work on the notorious Thai–Burma railway. A small museum and a replica chapel sit just inside the main entrance to the prison today.

6 CHANGI MURALS

Within Block 151 of the military camp at Martlesham Road is the former dysentery bay for the Changi POWs. An area of this was turned into St Luke's Chapel, and large murals by Bombadier Stanley Warren decorate the walls. Visitors are allowed during office hours: you are accompanied by a soldier across rough ground to the building.

7 CHANGI PHOTOGRAPHS IN LE MERIDIEN HOTEL

A series of photographs by George Aspinall, an Australian interned at Changi, are on permanent display on the fifth-floor lobby of Changi's Le Meridien Hotel. The images show the widespread dysentery and malnutrition of the prisoners of war, both in Singapore and at work on the Thai–Burma railway.

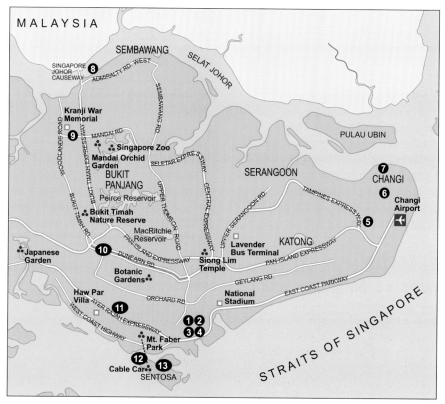

8 THE CAUSEWAY

The British troops managed to retreat rapidly across the Causeway on the night of 30–31 January 1942, Indian sappers blasting a 21-m (70-ft)-wide hole in the structure on the morning of 31 January. Sadly, the hole was made at the Malaya end of the Causeway, out of range of British gunfire, so that it was rapidly restored.

9 KRANJI WAR CEMETERY

The graves of Allied servicemen sits on a peaceful hilltop overlooking the Straits of Johor.

10 FORD FACTORY ON BUKIT TIMAH ROAD

The site of the British surrender to

Places connected with the Second World War.

General Yamashita on 15 February 1942.

11 ALEXANDRA HOSPITAL

Site of a massacre on 14 February 1942, when advancing Japanese troops bayonneted war wounded and nursing personnel to death.

12 SENTOSA ISLAND: FORT SILOSO

Site of Singapore's defence guns, sited to protect the island from sea-based offences. Fort Siloso is now a popular attraction on Sentosa Island, hosting various temporary wartime exhibitions.

13 SENTOSA ISLAND: SURRENDER CHAMBERS

The Japanese campaign, the fight for Singapore, details of life during the occupation, waxwork figures of both the surrendering British in 1942 and the surrendering Japanese in 1945 are all well displayed, with video footage, newspaper cuttings and a variety of mementoes.

Where to see the natural wildlife of Singapore.

Nature: Walks and Wildlife

Although it does at times seem like an urban jungle, there is a lot of wildlife and natural flora still to be seen in Singapore.

1 BUKIT TIMAH NATURE RESERVE

Monkeys are commonly seen, along with hungry mosquitoes, and recent reports of packs of stray dogs. Secondary forest and vegetation, with clearly signposted paths for walks. Nearby, training grounds for the armed forces and a quarry compromise the peace somewhat.

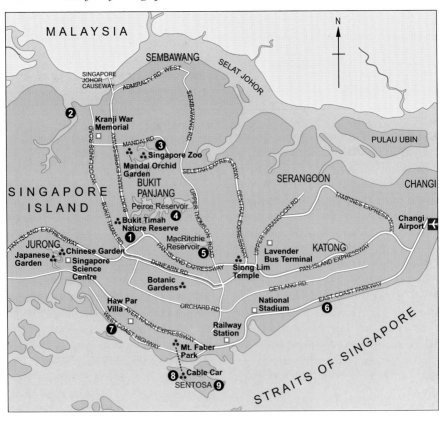

2 KRANJI RESERVOIR
Nesting ground for herons and bitterns. Binoculars needed.

3 SELETAR RESERVOIR
Monkeys, various birds including black-naped orioles, lush tropical vegetation; fishing is popular.

4 UPPER AND LOWER PEIRCE RESERVOIRS
Monkeys, often around the car park and along the approach roads, various birds, turtles.

5 MACRITCHIE RESERVOIR
Monkeys, turtles, jogging track and exercise stations, lush vegetation.

6 EAST COAST PARK
Various bird sanctuaries, sea eagles and terns; fishing is popular.

7 WEST COAST PARK
Turtles, occasional herons, fishing.

8 SENTOSA ISLAND:
SILOSO BEACH
The swimming lagoons are still under renovation, so the large stretch of clean sand of Siloso Beach is the main swimming area.

9 SENTOSA ISLAND:
COROLARIUM BEACH
Every afternoon, monkeys are fed with small bananas; turtle pool; also unspoilt and fairly empty beach.

10 SISTERS ISLANDS
Swimming lagoons marked out; access is by boat only to a quiet unspoilt island.

Flora and Fauna Attractions

On a fine day, Singapore, the Garden City, boasts many outdoor attractions which feature animal and plant life from around the world.

1 BOTANIC GARDENS
Extensive collection of local and imported trees, shrubs and plants, as well as lakes, gazebos, sculptures and sundials. Kingfishers are often seen, as well as the resident swans, on the lakes.

2 MANDAI ORCHID GARDEN
Haphazardly laid out, with erratic labelling, rows and rows of sun-, shade- and semi-shade-loving orchids grow up a hillside location in the centre of the island. Some species are for sale and export. A water garden completes the attraction.

3 SINGAPORE ZOO
Avoiding wire cages whenever possible, the zoo strives to create adequate living spaces for its wide range of species. A children's zoo has farm animals as well as a playground, the primate kingdom features islands of different monkeys, animal shows and rides are available.

4 JURONG BIRDPARK
A huge collection of different birds from all over the world are displayed in Jurong BirdPark. Bird shows are given daily in the large central amphitheatre, and a renewed and improved walk-through aviary is a recent addition.

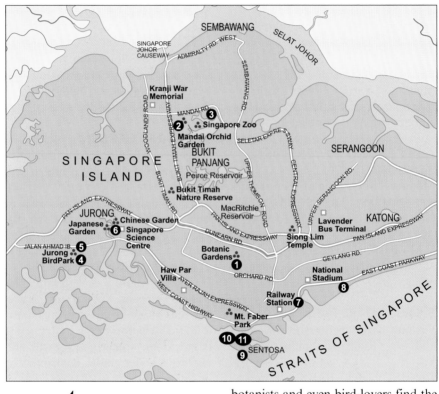

*A*ttractions featuring animals and plant life.

5 JURONG CROCODILE PARADISE

Many huge crocs lie overfed in uninspiring cages, barely interested in their next meal despite the entertaining safety notices.

6 JURONG: CHINESE AND JAPANESE GARDENS

Two adjoining and linked gardens sit beside a lake in Jurong: you can never ignore the nearby housing estates and the road noise, but garden-lovers,

botanists and even bird-lovers find the experience worthwhile.

7 MARINA CITY PARK

Bridges over streams, copious bougainvilleas, carefully placed pavilions and Chinese sculptures grace this park with a view of the East Coast Parkway Benjamin Sheares Bridge.

8 SINGAPORE CROCODILARIUM

Fewer crocs than in Jurong, in smaller cages, and instead of the wrestling, you can buy handbags and belts of crocodile skin.

9 SENTOSA ISLAND: BUTTERFLY PARK

Display cases of pinned-out butterflies and other insects; the most enjoyable part is the butterfly garden when you are surrounded by the fluttering creatures and a colourful display of plants.

10 SENTOSA ISLAND: NATURE WALK

A signposted circular walk through the trees, with occasional good views, some vegetation of interest.

11 SENTOSA ISLAND: UNDERWATER WORLD

A walk-through aquarium with small sharks and stingrays, as well as numerous smaller tanks, a touch pool to touch starfish, small turtles, a film show on corals—a good day out.

Things to Do with Children

There are several attractions for children particularly to enjoy as well as those that have been specially designed for them.

1 SENTOSA ISLAND: FORT SILOSO

The old fort now has sound effects of gunfire, triggered as you enter the various bunkers and tunnels and a variety of cannons and hideouts/lookout posts.

2 SENTOSA ISLAND: UNDERWATER WORLD

The walk-through aquarium is a thrill for all ages; the touch pool at the entrance area is both educational and direct.

3 SENTOSA ISLAND: CORALARIUM

Different types of coral, a turtle pool

and, perhaps the highlight for children, feeding the wild monkeys every afternoon.

4 SINGAPORE ZOO

A host of interesting animals, and a special children's zoo, complete with miniature train, two adventure playgrounds, pools for paddling and for toy boats, and of course, various milking and sheep round-up displays as well as the usual farmyard animals.

5 JURONG BIRDPARK

Have your photo taken with various macaws and parrots; watch a bird show to see the natural flight of hawks or macaws; a large choice of birds to see, and a walk through aviary to be opened late in 1992.

6 JURONG CROCODILE PARADISE

A chance to see as many crocodiles as you could want to, well caged in and still visible.

7 SINGAPORE CROCODILARIUM

Crocodiles again, quite close up—convenient if you're in the east as opposed to the west side of town.

8 HAW PAR VILLA

Chinese mythological theme park with a water-flume ride, a boat ride through the belly of a dragon, various theatrical performances of Chinese legends (in English or Mandarin), film shows, moralistic tableaux.

9 TANG DYNASTY CITY

Another Chinese theme park with film studios, pagodas, temples, food outlets and shops.

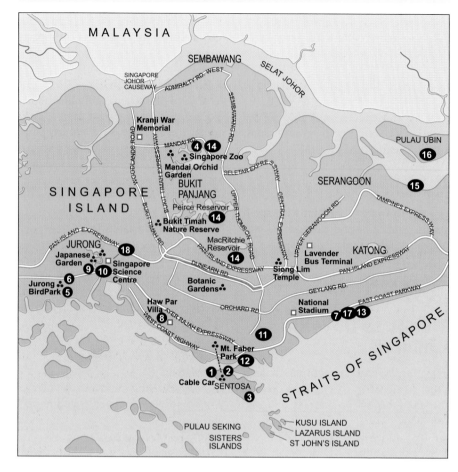

Places to take children.

11 NATIONAL MUSEUM

A children's section, modelled costumes, easy tableaux to show Singapore's history.

12 GUINNESS WORLD OF RECORDS

Singapore's own greatest, fastest, biggest feats and facts.

13 EAST COAST PARK

Good venue for a picnic and a swim, or even a barbecue, bikes can be hired, as can windsurfers and laser dinghies from the East Coast Sailing Centre.

10 SINGAPORE SCIENCE CENTRE

A hands-on treatment of various aspects of science: press knobs, dials, computer screens and pit your intelligence against a whole load of puzzles.

14 MACRITCHIE RESERVOIR PARK, UPPER PEIRCE RESERVOIR, SELETAR RESERVOIR

All good spots for a picnic and a walk, with views of reservoir and countryside. Seletar Reservoir has paddleboats for hire.

15 PASIR RIS PARK

An adventure playground divided into three different areas for different age groups; clean seaside beaches for swimming.

16 PULAU UBIN

A boat ride away from Changi Point, bicycles can be hired to explore the island, one with quarrying and some farming activity.

17 BIG SPLASH

A water slide into a large public pool on the east coast.

18 CN LEISURE PARK

Rather sleepy public pool, handy if you're in the west of the island, with a whirlpool and a water slide and some funfair rides.

Museums, Exhibitions and Palaces

Collections of artefacts, photographs and memorabilia are available in Singapore, and in Kuala Lumpur and Malacca on day excursions. As well as the public museums listed below, visitors interested in antiques and collectibles from the region should simply browse through the many shops in the Tanglin Shopping Centre, the Shaw Centre and further afield to Just Anthony in Payar Lebar or Tatiana on Upper Paya Lebar Road.

1 SINGAPORE MARITIME SHOWCASE

To be opened later in 1992, a hands-on display of Singapore's port and its traffic.

2 LEE KONG CHIAN ART MUSEUM

Hidden on the top floor of the Arts and Sciences Block 5 in the National University, an interesting collection of Chinese calligraphy, painting, porcelain and sculpture.

3 CHINAMAN SCHOLAR GALLERY

A small, friendly and interesting collection of household items, furnishings and clothes displayed and explained by the proprietor over a cup of Chinese tea.

4 NATIONAL MUSEUM

Dioramas of Singaporean history, interior furnishing styles, photographs and artefacts, porcelain, jade, children's section and temporary exhibitions.

5 REPUBLIC OF SINGAPORE AIR FORCE MUSEUM

Free-standing planes outside, three halls of models, photographs, radar mock-ups, history and anecdotes.

6 PERANAKAN SHOW HOUSE MUSEUM

A typical Peranakan-style house with furnishings and clothing in Emerald Hill.

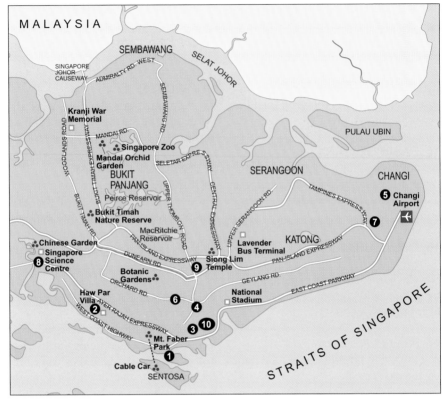

MALAYSIA

SEMBAWANG

SELAT JOHOR

SINGAPORE JOHOR CAUSEWAY

ADMIRALTY RD. WEST

SEMBAWANG RD.

WOODLANDS ROAD

Kranji War Memorial

MANDAI RD.

PULAU UBIN

Singapore Zoo

Mandai Orchid Garden

SELETAR EXPRESSWAY

BUKIT PANJANG

SERANGOON

CHANGI

Peirce Reservoir

UPPER THOMSON ROAD

5 Changi Airport

Bukit Timah Nature Reserve

MacRitchie Reservoir

7

CENTRAL EXPRESSWAY

TAMPINES EXPRESSWAY

Chinese Garden

PAN-ISLAND EXPRESSWAY

UPPER SERANGOON RD.

Lavender Bus Terminal

KATONG

Singapore Science Centre

DUNEARN RD.

8

9 Siong Lim Temple

PAN-ISLAND EXPRESSWAY

Botanic Gardens

ORCHARD RD.

GEYLANG RD.

EAST COAST PARKWAY

Haw Par Villa

2

WEST COAST HIGHWAY

AYER RAJAH EXPRESSWAY

6

4

National Stadium

3 **10**

Mt. Faber Park

1

Cable Car

SENTOSA

STRAITS OF SINGAPORE

BUKIT TIMAH RD.

7 CHANGI PRISON MUSEUM

A prefabricated hut by the entrance to Changi Prison containing photographs and drawings of POW life, as well as various medals and oddments. An adjacent replica chapel has regular remembrance services.

8 SINGAPORE SCIENCE CENTRE

A hands-on, have-fun approach to space, flight, mathematics, geology, biology—you name it.

9 SUN YAT SEN VILLA

Good example of a large villa, dedicated to the memory of the Chinese visionary and first provisional president of China. Upstairs there is, as well as

Where to see the old history of Singapore and Malaysia in museums, exhibitions and palaces.

a library, a small display of POW memorabilia and photographs.

10 EMPRESS PLACE EXHIBITION HALL

Well-staged displays of Chinese art and culture.

Malaysian Sites

JOHOR BARU SULTAN'S PALACE

European-style architecture, imposing ceremonial reception rooms, photographs and family trees, wide-ranging porcelain collection, Anglo-Malay furnishings, hunting trophies, silverware, materials, weapons.

KUALA LUMPUR NATIONAL MUSEUM
Historic vehicles including rickshaws, traditional furnishings, costumes, musical instruments, cultural accessories such as puppets, opera masks, stuffed birds, temporary exhibits, sporting history.

MALACCA SULTANATE'S PALACE
Costumes displayed on wax models, crafts, instruments, porcelain, teakwood finishing and furnishing.

MALACCA STADTHUYS
Dutch colonial building in central square housing colonial furniture, ceramics, weapons, bridal chamber, transport and historical museum of photographs and dioramas on the upper floor.

The Colonial Heart of the Island

The cluster of buildings on three sides of the Padang area itself, an attempt by colonial town planners to re-create a village green in their far-flung outpost, hark back to the island's days as a Straits Settlement and then as a Crown Colony. The City Hall and Supreme Court sit stolidly to the north, serving administrative purposes now as in former days; the Parliament building nearer the river is located in a former merchant's house; and the Empress Place Building and Victoria Memorial Hall, now both used for public entertainment, face the Singapore Cricket Club, no longer reserved for Caucasian members, but retaining much old-world style. To get there, take the MRT to Raffles Place or City Hall and walk.

The Singapore River

In many ways the Singapore River is the heart of the island, the key to its history and success. According to the 15th-century *Malay Annals*, it was here, at Kuala Teniagala (big river or estuary) that Sang Nila Utama, the 14th-century founder of ancient Singapura, first landed. It was also on its banks that in 1819 Sir Stamford Raffles disembarked to found the British trading station.

T he bright white painted St Andrew's Cathedral, now dwarfed by the Westin Stamford Hotel, was once the tallest building near the Padang.

One way to see the river is to take a boat ride up it. Boats leave regularly from Clifford Pier or from Raffles Place Landing Site on North Boat Quay (*see* page 271 for further details). A river trip will give you a good general initial orientation. From the boat you can see the vestiges of colonialism—the **Victoria Theatre** and **Memorial Hall, Parliament House**, the **Empress Place Exhibition Centre**, the various bridges constructed during the colonial period, and at the same time your guide will point out and identify the various soaring towers in the city and across the Padang. The contrast of the somewhat shabby but endearing Chinese shophouses, currently almost all undergoing renovation, right next to the site of the emerging 270-m

125

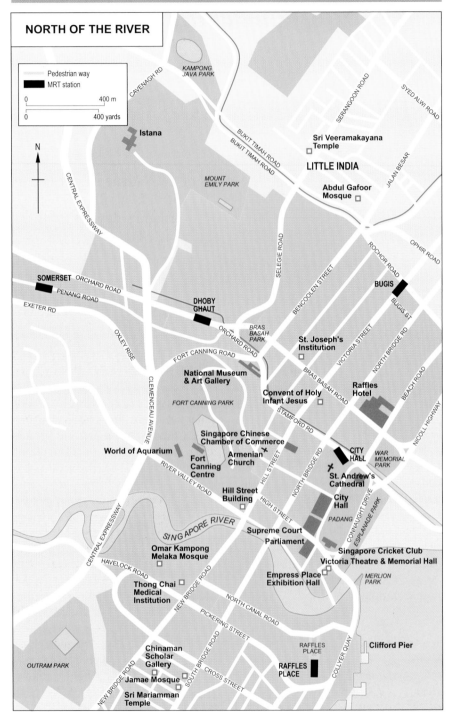

NORTH OF THE RIVER

Pedestrian way
MRT station

0   400 m
0   400 yards

N

KAMPONG JAVA PARK
CAVENAGH RD
SERANGOON ROAD
SYED ALWI ROAD

Istana
BUKIT TIMAH ROAD
BUKIT TIMAH ROAD

Sri Veeramakayana Temple
JALAN BESAR

LITTLE INDIA

MOUNT EMILY PARK
Abdul Gafoor Mosque

CENTRAL EXPRESSWAY

SELEGIE ROAD
ROCHOR ROAD
OPHIR ROAD

SOMERSET
ORCHARD ROAD
PENANG ROAD
EXETER RD

BENCOOLEN STREET

BUGIS
BUGIS ST

DHOBY GHAUT
BRAS BASAH PARK

St. Joseph's Institution
VICTORIA STREET
NORTH BRIDGE RD

ORCHARD ROAD
FORT CANNING ROAD

OKLEY RISE

National Museum & Art Gallery
FORT CANNING PARK
BRAS BASAH ROAD

Raffles Hotel
BEACH ROAD

Convent of Holy Infant Jesus
STAMFORD RD
NICOLL HIGHWAY

CLEMENCEAU AVENUE

World of Aquarium
Fort Canning Centre

Singapore Chinese Chamber of Commerce
Armenian Church

CITY HALL
WAR MEMORIAL PARK

HILL STREET
NORTH BRIDGE RD

St. Andrew's Cathedral

Hill Street Building
HIGH STREET

City Hall
PADANG
CONNAUGHT DRIVE
ESPLANADE PARK

RIVER VALLEY ROAD

SINGAPORE RIVER

Supreme Court
Parliament

CENTRAL EXPRESSWAY

Omar Kampong Melaka Mosque

Singapore Cricket Club
Victoria Theatre & Memorial Hall

HAVELOCK ROAD

Empress Place Exhibition Hall
MERLION PARK

Thong Chai Medical Institution
NEW BRIDGE ROAD

NORTH CANAL ROAD
PICKERING STREET

OUTRAM PARK

Chinaman Scholar Gallery
SOUTH BRIDGE ROAD
RAFFLES PLACE

Clifford Pier
COLLYER QUAY

Jamae Mosque
CROSS STREET
RAFFLES PLACE

Sri Mariamman Temple
NEW BRIDGE ROAD

Clean Waters

The river was home to numerous bumboats—small, wooden boats, moored along both banks—and its banks a lively but extremely dirty mélange of hawker stalls, foodstuffs and trading goods. In 1977 a Clean River Campaign was launched by the then Prime Minister, Mr Lee Kuan Yew, the bumboats were all relocated to Pasir Panjang, the hawkers all removed to the government-inspected food centres we see today, and fish returned to the river. Today you can walk along either side of the river, from Fullerton Bridge to Read Bridge, seeing the occasional turtle or fish. At Chinese New Year the Singapore River becomes the lit-up focal point of the island's festivities, and on other occasions such as the Mooncake Festival it is also lit up, with night markets lining its banks.

(886-ft) UOB tower is typical of Singapore: the very new and the old live side-by-side. You may also see the projected sculptures of the new tourist emblem, Kucinta, the Singapura cat, planned to grace the riverside.

On the north side of the river, the **Raffles Landing Site** has a polymarble replica of the bronze statue which stands outside the Victoria Memorial Hall. This statue is said to stand on the very site where Raffles stepped ashore in 1819.

*M*ap of the area north of the Singapore River.

Empress Place Exhibition Hall

1 Empress Place, Singapore 0617
Telephone: 336 7633
Opening Hours: 9 a.m–6 p.m. daily, including Sundays and public holidays

Regular, well-staged exhibitions are on display here, often for several months at a time, so do check with your hotel information desk or the tourist board to find the latest attraction. In addition to the main exhibition galleries, there are often lesser exhibitions of local art, often for sale, and a selection of boutiques and restaurants within the building.

The Georgian-style building (1864–65), built by the government engineer J. F. A. McNair, who also designed the *Istana*, was originally intended as a new court-house, and fulfilled a variety of government roles, most recently housing the Immigration Department and National Registration Office, before becoming an art gallery in 1988.

The Victoria Theatre and Memorial Hall

8 Empress Place, Singapore 0617

This handsome building, along with the next-door Exhibition Hall, dominates Empress Place. It comprises a theatre and a concert hall, and is the home of the Singapore Symphony Orchestra and a well-used cultural centre. Check the local press for details of performances.

The original building (half of the current building) was completed in

1862 by Chief Engineer John Bennett, and served as a Town Hall before becoming a theatre. The tower and additional memorial hall were added in the early 20th century in commemoration of Queen Victoria's Jubilee by R. A. J. Bidwell, who left his mark on several municipal buildings in Singapore. It is known in Chinese as *Tai Chung Lau*—Big Clock Tower.

The Empress Place Exhibition Hall (left) and the Victoria Theatre and Memorial Hall (right) viewed across the Singapore river.

Colourful Comments on Raffles
When the original Raffles Statue was unveiled on 27 June 1887, on the 50th anniversary of Queen Victoria's accession to the throne, people in the crowd were heard to exclaim with surprise that the great founder was a black man! This rumour was quickly dispelled, though may be a factor in the commissioning of the (white) polymarble replica now located by the Singapore River. The (black) Raffles statue originally had an Italian-style colonnade and a pool surrounding it, which were destroyed during the Second World War. The statue was firstly located on the Padang until being moved to its present position in 1919.

In front of the Victoria Memorial Hall stands the bronze statue of Sir Stamford Raffles, erected on the Padang in 1887 and moved to its present position after the First World War. Its original semicircular marble colonnade was destroyed during the Second World War. The obelisk-shaped monument nearby is dedicated to the brief visit in 1850 of the Marquis of Dalhousie, then Governor-General of India, and was designed by the prolific Government Surveyor John Turnbull Thomson.

After sightseeing or visiting the exhibitions at Empress Place, stop off for a fruit juice, or a plate of *mee goreng* at the Empress Place hawker centre. (For details of local food terms, *see* page 258.)

The Cricket Club

Connaught Drive, Singapore 0617

The Cricket Club is a private club, and only members and their guests

Cricket being played outside the Singapore Cricket Club on the Padang.

may enter. You can, however, see the pavilion from the Padang and from the Empress Place side.

The club was founded in 1852 and various pavilions occupied a site to the south before the 1884 pavilion which is the central part of today's building to which side wings were added in the 1920s.

The Padang

St Andrew's Road/Connaught Drive, Singapore 0617

The green open space between the Singapore Cricket Club and the Singapore Recreation Club was originally known as Raffles Plain or the Esplanade. The first Resident of Singapore, Colonel Farquhar, first encouraged Europeans to settle and build houses on the site of today's City Hall, and reserved this open space for recreation. The island's first land reclamation project entailed widening this area to reclaim what is now Connaught Drive in the 1890s.

Members of the cricket and recreation clubs regularly use the Padang for sports activities, and National Day parades and celebrations likewise on occasion use this central area. A footpath bisects the Padang, from Coleman Street across to the (First World) War Memorial on the Esplanade.

The Esplanade

Connaught Drive, Singapore 0617

The original waterfront in Singapore followed the path of today's Connaught Drive, just to the south of the Padang, and across the river followed the line of today's Shenton Way. The Esplanade, the whole complex of Marina Square and its hotels, the Marina South development and a large swathe of land over which the ECP (East Coast Parkway) expressway now passes is all reclaimed land.

If it is not too hot, you can have a pleasant walk along the Esplanade from Empress Place. As well as a view of the boats and general marine activity in Marina Bay, the walk is graced with a variety of monuments. As you walk away from Empress Place, the first you see is the pagoda-shaped Lim Bo Seng Memorial, to a Chinese war hero and member of the resistance Force 136 during the Japanese Occupation who was captured and tortured to death. Next is the large and rather brash wavy steel

*T*he statue of an elephant outside the Parliament Building donated by King Chulalongkorn of Siam during his visit to Singapore in 1871.

monument to celebrate the 1977 Clean River Campaign. The Cenotaph looks across the Padang, and commemorates the victims of the First World War. The "chopsticks" memorial to the civilian victims of the Japanese Occupation is the towering monument which sits on its own in War Memorial Park across Stamford Road.

Parliament House

High Street, Singapore 0617

Built as a private house for the merchant John Argyle Maxwell by G. D. Coleman in 1826, with various additions and extensions during the 1870s and 1900s, Parliament House is rather a delightful small building. You can visit when Parliament is in session: check the local press for details.

The next-door building on High Street is another example of Singapore's colonial neo-classical architecture, constructed in 1864 by the Public Works Department to house the Court House, but used instead as the public offices of the judiciary. It was formerly known as the Secretariat, and more recently used as the Attorney-General's Chambers, though Parliament has now taken it over as additional space for meeting rooms. It is scheduled to house a mini museum displaying artefacts and memorabilia.

The Supreme Court

St Andrew's Road, Singapore 0617

This was the last classical-style building built in Singapore, completed in 1939, designed by Frank Dorrington Ward, the then Municipal Architect. It stands on the site of the former Hotel de L'Europe. The circular dome recalls London's Old Bailey, and the whole façade is clearly intended to inspire confidence in the majesty of the (then) British legal system. Its registry has now shifted next door to City Hall.

City Hall

St Andrew's Road, Singapore 0617

This rather heavy classical-style colonnaded building has now assumed a dirty brownish colour. Events of national importance have taken place on its steps, from the Japanese surrender on 12 September 1945 to the Proclamation of Independence in 1965.

Today, its steps are occasionally graced by wedding parties posing for photography.

St Andrew's Cathedral

St Andrew's Road, Singapore 0617

Built by Indian convict labour and completed in 1861, St Andrew's Cathedral is modelled on an Early English-style abbey in Hampshire. Its plain white spire is now dwarfed by The Westin Stamford tower, though it retains the peaceful and timeless feel of English Gothic despite its tropical setting. Inside, the soaring arches and plain Anglican-style furnishings are particularly reminiscent of English cathedrals.

Various memorials and graves are in the cathedral, including a memorial to 23 people killed during the 1915 sepoy mutiny (*see* page 44). Service times are listed by the entrance.

Raffles Hotel

1 Beach Road, Singapore 0718
Telephone: 337 1886

A $160-million restoration programme was carried out at the Raffles Hotel from 1989–91, with research worldwide into mementoes, souvenirs and details to ensure a faithful reproduction of the grand hotel in its prime. It now has 104 suites, each with teakwood floor, *en suite* bathroom, and the whole range of luxury facilities. The renovation includes a replica of the original 4-m (13-ft)-high cast-iron entrance portico as it was in 1910–20, as well as stained-glass commissions,

RAFFLES HOTEL

and 400 existing pieces of furniture have been restored for reuse. Many of the original mouldings for pillars and cornices have been reconstructed, with over 700 new mouldings and templates made from designs shown on old postcards and photographs. Some of the original china and silverware has been saved and will be used again.

Entering the expansive lobby is like taking a walk back through time: doors are opened courteously by uniformed doormen wishing you welcome; stunning floral displays and period-style armchairs sit invitingly to either side of the marble floored lobby. The interior balconies on the two storeys around the main lobby lead your eye up to the soaring skylight roof; the inviting carpeted stairways are for hotel guests only and casual tourists will be politely prevented from intruding.

The **Tiffin Room** is on your left as you enter; the **Raffles Grill** to your right; the tiny **Writers' Bar** is also

*T*he Raffles Hotel,
newly restored to its 1920s glory.

tucked away on your right. Leaving through the main lobby, a right turn will take you to the **Bar and Billiard Room** (beneath which the last tiger to be shot in Singapore was reputedly shot in 1902), which has the original Raffles billiard table at the Beach Road end, and one donated by the government from the *Istana* at the far end. Next to the Bar and Billiard Room is the **Palm Garden**, and you can follow a small path by the hotel to the **Fern Court** which is lined by a row of Raffles Hotel merchandising shops opening also on to Bras Basah Road. To enjoy the hotel at leisure, have a meal, a cup of afternoon tea, or even a Singapore Sling at the Bar and Billiard Room or the Long Bar.

Adjoining the hotel on the North Bridge Road side, an up-market retail development of 70 shops on three floors, known as "Raffles" which includes the jeweller Tiffany, Hardy Amies and the Japanese designer Mori. It is linked to the rest of the Raffles Hotel by the **Raffles Courtyard** and **The Lawn**, an outdoor function and restaurant area where you can listen to caged songbirds during breakfast or eat grilled seafood for dinner. **The Empress Cafe**, a late-opening coffee shop, and **Ah Teng's Bakery** face the Raffles City complex across Bras Basah Road, with the famous **Long Bar**, its tiled floor strewn with peanut shells, located on the second and third floors above them.

The Raffles Hotel Museum, located on the third floor of this wing, contains all kinds of photographs, menus, luggage labels, porcelain, silverware, and newspaper cuttings from the late 19th century onwards, as well as architectural drawings of the hotel. Some photographs of other great hotels of the time, such as the Grand Hotel de L'Europe or the Sea View give a feeling of what Singapore must have looked like during the Golden Age of Travel, the period from 1880–1939, when popular tourism was beginning. There are few captions, sadly, but artistically displayed mementoes—and an adjacent gift shop selling everything from coasters and reproduction prints to cuddly toys, key rings and mugs so that visitors can take home a little bit of history.

This wing also houses the **Jubilee Hall playhouse**, with five multi-media shows on Singapore history, cultural revues and a variety of short plays, lectures and films. The 300-seat **Ballroom**, the **Empress Room Chinese Restaurant** and the **Seah Street Deli** serving American-style fare are popular eating venues.

The Raffles Hotel first opened on 1 December 1887 in a house leased by the three Sarkies brothers—Tigran, Arshak and Aviet—from the Arab merchant Syed Mohammed Bin Ahmed Alsagoff. The main neo-classical building was opened in 1899, designed by the prolific R. A. J. Bidwell, with Singapore's first electric lights and fans, as well as en suite bathrooms. It swiftly became the stuff of legends, with Singapore's last tiger reputedly shot in the billiard room in 1902, and the renowned Singapore Sling invented by the Barman Ngiam Tong Boon and first served in the Long Bar in 1915. Its many famous patrons over the years have included Rudyard Kipling, Somerset Maugham, Noel Coward, Charlie Chaplin, Herman Hesse and many, many more.

Just before the surrender to the Japanese during the Second World War the Raffles Hotel silver treasures were buried under the Palm Court, to be retrieved once more in 1945. The last of the Sarkies brothers died in 1931, and the hotel was taken over by a public company, Raffles Hotel Ltd.

Things Left Unsaid
Much of the highly tasteful revamped Raffles Hotel merchandising focuses on Rudyard Kipling's phrase: "feed at Raffles when visiting Singapore". What it doesn't add, is the rest of his suggestion, that one should stay at the Hotel de L'Europe rather than at the Grand Old Lady. The Raffles Hotel Museum shows photographs of this and other grand hotels which have now disappeared, from which you gain a real insight into the city's former glory.

The Convent of the Holy Infant Jesus

Victoria Street, Singapore 0718

This building is scheduled to be converted into yet another up-market shopping and dining complex, retaining the architectural framework since this is a gazetted national monument. At present there's little to see over the wall.

St Joseph's Institution

Bras Basah Road, Singapore 0718

This building is currently earmarked for renovation as part of the National Museum, (see page 136) and, like the Convent of the Holy Infant Jesus, is closed to visitors, though you can peep through the ironwork gates.

On the corner of Hill Street and Stamford Road, is the **MPH building**, a 1908 red and white Edwardian façade recently renovated and housing an excellent bookshop. Stamford House, on adjoining Stamford Road, likewise is undergoing restoration.

The Armenian Church

Hill Street, Singapore 0617

The charming little Church of St Gregory the Illuminator is well worth a visit. It stands below Fort Canning Rise, on Hill Street, between the red and white striped Central Fire Station and the American Embassy, and is the oldest church in Singapore.

The church was built by the architect G. D. Coleman in 1835, and is circular with a wide verandah encircling it to protect the windows from heat and rain. The tower and spire were added in 1847. Buried in the graveyard are members of prominent Armenian families, including Miss Agnes Joaquim, who discovered the Vanda Miss Joaquim Orchid, which is now Singapore's national flower. The spot is an oasis of tranquillity in the heart of the city.

Singapore Chinese Chamber of Commerce and Industry

47 Hill Street, Singapore 0617

The colourful Chinese Chamber of Commerce and Industry, on Hill Street opposite the Armenian Church, hosts the occasional art exhibition—check in the newspapers for details. Otherwise, you can simply admire the green roof tiles, mock Chinese-style architecture, the two South China entrance lions and the colourful porcelain dragon murals on each side of the entrance.

On Armenian Street you will find the recently opened "alternative" cultural centre at the **Substation**. Here you can have a snack or a drink in the *Kopi* (coffee) Garden, join various courses in drama, photography, dance or music, listen to a wide variety of musicians performing, and look at whatever is currently on display in the art gallery. On Sundays there is a small flea market, where you can browse through a variety of stalls to pick up local bargains and bric-à-brac. Frequent "fringe" theatre performances are staged at the **Guinness Theatre** here, as well as a range of creative workshops—check the press for details. Funded by private sponsors, the Substation's future remains a little doubtful, but its very existence (since 1990) is a new and exciting departure in the cultural life and broadening outlook of the city.

At the corner of River Valley Road and Hill Street is the pale blue, six-storey neo-classical **Hill Street Building**. It was a police station from 1934–80, and since 1983, after renovation, it has housed the Archives and Oral History Department. When it was built it was believed to have bad *feng shui*, since it destroyed the fish shape the area had previously had, and many Chinese traders blamed trading difficulties on this.

World of Aquarium

River Valley Road, Singapore 0617
Telephone: 334 3762
Opening Hours: 9.30 a.m.–8.30 p.m. Monday–Friday; 9.00 a.m.–9.00 p.m. weekends and public holidays

This ungrammatically named aquarium is the former Van Kleef Aquarium, which closed down shortly after Sentosa's Underwater World (*see* page 223) opened in 1991, but is now under new ownership. Not much has changed apart from the name, some colourfully painted fish panels on the entrance, a marginally increased entrance fee, and a better souvenir shop selling fish earrings, teeshirts and arty postcards.

There is a total of 68 tanks, of which 37 contain freshwater species and the balance marine water species—

according to the accompanying notices, that is. The tanks are comparatively small, often only a square metre (yard) or so large, yet the overhead captions very often picture completely different fish species from those you can see, which makes the visit rather frustrating. Doubtless somewhere within the aquarium there will be a picture and details about the fish or coral you are looking at, but you may have to walk some way to find it. Some spectacular corals are there, including the aptly named durian coral (I couldn't smell it through the glass!), and various fish species ranging from the huge Electric Eel, to Catfish, Shark Suckers and Stingrays, to smaller Tiger Barbs, Guppies, Latticed Butterfly Fish, Long Horned Cowfish and Sea Horses, to name a few of those I managed to identify. You do see the fish close-up in these small tanks—those without corals seem an extremely bare habitat for fish—but in my opinion the aquarium comes a definite second to Underwater World.

Fort Canning Park

Fort Canning Road, Singapore 0617

This hill in the centre of the city was originally called *Bukit Larangan* (Forbidden Hill), possibly because of the rumours that the Malay Kings of the 14th century (*see* page 41) were buried here. Archaeological findings from the site are displayed in the National Museum. The first Resident of the East India Company, Colonel Farquhar, cleared the hill and Raffles' first house stood on the top as the first Government House, until this was relocated to its Orchard/Cavenagh Road site. A fort was subsequently constructed there in 1860 (hence its name), and then destroyed to make space for the reservoir. Raffles also sited Singapore's first Botanic Gardens on this hill, though they were closed in 1829 due to costs.

There are two white Gothic-style gateways, built in 1846, to the Christian cemetery at the bottom of the hill. Tombstones are set into the two brick walls leading up the hill and there is a small area of gravestones and monuments. Halfway up the hill is the reputed **Tomb of Iskandar Shah**, covered by a Malay-style roof to protect it from the elements. The building on the top is the **Fort Canning Centre**, which houses the Singapore Dance Theatre's studios and the Black Box, the theatre used by the TheatreWorks company. Check the press for performance details: some outdoor performances are held in the park.

From the top of the hill you can walk round the reservoir, to see good views of the Singapore river, the Hill Street building and the city. The park itself is a peaceful spot, including an old fort and a small playground. The wartime control bunkers beneath the reservoir were opened to the public in 1992.

National Museum and Art Gallery

Stamford Road, Singapore 0923
Telephone: 337 7355
Opening Hours: 9 a.m.–4.30 p.m. Tuesdays–Sundays, closed Mondays
To Get There: MRT to Dhoby Ghaut;

buses 139 and 198 from Havelock Road; SBS buses 7, 13, 14, 16, 124, 171, 173 and 174; CBD bus 1 and TIBS buses 167, 182 and 850 from Orchard Road; buses 61, 124 and 166 from Raffles City.

The National Museum, formerly the Raffles Museum, was substantially restored and renovated in 1985, only opening at the end of 1989. It originally housed the Raffles Library and a large zoological collection from various colonialists' travels in the region, as well as a growing ethnographic display from the early 1900s onwards. As a colonial institution, the museum provided mainly for colonial tastes; now the museum obviously has Singaporean staff, public and aims. The library was separated from the museum in the 1950s and most of the zoological collection is now in the NUS Zoology Department as the Zoological Reference Collection.

The classical-style building was designed by Majors H.E. McCallum and J.F. McNair and opened by the then Governor, Sir F.A. Weld in 1887. An extension parallel building, built from 1904–1907, now houses the Art Gallery. Architecturally the museum is a prime example of Victorian and Edwardian Classical revivalist architecture, with examples of all three Greek orders united skilfully. The series of rounded arches on the ground-floor end with pedimented arches and Doric pilasters; the second-level windows have semicircular and triangular pediments separated by Ionic pilasters; while the large 27.4-m (90-ft) dome over the entrance rotunda is decorated with Corinthian columns and topped with silver fish scale tiles. The dome creates an imposing internal space, with colourful shafts of light entering through its stained-glass skylights, and attractive cast-iron balusters within the open arches of the upper rotunda. Recent restoration was necessitated by extensive termite damage to the tiles (all of which were individually numbered before removal and termite treatment), as well as to the timber roof trusses now replaced by aluminium structures.

It's well worth a visit for an hour or so, both to enjoy the building itself and the various exhibits and collections on display. As you enter, the ground-floor level of the domed area or lower

*F*loor plan of the National Museum and Art Gallery.

rotunda features four large oil portraits of influential men in Singapore's history from the museum's large collection of such portraits. These are changed periodically. Behind the rotunda, to the right of the entrance, is a copy of the famous portrait of Sir Stamford Raffles by G. F. Joseph in 1817 (the original hangs in London's National Portrait Gallery). A display of reproductions of old maps of the area and Singapore's—or rather, Temasek's—early history is set out around the outside of the dome, together with some early models of the island's habitation, archaeological finds from Fort Canning Hill, a collection of bells including the Revere Bell given to St Andrew's Cathedral in 1834 by Mrs Joseph Balestier, the wife of the then American Consul, copies of

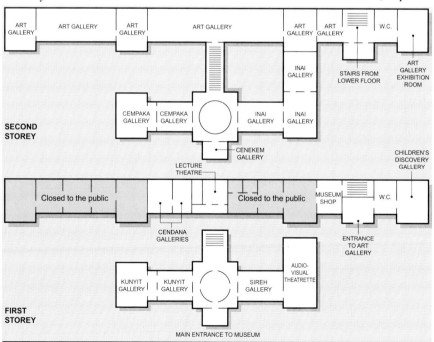

Singapore's National Museum, formerly the Raffles Museum, an architectural jewel in its own right.

documents relating to Singapore and Malaysia's independence, and Raffles' treaties of 1819 and 1823 confirming Singapore's colonial status.

To the left of the main entrance are two darkened galleries—the *Kunyit* (turmeric) Galleries—which contain 20 dioramas of Singapore's history, from the arrival of Raffles in 1819 through to the first session of an independent Parliament in 1965. These were made by craftsmen from the Ayak Museum in the Philippines. To the right of the main entrance the *Sireh* (betel) Gallery is arranged as a Straits Chinese (*Peranakan*) home, with highly ornate opium chairs, an

altar for ancestor worship, planter's chairs and a wealth of elaborate furniture, photographs, ornaments and costumes. Through the Sireh Gallery is a small "theatrette" with regular audio-visual slide shows on Singapore's history. Check the daily papers for exact details of showings, or check as you enter the museum.

Up the stairs (no sign of a lift for the disabled) you can turn right to the six galleries of the National Art Gallery, opened in 1976, which hosts a permanent display of over 600 local works as well as a regular stream of exhibitions sponsored by local businesses. (There is a separate entrance to the Art Gallery, which is free, next to the Museum Shop at the back of the Museum.) If you want to continue within the Museum, turn left to regain the domed central area. Around the balconied upper rotunda are examples of Chinese ceramics donated by the Shaw Foundation. Above the Straits Chinese House (right of the main entrance on ground level) are the three *Inai* (henna) Galleries, wed for temporary exhibitions as well as displays of Singapore's multi-cultural heritage. The *Cengkeh* (cloves) Gallery, above the main entrance, houses temporary collections of pottery and artefacts.

Across the upper rotunda, above the dioramas, are the *Cempaka* galleries. You come firstly to an exhibition room, most recently displaying historical garments. Beyond this gallery is the renowned Jade Collection of over 300 pieces, much of which was donated by the Aw family of Tiger Balm fame in January 1980. As well as jade, carvings and pieces are shown of rose quartz, adventurine, smoky quartz, jasper and agate.

Downstairs once more, there are two more galleries to visit, located beneath the Art Gallery in the second wing further from the main Stamford Road. There are the *Cendana* (sandalwood) Galleries, which are again used for temporary exhibitions—most recently an impressive display of Singapore during the Japanese occupation. Also in this second wing is another lecture theatrette, the museum shop (with access to the National Art Gallery), and at the extreme right the Children's Discovery Gallery with hands-on exhibits, open to organized school parties by prior arrangement.

With so much of interest to see, it is rather surprising that the museum is a little chaotic compared with other tourist attractions. You pay your one dollar entrance fee as you enter, which has to be a note rather than a coin to use the highly technical ticketing machine (don't panic—the lady on the door has change). At the time of writing there were no plans or leaflets about the museum available—hence my inclusion of one—and the little book shop you can find at the entrance to the Art Gallery features postcards of the dioramas and jade carvings, some reproduction cards of old engravings, and a selection of well-worn, rather academic journals which are probably not for sale. There are toilets, yet there are only squat-style lavatories for the ladies, a misjudgment for the potential number of Western tourist visitors. And no inviting coffee shop or even snack bar either—so if you need refreshment and rest after absorbing photographs, artefacts and displays for an hour or so, you have to keep going, either down Stamford Road to a small hawker centre outside the National Library, or up to the YMCA complex where you can at least grab a McDonalds!

Outside the museum is a two-storey high, coffee-brown, carved ceremonial ironwood pole, a gift from the people of Sarawak in Borneo. Traditionally this type of pole would be in front of a headman's home at the centre of a longhouse, and would mark the capture of an enemy's head in battle or the safe return of villagers from a long journey. There have been close links between Singapore and Sarawak since colonial times. There is also a rather curious raggedy doll-type sculpture of seated figures outside the museum.

There are ambitious plans for the future development of the National

Museum as a cultural centre of Singapore. Two nearby buildings, the Tao Nan School in Armenian Street, and the St Joseph's Institution (*see* page 134) on Bras Basah Road, are projected to house the new Children's Museum and expanded Art Gallery respectively, as well as providing the Museum with much-needed storage facilities for vulnerable exhibits in a tropical climate. The National Library, currently next door to the Museum, is to be relocated to a new site on nearby Queen Street, and a new 6,000-sq m (5,000-sq yd) gallery of Asian art, to display Chinese ceramics, Indian sculptures and examples of Islamic art, is planned on the vacated site within the 1990s.

Orchard Road

Singapore 0923

The area along Orchard Road from Dhoby Ghaut to Tudor Court, and along Scotts Road from Orchard Road to the **Goodwood Park Hotel** (like its rival Raffles Hotel, also designed by R. A. J. Bidwell), is the main shopping area of Singapore. For a detailed guide to shopping malls, *see* page 272. The whole road is currently (1991) undergoing an ambitious improvement scheme, whereby the road level in some places is being raised by as much as 1 m (3 ft), to keep it level with the improved pedestrian walkways. Underpasses are also being constructed to ease congestion at traffic lights. This improvement, costing $26 million, will widen the walkways from 1.5 m (5 ft) to between 6 and 10 m (20–33 ft), and is geared to improve

pedestrian safety. A colourful planting scheme has been contributed by the Parks and Recreational Department, with big beds of bougainvilleas, heliconias, cats whiskers, *Plumbago Capensis*—all chosen to give a really colourful effect. Until the scheme is completed, however, there is a considerable amount of construction work throughout this area, with nightly roadworks on those sections of the road being raised.

Next to the Cockpit Hotel on Penang Road, and now owned by that hotel, is the **House of Tan Yeok Nee**. This used to be the Salvation Army Headquarters for Singapore. It was built in 1885, and is the only remaining southern-Chinese-style mansion, with porcelain roof decoration and further decorations inside.

The Istana

Cavenagh Road, Singapore 0923

The former Government House was built in 1869 in a colonial Classical style, with Ionic, Doric and Corinthian columns and an impressive square central entrance. It sits majestically within its extensive grounds (part of a former nutmeg estate) to the north of Orchard Road, completely shielded from view from surrounding buildings by a thick row of trees.

The only nearby building which could overlook it, Plaza Singapore, has the windows of its top floor blocked on the side overlooking the *Istana* grounds. The *Istana* is the official residence of the President of the Republic of Singapore, President Wee Kim Wee, and the Prime Minister also has an office in the annexe and uses the building for official visits and receptions. The spacious grounds contain a private 9-hole golf-course, a small lake, lily ponds and landscaped Japanese and Marsh Gardens. Prominently displayed in front of the *Istana* is the gun presented to Lord Louis Mountbatten by the defeated Japanese in 1945.

The grounds are open to the public at the President's discretion, generally on four public holidays: New Year's Day (1 January), one day of the Chinese New Year, Hari Raya Puasa (the end of Ramadan), and Deepavali (the Hindu festival of lights, in September or October). Check in the newspapers or at your hotel reception if you are visiting during one of these times. In addition there are changes of the guard at the main entrance on Orchard Road, again advertised in the What's On section of *The Straits Times*.

Emerald Hill and Peranakan Place

Orchard Road, Singapore 0923

On the site of a nutmeg plantation owned by a William Cuppage in the 1830s, the recently renovated Peranakan Place on Orchard Road reopened for business in mid-1991. A small air-conditioned shopping complex in a Peranakan-style building allows tourists to browse in comfort for cameras, watches and souvenirs, or to eat at Delifrance or at a Japanese restaurant. Next to Peranakan Place is the Emerald Mall Side-Walk Cafe Restaurant, a somewhat pricy outdoor cafe open from 8 a.m. to 1 a.m. daily, where you can sit amidst palm trees and sip a beer or a coffee, or eat Western or local food. Take the time to walk through Emerald Mall up Emerald Hill to see further examples of Peranakan architecture, mostly now private homes or restaurants. The Show House Museum of Peranakan furnishings is open from Monday to Saturday 10.30 a.m. and 3.30 p.m. and gives an authentic feel of a typical Peranakan home. If the museum is shut during these hours ask at the adjacent Emerald Hill Restaurant for Helen, or telephone 732 6966 beforehand. The museum also stages Peranakan wedding shows on request.

Further up Orchard Road, Orchard Emerald shopping centre has several small crafts stalls where you can watch batik makers or teeshirt painters. Further up again, the **Al Falah Mosque**, at Cairnhill Place, is a modern mosque beneath the Cairnhill Plaza multi-storey car-park.

Skyscrapers, Shophouses and Songbirds

Raffles having reserved the area to the north of the Singapore River for European settlement, the early Chinese traders who arrived in Singapore settled to the south of the river, building *godowns* (warehouses) along the upper reaches, and shophouses as near the river as they could. Early land reclamation schemes increased the land area at the south, seaward side, and this area today presents a striking contrast between the old and the new: tatty shophouses and old Chinese temples sit cheek-by-jowl a street away from high-rise office blocks.

Raffles Place

Singapore 0104
To Get There: Raffles Place MRT
This used to be the commercial and shopping centre of Singapore, centred on the prestigious colonial-style store Robinsons until it burned down in 1972. Now many businesses and offices have relocated from Shenton Way to the high-rise office space built in its

The entrance to Hock Teck Ch'i Temple, a tiny temple dating from the 1820s, on Telok Ayer Street. Religious observation continues here in an unassuming manner.

place. The **OUB Centre** on Raffles Place, at 270 m (886 ft) high, is currently the highest block in Singapore, though a rival Singapore bank, UOB Bank, has commissioned the same architect, Kenzo Tange, to design an equally tall tower for them, due for completion by 1993.

Merlion Park

Fullerton Road, Singapore 0104
Immediately across the Singapore River, if you use the **Fullerton Bridge,** is the **Merlion Park**. Since 1972 this park has housed the city's 8-m (26-ft)-high lion's head and fish body mascot (hence the name) and gives a good view on to the bumboats on **Marina**

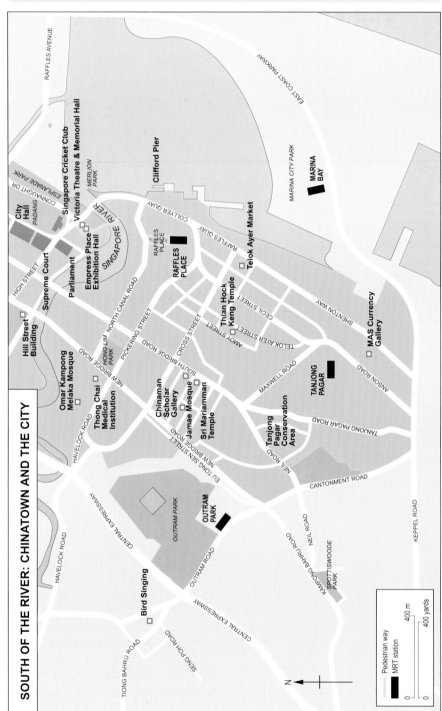

SOUTH OF THE RIVER: CHINATOWN AND THE CITY

RAFFLES AVENUE

CONNAUGHT DR

ESPLANADE PARK

City Hall

PADANG

Singapore Cricket Club

Victoria Theatre & Memorial Hall

MERLION PARK

Clifford Pier

MARINA CITY PARK

EAST COAST PARKWAY

MARINA BAY

Supreme Court

Empress Place Exhibition Hall

Parliament

SINGAPORE RIVER

COLYER QUAY

RAFFLES QUAY

HIGH STREET

RAFFLES PLACE

RAFFLES PLACE

Telok Ayer Market

Hill Street Building

Omar Kampong Melaka Mosque

HAVELOCK ROAD

NEW BRIDGE ROAD

HONG LIM PARK

NORTH CANAL ROAD

PICKERING STREET

SOUTH BRIDGE ROAD

CROSS STREET

Thian Hock Keng Temple

AMOY STREET

TELOK AYER STREET

CECIL STREET

SHENTON WAY

MAS Currency Gallery

ANSON ROAD

Thong Chai Medical Institution

Chinaman Scholar Gallery

Jamae Mosque

Sri Mariamman Temple

EU TONG SEN STREET

NEW BRIDGE ROAD

MAXWELL ROAD

Tanjong Pagar Conservation Area

NEIL ROAD

TANJONG PAGAR

TANJONG PAGAR ROAD

CANTONMENT ROAD

HAVELOCK ROAD

CENTRAL EXPRESSWAY

OUTRAM PARK

OUTRAM PARK

OUTRAM ROAD

Bird Singing

KAMPONG BAHRU ROAD

NEIL ROAD

SPOTTISWOODE PARK

KEPPEL ROAD

TIONG BAHRU ROAD

SENG POH ROAD

CENTRAL EXPRESSWAY

N

Pedestrian way

MRT station

400 m

400 yards

144

Bay and the sweeping reclaimed land of the Esplanade, but apart from these points of interest, this tiny park is really not worth a special trip. The Merlion itself—or themselves, since as well as the larger version overlooking the entrance to the Singapore River, there is also a baby sculpture within the small park facing away from its parent—has become somewhat grubby, stained over time by the water that pours from its mouth, so it really only looks its best at night. The creature was designed by a Mr Kwan Sai Kheong, and appeared originally on some postage stamps and one of the first $1 dollar coins. The sculptures were executed by Lim Nang Seng. The symbol appears on a variety of souvenirs and tourist trinkets and is also the STPB's emblem, appearing in red at stores which are deemed reputable and are unlikely to sell you faulty goods. (Whether it will continue to be their mascot with the 1991 launch of Kucinta, the Singapura cat, in tourist promotional campaigns worldwide, remains to be seen.)

Clifford Pier

Collyer Quay, Singapore 0104

Built in the early 1930s, as is clear from its style, this is the current departure point for island and river cruises. The walk along **Collyer Quay** from **Fullerton Bridge** takes you along the historic waterfront as seen and described in books by Joseph Conrad.

Map of the area south of the river.

Shenton Way

Singapore, 0104

The city, the stock exchange, and Singapore's financial and banking institutions are all located in the area from **Raffles Place** to **Shenton Way,** a maze of one-way streets, office blocks and car parks, that looks much the same as modern capital cities worldwide. There is little for the tourist within the city itself, except the haphazard juxtaposition of modern and not-so-modern blocks with well-frequented coffee shops and small-scale shops, and the **Currency Gallery** in the MAS Building, but you will have to pass through this area in order to reach **Telok Ayer Festival Market**.

Currency Gallery

MAS Building, Shenton Way, Singapore 0104
Telephone: 229 9582
Opening Hours: 10 a.m.–4 p.m. Mondays–Fridays, 10 a.m.–1 p.m. Saturdays, closed Sundays

This free museum has a permanent display on the ground floor of the history of Singapore currency, from 1819 to the present day, as well as explaining the minting process. The local notes gallery contains Straits Settlements, Japanese Occupation, and Malaysian notes, and then the three series of Singapore's own notes: the first orchid series from 1965; then the bird series from 1976; and the ship series in circulation since 1984. An exhibition space is available for temporary displays: during my visit there was an exhibition of gold coins from Malaysia and Canada, nuggets from Australia and some US bullion and gold dust.

Upstairs is a foreign currency gallery arranged alphabetically, with a mixture of real and specimen notes and coins, largely depending on the denominations. Disappointingly, the impressive-looking display screen and computer, which is supposed to give today's exchange rate for various currencies as well as population numbers and other statistics, was not fully functional. That aside, the Currency Gallery is a much more switched on and enjoyable place than the Mint Coin Gallery in Jurong (*see* page 174).

Telok Ayer Festival Market

Singapore's first fish market was built near this site in the 1820s, which is why it is also known as *Lau Pa Sat* (old market). The building we see today was rebuilt in 1894 on the reclaimed land of the Telok Ayer Bay (reclaimed in 1879), designed by the then municipal engineer James MacRitchie. The typically Victorian cast-iron structure was shipped out from Glasgow, and the building remained a market until a renovation in 1972–73, when it was gazetted as a national monument and turned into a food centre. The market was dismantled in 1986 during the MRT construction work, when there was concern that train vibrations could damage the structure.

The recent renovation was carried out by a subsidiary of Scotts Holdings, who also run Scotts building on Scotts Road. They spent a considerable time researching open markets and their attractions throughout the world, in order to design a festive and vibrant marketplace with numerous self-service food outlets, two levels of seating, trolleys selling all types of goods, live and varied entertainment, all open from 7 a.m. to 3 a.m. Attractions include a central fountain, which can be converted into a stage for performances, and 23 specially commissioned Dutch bronze bells in the clock tower, complete with mechanical figurine to ring them. In addition, weekends the hawker trolleys and flea market should attract Singaporeans and tourists alike as it spills over on to the adjoining section of **Boon Tat Street**, closed to traffic from 7 p.m. Despite overhead fans, the market is warm to eat in at lunchtime, though pleasant in the evening. Shops and stalls built into the pastel shades of the exterior sell numerous souvenir goods and trinkets.

Chinatown

A short walk up **Boon Tat Street**, across Robinson Road, brings you to **Telok Ayer** (literally water bay) **Street**, originally the road along the sea front until the land to the south of it was reclaimed in the 1880s. Here you are immediately in Singapore's Chinatown. It may seem odd that an island with 76 per cent of its population being Chinese should have a Chinatown, but this area remains special and worth a visit. Bordering on the financial and business district's high-rise towers is an older network of streets of low-level shops, medicine halls, temples and homes which has changed little in recent years. Souvenir and tourist shops offering discount clothing, silks, kites and postcards now crowd into the maze of streets near the **Sri Mariamman Temple**, but if you wander just a block away from a major tourist site you can find traditional calligraphers or funeral shops still practising a trade that has a much longer history. It really is an area to explore slowly, on foot.

Telok Ayer Street is home to a number of temples and mosques, the best known of which is the Thian **Hock Keng Temple**.

A small and very typical fruit shop in Chinatown near the Sri Mariamman Temple on South Bridge Road.

Thian Hock Keng Temple

Telok Ayer Street, Singapore 0106

This showpiece temple was built by Hokkien sailors on the site of a joss house (a makeshift temple where joss sticks could be burned as offerings) established in the early 1820s as a place to give thanks for their safe arrival in Singapore, and completed in 1842. It is dedicated to Ma Zu Po, the goddess of the sea and protector of sailors, and is built to a traditional design by craftsmen from mainland China using materials imported from China. There are various lesser shrines as well as that to Ma Zu Po in the central temple. Notice the dragon panels on the doorways, as well as the entrance gods.

Early benefactors to the temple included Tan Tock Seng and Tan Kim

Seng. The temple, reputedly the oldest still in existence in Singapore, is now owned by the Hokkien Huay Kan clan association and is listed as a National Monument.

At the city end of Telok Ayer Street is the **Hock Teck Ch'i Temple**, started in the 1820s when it was only reachable by boat, and now used by Hokkiens, Teochews, Cantonese and Kheks (Hakkas). Between that and the Thian Hock Keng Temple you see the pale blue **Nagore Durgha Shrine**, built in the 1830s by Chulias, South Indian Muslims, which combines Classical and Indian Muslim motifs in its stunning façade. It is similar in design to the Jamae Mosque on South Bridge Road (*see* below). Past the Thian Hock Keng Temple is the **Al Abrar Mosque,** again constructed by Chulia Indians, built on a simple Indian Islamic plan. Its front has two minaret-type towers, each topped by a small onion-shaped dome or *chatri*. It is also known by its Tamil name *Kuchu Palli* (mosque hut) and after its founders as *Masjid Chulia.*

Still (just) on Telok Ayer Street, is the tiny **Fuk Tak Ch'i Temple**, with only one small courtyard. This also dates from the earliest Chinese immigrants, although it seems almost gaudily restored today. Its main deity is Tua Peh Kong, the god of wealth, and it is patronized mainly by Hakkas and Cantonese.

From this temple you can double back, parallel to Telok Ayer Street along **Amoy Street**, past small shophouses and a small park until you meet **Cross Street**. Turn left and then take the first left again along **Club Street**, an opportunity to follow a winding street of two- and three-storey shophouses still bustling with life. Many such houses were designed in the 1930s by a Frank W. Brewer, and are still shops and homes. If you can resist diving down the inviting side streets, Club Street will lead you to South Bridge Road, just opposite the famous **Sri Mariamman Temple**.

Sri Mariamman Temple

South Bridge Road, Singapore 0105

Dedicated to the goddess Mariamman, who is known for curing epidemic diseases, this is the largest Hindu place of worship in Singapore. A temple has stood on this site since 1827, the first one put up by Naraina Pillai, the first Indian immigrant to Singapore, who arrived with Raffles himself. The present structure dates from 1843. The *gopuram*, the tower, was built in the early 20th century, and thoroughly restored in 1984. It features a host of deities, including the divine trinity of Brahma, Vishnu and Siva, and animals, of which the cow features prominently.

A lively centre at all times, this temple is particularly striking during the Thimithi festival in November/December, when devotees process barefoot from the Serangoon Road temples to walk over burning coals as a sign of their devotion.

Jamae Mosque

South Bridge Road, Singapore 0105

Next to the Sri Mariamman Temple,

*T*he goporam
(entrance gateway) to the Sri Mariamman Hindu temple on South Bridge Road.

though not itself frequented by tourists, this unusual twin-towered mosque dates from the 1830s. Like the Al Abrar Mosque and Durgha Shrine on Telok Ayer Street, it was constructed by Chulia Indians. Stylistically it is a mixture of Chinese, Anglo-Indian and Malay architecture, with square, tiered pagodas and a large prayer hall within its spacious courtyard.

Walking north from South Bridge Road, up Smith, Mosque or Pagoda Streets will show you more of the typical bustle of Chinatown where there is now much renovation work. You can see dried goods shops, medicine halls, and fruit and vegetable stalls; you may also see calligraphers, funeral parlours with their paper models of the deceased's favourite car or house; and you will certainly see trishaw drivers hawking for your trade, and souvenir shops doing likewise. In the basement of the HDB building on **Smith Street** there is a lively wet market, where you can pick up some refreshing fruit, or watch as people haggle over and eventually buy an enormous variety of fish.

On **Trengganu Street**, parallel to both South Bridge and New Bridge Roads, you can have a deeper sightseeing stop if you visit the Chinaman Scholar Gallery.

The Chinaman Scholar Gallery

14B Trengganu Street, Singapore 0105
Telephone: 222 9554
Opening hours: 9 a.m.–4 p.m. daily
Monday–Friday

Tucked away on the third floor of a restored shophouse behind the Sri Mariamman Temple, this house has been lovingly filled with furnishings, photographs and silk hangings typical of a Cantonese family living in the area in the 1930s. The building is owned by the URA (Urban Redevelopment Authority) but rented and managed by antique dealer and local historian Vincent Tan, who has collected many family pieces together, as well as digging into his own porcelain collection for particular favourites.

As you enter the gallery, portraits of Vincent Tan's great-grandparents from China face you over the

Extraordinary Potions and Remedies
Walking through any part of Chinatown you will often come across Chinese Medical Halls and shops dispensing a variety of herbs and substances for different ailments.

Chinese medical practitioners believe that disease is the result of an imbalance in the whole body rather than being caused by a particular germ, an imbalance between the geomantic *yin* and *yang* elements, or between the five elements of wood, fire, earth, metal and water. Different herbal teas, pills and dietary adjustments are prescribed, depending on whether the patient is full or empty *yang* or *yin*, and whether the symptoms suggest a water, blood or "*chi*" (literally life-force) disease.

Some examples of medicinal herbs and prescriptions include donkey skin, dried cicada shells, dried seaweeds, malted barley, licorice, chrysanthemum flowers, apricot kernels and magnolia buds.

traditional altar, also featuring the Buddha and other gods and relatives, with offerings to the house spirit under this table. In front of this is a Victorian-style table covered with a heavy carpet-like cloth, and several *tingat* sets (tiffin carriers, multi-layered baskets enabling you to carry your picnic lunch)—curiously, made in Czechoslovakia!

An opium bed, porcelain head pillows (different sizes for men and women), loads of photographs showing the gradual transition from pig-tailed traditional Chinese costume to the Western style of dressing, a wardrobe filled with traditional clothes, and examples of Chinese shampoos, hair oils and other ointments all is arranged as it would have been in a Chinese home of the period.

The writing desk has its brushes for calligraphy and abacus; a large Chinese zither is displayed, along with glorious silk hangings, and a songbird twitters casually in a bamboo cage suspended from the ceiling.

Above all, the homely atmosphere you experience as you are offered tea and learn about the history of the area, makes it well worth a visit. Double-check it's open if you plan to go, either phone, or call back later if there's no answer when you first try.

If you continue down South Bridge Road past the Sri Mariamman Temple, you come to the Tanjong Pagar Conservation Area.

Tanjong Pagar Conservation Area

Tanjong Pagar and Neil Roads, Singapore 0208

Singapore's recent policy of conservation and restoration has its landmark and prestigious flagship in the now Senior Minister's (Lee Kuan Yew's) constituency. Traditional shophouses, complete with covered 5-ft ways to protect pedestrians from rain and sun alike, have been restored and renovated in pastel shades, looking almost like children's model houses. Souvenir, antique and handicraft shops, together with a variety of restaurants and "pubs" have moved into the new area, which is keen to attract tourists and locals to create an ambiance similar to Boston or Sydney's waterfront or London's Covent Garden.

At the junction of Tanjong Pagar and Neil Roads is the triangular-shaped **Jinrickshaw Building**, built at the turn of the century as a station for rickshaw drivers and now housing an up-market Chinese restaurant. Passing along Tanjong Pagar Road, a first right takes you to Duxton Road, on which you will find a variety of antique and arts shops as well as various food and drink venues. **The Pewter Museum** at 49A (Telephone: 221 4436 Opening Hours: 9.00 a.m.–5.30 p.m. daily), is a small outlet for Selangor Pewter, with a gallery of vases, medals and other items for sale on the ground floor, and an exhibition of pewter-making and its history in Malaya upstairs. About 75 antique pieces are also displayed, including huge domestic altar pieces commissioned by wealthy Chinese families in the early 20th century. There is no obligation to buy, and staff will readily explain the processes shown to you.

Continuing along Duxton Road, you rejoin **Neil Road**, another road of tourist and art shops. At the top of the incline is **Number 51**, developed and run by the Raffles Management Company. This houses an air-conditioned mini food court, handicrafts bazaar (mainly earrings, souvenirs and tee-shirts), several caneware and furnishing outlets, 25 offices, and the **Emmerson Tiffin Rooms** (Telephone: 227 7518 Opening Hours: 12 noon–2.30 p.m., 7 p.m.–11.00 p.m. daily). These offer a traditional curry tiffin (lunch) or a Western menu in a mock colonial setting, complete with pre-programmed piano-playing and attentive service—at a price, obviously. The Emmerson connection was discovered during the recent renovation work at the Raffles Hotel. An old plate was found

there, with The Emmerson Tiffin Rooms inscribed just as those are in today's reconstruction, and this was found to be from a tearoom opened near Cavenagh Bridge in 1866 by one Charles Emmerson, an English vet who operated a hotel on Beach Road in the 1860s. Joseph Conrad, amongst others, reputedly frequented the tearooms. A small exhibition, **Glimpses of Tanjong Pagar**, mainly consisting of photographs and some small artefacts from the area is located at the entrance to the food court.

The **Maxwell Road** hawker centre opposite the Jinrickshaw Building is an alternative refreshment stop; so too are the various restaurants along the nearby **Murray Street**, between Maxwell and Tanjong Pagar Roads. Further up Neil Road, across the junction with Cantonment Road, you can find the charming area of **Spottiswood Park**, overlooking the Keppel Road railway station. Designated to become another conservation area, turn left to find the peaceful backwater of **Blair Road**, featuring traditional Peranakan houses.

Doubling back, opposite Number 51 Neil Road, **Keong Saik Street** leads you to New Bridge Road, itself bordered by HDB estates, though the roadside shops still supply Chinese curiosities. A 15-minute walk, or a couple of stops by bus or a quick cab ride, will take you along to the **Old Thong Chai Medical Institution** on Eu Tong Sen Street, now the Seiwaen Arts Centre. This private house, built in 1897, was used as a hospital before becoming a medical institution. Funded by public subscriptions and private benefactors, low-cost or even free medical advice and herbal medicines were handed out to the poor, including quinine treatments for a malaria outbreak in 1911.

It is two storeys high, with two internal courtyards shaded from rain and sun but allowing light to penetrate. Its unusual curly-style roof and vibrant colour mural along the façade show how domestic Chinese architecture may have looked at the turn of the century. The only comparable building still standing in Singapore is the House of Tan Yeok Nee on Penang Road, sold in 1991 by the Salvation Army to the next door Cockpit Hotel.

Today the Thong Chai building stands between two demolition sites, looking rather precarious although it is a listed monument. It houses an antiques shop, selling jade and precious stones, earrings and jewellery, porcelain and silk paintings.

Behind the Thong Chai Building is the elegant minaret of the **Omar Kampong Melaka Mosque**, on the site of the island's first mosque built by the pioneering Arab merchant and community leader Syed Omar bin Ali Al-Junied. The present building was completed in 1920, with the minaret added after substantial renovation in 1985. A charming Chinese temple is located nearby.

Returning to Eu Tong Sen Street, buses 2, 3, 12, 28, 41 will take you along to Victoria Street, whence it is a short walk to City Hall MRT station; alternatively a taxi or trishaw could take you direct to your next stop.

Bird Singing

To Get There: MRT to Tiong Bahru and walk

Rather off the beaten track, and outside the oldest and most picturesque part of Chinatown, you can see a tradition continuing. Every Sunday morning, between about 7.30 and 9.30, is a bird singing competition

outside a small coffee shop on **Tiong Bahru Road** near the crossing with Outram Road. Bird fanciers bring their bamboo-caged merboks (small green birds with white rings around their eyes) and sharmas (larger, blacker birds more like the ubiquitous myna) to join the 50 or so suspended from a metal scaffolding frame overhead, while fellow fanciers discuss birds and their merits. Cages are moved up and down along the numbered pegs as judges assess the qualities of the various birds. You can just sit and listen to the strangely melodious sounds, with no need to buy even a coffee—unless you need waking up!

Across Tiong Bahru Road is a small Chinese temple which benefits from good *feng shui*, and a bird shop. As well as birds, including sparrows, merboks and mynas, there are cages and porcelain drinking and feeding bowls, plus the material covers used to transport the birds by car, bus, trishaw or even bicycle between competitions. A large covered wet market, selling fresh fish, meat, fruit and vegetables, as well as clothing, and an adjoining hawker centre is across the road.

Tiong Bahru itself was Singapore's first housing estate, built over an old cemetery by the Singapore Improvement Trust in 1954. In the international style of the time, the housing blocks are simple expressions of lines and planes in shades of white, and the area is a successful community development.

The regular Sunday morning bird singing competition at Tiong Bahru.

Marina South

To Get There: MRT to Marina South and longish walk, taxi

Certainly not within walking distance, in fact a stop on the tube from Raffles Place, or two stops from Tanjong Pagar, is Marina Bay, the reclaimed area to the south of the city. This area has so far been reserved for leisure activities providing, in the words of Mr Lee Yock Suan, Minister for Labour and Deputy Chairman of the People's Association, a "green lung for the city". Its 30-hectare (74-acre) **Marina City Park** has a 30-m (98-ft)-high jet fountain—currently the highest in South-East Asia, designated theme areas, as well as various sculptures including eight legendary Chinese hero statues, commissioned from craftsmen in China. The characters are Hua Mulan, Zheng He, Guang Gon, Qu Yuan, Yue Fei, Wen Tianziang, Zheng He and Lin Zexue. Also at Marina Bay is the formerly prestigious and expensive Marina Village restaurant area, now virtually deserted except for the Khameleon nightclub as the developer's financial difficulties unfold. For those with less to spend, there is the Marina Bay Hawker Centre, which does a busy trade from patrons of the two bowling alleys, various sports facilities, and those who come to fly their colourful kites in the relatively tree-free open space. Plans for extending the financial district out to Marina Bay are currently being discussed, since the reclaimed land will have settled. Hence all the current development is on fairly short-term land leases from the government, so that the area can be developed after the year 2000.

153

Sarongs, Saris, Silks and Spices

Two distinctly different quarters lie to the east of the city centre, with shophouse architecture similar to that in parts of Chinatown, but a totally distinctive flavour. In the Arab Street area silk and fabric traders display their wares across the 5-ft ways, while nearby the Sultan Mosque and the old Istana Kampong Glam remain the centre of Muslim life. Little India is precisely that: Indian music, books, magazines, fabrics, jewellery and clothing are all displayed along with a dazzling collection of flower garlands, betel nuts and spicy curries for those with an appetite.

To get to Arab Street or Little India: MRT to Bugis or Lavender, buses along Beach, North Bridge Roads and Victoria Street

Sultan Mosque

North Bridge Road, Singapore 0719
The Sultan Mosque on North Bridge Road is the centre of Singapore's Muslim religion. Situated in the

A street vendor, Little India, selling religious pictures. Within the crowded 5-ft ways are numerous stalls selling magazines, cassettes, flower garlands and betel nuts.

heart of Kampong Glam, it dominates the maze of surrounding streets. Good views can be had from Bussorah Street to the south or from Jalan Pinang to the north. Bussorah Street itself is being renovated in order to become a pedestrian mall giving a spectacular view of the rear of the mosque.

The first mosque on this site was built in 1824. The East India Company contributed towards its foundation, and diverted North Bridge Road around it when the road was extended. The current building dates from 1924 and was built by the architects Swan and Maclaren, with a mixture of classical, Persian, Moorish and Turkish elements. Impressive from the outside as well as from inside the spacious prayer hall (do be sure to visit properly

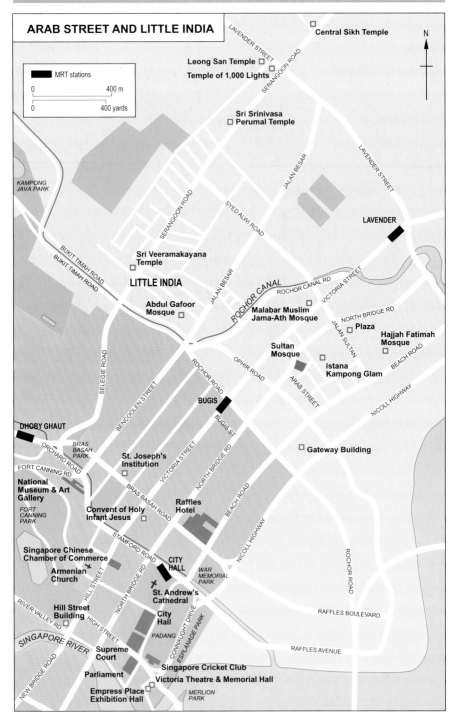

ARAB STREET AND LITTLE INDIA

■ MRT stations

0   400 m
0   400 yards

LAVENDER STREET

Central Sikh Temple

Leong San Temple
Temple of 1,000 Lights

SERANGOON ROAD

N

Sri Srinivasa
Perumal Temple

JALAN BESAR

LAVENDER STREET

KAMPONG
JAVA PARK

SYED ALWI ROAD

LAVENDER

BUKIT TIMAH ROAD
BUKIT TIMAH ROAD

SERANGOON ROAD

Sri Veeramakayana
Temple

LITTLE INDIA

Abdul Gafoor
Mosque

JALAN BESAR

ROCHOR CANAL

ROCHOR CANAL RD

VICTORIA STREET

Malabar Muslim
Jama-Ath Mosque

NORTH BRIDGE RD

JALAN SULTAN

Plaza

Hajjah Fatimah
Mosque

BEACH ROAD

SELEGIE ROAD

ROCHOR ROAD

OPHIR ROAD

Sultan
Mosque

Istana
Kampong Glam

ARAB STREET

NICOLL HIGHWAY

BENCOOLEN STREET

BUGIS

BUGIS ST

DHOBY GHAUT

ORCHARD ROAD

BRAS
BASAH
PARK

St. Joseph's
Institution

VICTORIA STREET

NORTH BRIDGE RD

Gateway Building

FORT CANNING RD

National
Museum & Art
Gallery

FORT
CANNING
PARK

Convent of Holy
Infant Jesus

BRAS BASAH ROAD

Raffles
Hotel

BEACH ROAD

NICOLL HIGHWAY

ROCHOR ROAD

RIVER VALLEY RD

Singapore Chinese
Chamber of Commerce

Armenian
Church

Hill Street
Building

HILL STREET

HIGH STREET

STAMFORD ROAD

NORTH BRIDGE RD

CITY
HALL

WAR
MEMORIAL
PARK

St. Andrew's
Cathedral

City
Hall

PADANG

CONNAUGHT DRIVE

ESPLANADE PARK

RAFFLES BOULEVARD

SINGAPORE RIVER

NEW BRIDGE ROAD

Supreme
Court

Parliament

Empress Place
Exhibition Hall

Singapore Cricket Club

Victoria Theatre & Memorial Hall

MERLION
PARK

RAFFLES AVENUE

A selection of silks and other fabrics spilling out on to the pavement in Arab Street.

attired—no shorts, teeshirts, or short skirts), the architecture is an Islamic fusion of styles, somewhat reminiscent of Kuala Lumpur's Railway Station.

Follow North Bridge Road along in front of the mosque, and an appetizing array of Muslim eating houses presents itself. For a step back in time—to the 1930s, when the restaurant was opened, and I doubt anything's changed since then at all—have a biryani or a murtabak at the **Jubilee Cafe and Restaurant**. The ceramic tiling, tablecloths, cooling revolving fans, and tables and chairs are of another age—a sight in themselves.

Map of Arab Street and Little India.

Arab Street

Singapore 0719

Raffles encouraged the first Arab traders to settle in the area near the sultan's residence in the early 1820s, and the resulting mixture of street names in this area shows how far they spread. The 5-ft ways on both sides of this busy street are packed with materials, spices and condiments, baskets and clothing bargains so that it is hard to wend your way along without browsing through the goods. The shopkeepers pull down their shutters during the heat of the day, thus each claims his part of the walkway as an extension to his shop and you can brush past scarves, batiks, silks, basketware and a host of unidentifiable spices and substances. A friendly and bustling area of low shophouses, no one minds if you just look at their wares, or even take their photograph.

*T*he stately Sultan Mosque on North Bridge Road, the focal point of Singapore's Muslim community.

Famous Names

Influential Arab traders have left their mark on Singapore today. Syed Omar bin Ali Al-Junied commissioned Singapore's first mosque in 1820, the Omar Kampong Malacca Mosque near Havelock Road (today's building is the third on the site). Syed Mohammed bin Ahmad Alsagoff founded the Alsagoff Arab School on Jalan Sultan; while the Alkaff family mansion is now a pricey restaurant with attractive views over the harbour. Moe Alkaff is one of Singapore's most popular disc jockeys and media personalities today.

This area was always the centre where Arab traders congregated, near to the predecessor of today's Sultan Mosque, and remains so today.

Gateway Building

Beach Road, Singapore 0719

I. M. Pei's latest and most controversial building yet: two facing triangles of glass reaching up 37 storeys high to look over the Nicholl Highway to the East Coast Parkway and the South China Sea beyond.

Istana Kampong Glam

Sultan Gate, Singapore 0719

The former residence of Sultan Iskandah Shah dates from the 1840s, and may have been a private commission from the then municipal architect, G. D. Coleman. Somewhat unprepossessing, the building and surrounding area is, at the time of writing, subject to a government-sponsored conservation plan, which will—inevitably for Singapore—result in a further shopping centre/arcade and a theme park treatment of the history of the sultan and Malay furniture and architecture. Before it is covered in scaffolding for such "renewal" it is worth a quick look through the overgrown main gates to see a square-set, plain colonial style house. Next door, on Sultan Gate, the yellow house was once occupied by the sultan's heir, but was sold on his death.

The Glam tree (*melaleuca leucadendron*), after which the area is named, can grow up to 30 m (98 ft), and provided medicinal oil, while its bark was used by the Bugis traders to caulk their ships. Wander along the various back-streets, noting the between-the-wars terraces, and on nearby Jalan Sultan the rather crumbling yet still grandiose Alsagoff Arab School with its fine façade—now facing two multi-storey shopping complexes and an HDB (see page 214) estate.

Hajjah Fatimah Mosque

Beach Road, Singapore 0719

Hajjah Fatimah, a Malaccan businesswoman and the wife of a Bugis merchant, built this mosque in the 1840s. Her daughter Raja Sitti married Syed Ahmed A. Rahman Alsagoff. It is a successful hotchpotch of styles—classical pilasters, Chinese grilles and an Islamic minaret and dome—executed by builders and craftsmen from different backgrounds. The minaret and central building were possibly designed by J. T. Thomson. The main mosque was rebuilt in the 1930s by Malay builders trained by the French contractors Bossard Mapin, to the designs of Chung and Wong. It was gazetted a national monument in 1973 shortly after further restoration. Despite these two restorations it still tilts at an angle of approximately 6 degrees.

It is a very peaceful spot, surrounded by trees bearing jackfruit and other fruits, tucked a block away from Beach Road and well worth the walk along Jalan Sultan. A few Malay graves lie tranquilly in the small mosque gardens, enclosed within stone walls. The mosque opens at 12 noon, and the public can visit it and walk along the shady verandahs, though they cannot enter the prayer hall.

On Victoria Street, parallel and to the north of North Bridge Road, is the Malabar Muslim Jama-Ath Mosque, built by A. H. Siddique, an immigrant from North India in the 1920s.

Bugis Street

Queen Street, Singapore 0718

In the 1960s and 70s, Bugis Street was the "sin" centre of Singapore, with nightly parades of transvestites, as well as prostitutes, touting for business. Many who remember it in those days do so fondly, for it was a bustling, crowded and generally good-humoured, tolerant place—but not one in keeping with the new, PAP-inspired, squeaky-clean Singapore. In 1980 the area was knocked down in preparation for constructing the MRT station of the same name, while the prostitution relocated to certain lorongs (lanes) off Geylang Road, much less obtrusive than the previous site.

In 1991 a new Bugis Street area emerged, an attempt to re-create a somewhat sanitized and stylized part of Singapore's past—and make money out of it! Six blocks of re-created Chinese shophouses, styled after some original Bugis Street buildings—including a three-storey hotel and a famous public toilet (not for general use any longer)—enclose an open area where food and drink stalls compete for business with a night market (pasar malam) of hawker trolleys bearing delicacies, souvenirs, the inevitable tee-shirts, toys, jewellery and the like. The

850 daytime seats for diners and visitors double to 1,600 in the evening, as nearby pavements are colonized, and the area is open throughout the night—for that late-night snack or whatever you fancy in the small hours! Retail shops within the shophouses and an indoor air-conditioned dining hall and English-style pub complete the first stage opening.

The reopened Bugis Street is predominantly an eating area. Although the STPB has taken local transvestites on foreign sales drives, transvestites found soliciting or giving impromptu cabaret performances have been quickly removed—though a few "hostesses" are employed in the area, who are never allowed to depart with guests or diners.

A walk along Waterloo Street, to the north of Queen Street will show the small Sri Krishna Temple with its vibrantly coloured *gopuram* (gateway), as well as a large Chinese temple.

Little India

The area east of **Rochor Road**, bordered by Race Course Road to the north and Bencoolen Street to the south, is a fascinating one to explore, though both sides of Serangoon Road itself are currently undergoing fairly extreme renovation work. Down adjacent side streets, shopfronts offer a variety of flower garlands, betel nuts, dried and fresh chillies, saffrons and spices, Indian cassettes and discs, newspapers and books, jewellery, saris, other clothing, and of course, food. Rather than a definite itinerary, I would advise simply following your nose down the back-streets to discover your own delights: cafe scenes, trishaw

A stall-holder making garlands of fresh flowers for sale as decorative ornaments or religious offerings.

Chewing Habits

Numerous roadside stalls and shops in Little India sell betel nuts, wrapped in betel leaves, which the adventurous tourist may wish to sample: it's bitter, malodorous and I'm told rather like chewing tobacco. Betel nut has a strong brown dye, used in colouring batiks and other fabrics; regular betel chewers can be identified by this colouring, rather like nicotine, on their fingertips and teeth.

drivers, motor mechanics, even caged snakes—enough to reassure you that authentic old Singapore is alive and kicking, despite the advances of high-rise condominiums and shopping centres. The side streets offer delightful examples of Singapore baroque architecture, often terraced houses painted in blue or green, with decorated façades, windows, even Doric columns or pilasters. **Petain Road** has houses decorated with colourful ceramic tiles; **Syed Alwi Road** boasts some extremely ornate, almost Mannerist-style, oval windows; **Desker** and **Upper Weld Roads** as well as **Jalan Besar** offer further such delights.

Some attractions of the area have disappeared. The Kandang Kerbau wet market was demolished in 1981, and is now housed and somewhat sanitized in the ZuZhou complex. The Sungei Road flea market has also been moved along to the small streets just south of Bencoolen Street, Pasar Lane, Larut Road and Pitt Street, where you can find a selection of second-hand electrical goods and half-repaired motorbikes. Some restoration programmes are under way in this conservation area, including a stretch of Buffalo Road recently renovated and released on sale to the public. So far,

such schemes have been sympathetically carried out, and have in no way destroyed the innate charm of the area.

The area was originally swampland, then in the 1820s government brick kilns and lime pits were sited here. This in turn attracted Indian settlers to the area, many of whom lived initially in large bachelor colonies, many pursuing the traditional *dhoby* (laundryman) trade. The Indians remained in the area after the original kilns were removed in the 1860s, along with the European and Eurasian settlers—the road names Dunlop, Norris and Desker, for example, describe the areas these families lived in. Cattle traders, such as I. R. Belilios settled here—his original bungalow, with quarters for cattle as well as his family, has recently been renovated and put up for sale—and cattle- and goat-rearing took place in the area until 1936. Chinese goldsmiths arrived shortly after the Indian labourers, since gold is used in various Indian religious ceremonies.

On Dunlop Street, look at the **Abdul Gaffoor Mosque**, with its imposing façade of classical, Saracenic and Roman themes. The first wooden mosque on this site was built in 1881; the current building was erected between 1909 and 1927 and has an interesting central green dome and lesser turrets or minarets, with South Indian finials reaching up to the sky, mock Mogul arch heads opening on to the main prayer hall, and mock Corinthian columns hugging the wall by the main entrance. The Arabic calligraphy over the entrance bears the names of the prophets of Islam. It is distinctly South Indian Muslim in design (compare this

Elaborate carved figures from the Sri Veeramakayama Temple on Serangoon Road.

with the Durgha Shrine or Masjid Jamae in Chinatown, *see* page 148). In the peaceful enclave off the bustle of Dunlop Street, notice the nearby terraced houses, neatly kept, which remain largely populated by Malay or South Indian members of the Muslim community.

The Sri Veeramakayama Temple, on Serangoon Road opposite Dunlop Street, was founded in 1835 but this resplendent building was only recently (1987) renovated. You can admire the detailed figures carved on its *gopuram* from across the road, and can enter the cool interior to see Hindus at prayer or preparing foods for a special occasion—for example during the festival month of Deepavali. On the waste ground next to the temple there are occasional trade fairs, when saris, dhotis and other Indian cloths, as well as brasswares and assorted bits and pieces can be bargained for at leisure. At the far (eastern) end of Serangoon Road you will see the **Sri Srinivasa Perumal Temple**, currently undergoing restoration on its *gopuram*. The original temple on this site was built in 1855, though it was completely rebuilt in the 1960s. The marriage hall and *gopuram* were added by P. Govindasamy Pillai, the latter in 1979. Devotees leave from this temple on that most arduous of festivals, Thaipusam (*see* page 87), carrying their steel *kavadis* the three km or so (2 miles) to the Chettiar Hindu Temple on Tank Road. This temple dates from 1855, though it was extensively restored in the 1960s, and is now gazetted as a National Monument. Across Lavender Street, further up Serangoon Road is the Central Sikh Temple of Singapore, completed in 1986. The whole complex includes various community facilities, as well as a large prayer hall topped by a 13-m (43-ft) dome.

On Race Course Road, which runs parallel to Serangoon Road to the north, you can see the impressive 15-m (35-ft)-high Buddha in the **Sakya**

Muni Buddha Gaya, the **Temple of A Thousand Lights**. One of the very few Theravada Buddhist temples in Singapore (another, Burmese, is next to the Sun Yat-Sen Villa, *see* page 198), this Thai temple is a massive structure to contain the vast sitting Buddha— which you can, surprisingly for a Thai-style, *wat*, photograph. The numerous coloured lights illuminate the 300-tonne (295-ton) Buddha.

Opposite this temple, amidst colourful Chinese houses, is the **Leong San Temple**. Built in 1917, and restored and widened on several subsequent occasions, the temple has fine ceramic carvings, a main altar to Guan Yin, and a very elaborately decorated roof. Back towards the city, at the western end of Race Course Road, are some renowned eating houses, particularly the fish-head curry specialists, Muthu's and the Banana Leaf Apolo. The race-course, after which the road is named, has long since relocated to Bukit Timah (*see* page 190), but was situated on Farrer Park, where today's sports facilities stand.

Fantasy, Flamingoes and Fun

Several of Singapore's attractions lie to the west of the island, sited amidst industrial areas and new towns which are responsible for so much of Singapore's economic prosperity. In Jurong are the BirdPark, the Crocodile Paradise, the Chinese and Japanese Gardens, the Tang Dynasty City, and the Singapore Science Centre, as well as lesser sites of interest. On the way, Haw Par Villa Chinese mythological theme park is a colourful introduction to Chinese mythology, Singapore's biggest, fastest and greatest feats are recorded in the Guinness World of Records, and an intriguing collection of Chinese ceramics, scrolls and other artefacts is displayed within the National University.

Mount Faber

Mount Faber Road, Singapore 0409

To Get There: taxi is the only direct option apart from tour coaches; alternatively take a bus to the World Trade Centre (*see* below) and catch the cable car

Mount Faber looks out over **Keppel Harbour** to **Sentosa Island** and the Singaporean and Indonesian islands beyond. Most visitors come to take the cable-car ride over to the World Trade Centre and thence to Sentosa (*see* page 217), but the park itself is a pleasant spot, rising to 116 m (380 ft) high, with 73 hectares (180 acres) planted with a variety of trees and shrubs. Bird spotters may see sea eagles circling. At the cable-car station at the top there's a restaurant, a small cafe and souvenir shops.

Across Telok Blangah Road from the mosque, is Singapore's World Trade Centre. This large complex is home to various temporary exhibitions throughout the year, a high proportion of which are furniture and interior decoration items. It is a midway station on the cable-car route from Mount Faber to Sentosa Island, as well as the departure point for the regular Sentosa Island ferry it houses the Singapore Cruise Centre, departure point for

A peaceful scene at West Coast Park—a contrast to the busy highway and the bustling new towns beyond.

165

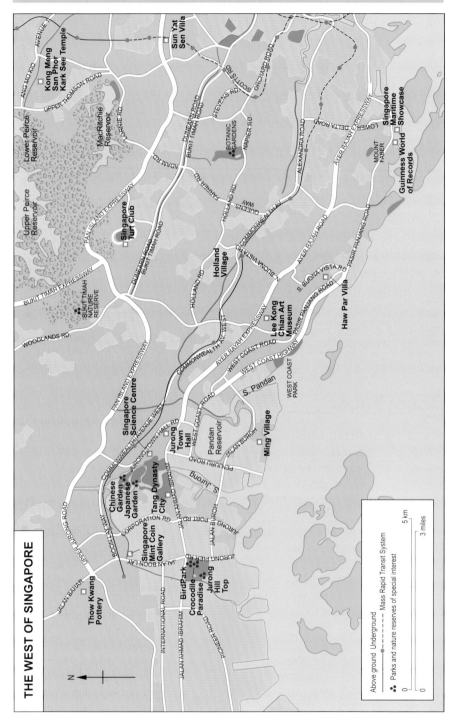

THE WEST OF SINGAPORE

N

Kong Meng San Phor Kark See Temple

Sun Yat Sen Villa

Singapore Maritime Showcase

Guinness World of Records

Lower Peirce Reservoir

MacRitchie Reservoir

Upper Peirce Reservoir

BOTANIC GARDENS

MOUNT FABER

Singapore Turf Club

BUKIT TIMAH NATURE RESERVE

Holland Village

Lee Kong Chian Art Museum

Haw Par Villa

Singapore Science Centre

WEST COAST PARK

S. Pandan

Jurong Town Hall

Pandan Reservoir

Ming Village

Chinese Garden
Japanese Garden

Tang Dynasty City

Singapore Mint Coin Gallery

Thow Kwang Pottery

BirdPark

Crocodile Paradise

Jurong Hill Top

Roads (labels)

AVENUE 1
ANG MO KIO
UPPER THOMSON ROAD
DUNEARN ROAD
STEVENS RD.
SCOTTS RD.
ORCHARD ROAD
BUKIT TIMAH ROAD
NAPIER RD.
FARRER RD.
HOLLAND RD.
ADAM RD.
LORNIE RD.
LOWER DELTA EXPRESSWAY
QUEENS WAY
COMMONWEALTH AVE
BUONA VISTA RD.
AYER RAJAH ROAD
ALEXANDRA ROAD
DUNEARN ROAD
PAN ISLAND EXPRESSWAY
BUKIT TIMAH EXPRESSWAY
WOODLANDS RD.
HOLLAND RD.
S. BUONA VISTA ROAD
PASIR PANJANG ROAD
COMMONWEALTH AV. WEST
AYER RAJAH EXPRESSWAY
WEST COAST ROAD
WEST COAST HIGHWAY
PASIR PANJANG RD.
COMMONWEALTH ROAD
JALAN BUROH
JURONGTOWN HALL ROAD
PENJURU ROAD
S. Jurong
WEST COAST ROAD
JALAN AHMAD IBRAHIM
CORPORATION RD.
JALAN PORT ROAD
JURONG PIER RD.
BOON LAY WAY
UPPER JURONG ROAD
JALAN BAHAR
INTERNATIONAL ROAD
JALAN AHMAD IBRAHIM
PIONEER ROAD
JALAN BOON LAY

Legend

Above ground   Underground
Mass Rapid Transit System

Parks and nature reserves of special interest

5 km

3 miles

Historical Perspectives
The original name for Mount Faber was Telok Blangah—literally cooking pot bay—Hill, and on the southern slope of the hill is the site where two of the early *temenggongs* (see page 41) are buried, next to the site of the 130-year-old Masjid Jamek Jarahaan Johor, which was recently pulled down in order to be replaced with a brand-new mosque by 1993, in view of the high cost of further renovation. The *Temenggong* Abdul Rahman was moved from his original central site to here in 1821, to allow G. D. Coleman to develop the European centre of town, and from here he and his son Daeng Ibrahim loosely oversaw the piracy ventures of their co-Bugis followers, and engaged in the increasingly profitable gutta-percha trade and the general development of the port. It was Daeng Ibrahim's son, Abu Bakar, who left Telok Blangah to build the spectacular European-style *Istana* across the Strait in Johor Baru (see page 228), and it is his great grandson, the present Sultan of Johor, who is funding and overseeing the construction of the new mosque.

ferries to Batam and Bintan. Other boat trips leave from the adjacent Jardine Steps pier. The World Trade Centre houses two major tourist attractions: *see* below.

Guinness World of Records

1 Maritime Square, #02–70, World Trade Centre, Singapore 0409

Map of the west of the island.

Telephone: 271 8344
Opening Hours: 10 a.m.–9 p.m. daily.
To Get There: SBS 65, 143, TIBS 167 from Orchard Road; SBS 61, 84, 100, 143, 145 from Chinatown; SBS 10, 30, 97, 100, 125 from Collyer Quay; SBS 10, 30, 97, 100 from Shenton Way; MRT to Tanjong Pagar and then taxi

Singapore's own branch of the worldwide biggest and greatest starts off with superlative statistics about weather, space, animals, vegetables and agriculture. There are a couple of hands-on exhibits—a space suit children can stand inside for photography, an exhibit to test how steady your hand is, and several computers of statistics on the biggest this or that don't necessarily quite work. All the various statistics on people—the biggest, fattest, heaviest, etc.—as well as a gross gobbling display of speed eating records.

The exhibition is all it sets out to be, a hotchpotch of superlatives appealing to young statistics gatherers, and is worth a quick look if you're passing.

Singapore Greats
Within the Asian gallery Singapore boasts the world's highest hotel (The Westin Stamford, 221 m/741 ft), the longest-serving prime minister in the world (Lee Kuan Yew), the world's busiest port in 1988, the world's biggest pizza (33.9 m/111 ft diameter), the world's vertical marathon record (up The Westin Stamford's 1336 steps in a record of 6 minutes 55 seconds, the world's smallest origami crane (4 mm/0.16 inch), and the world's longest dancing dragon (in August 1988, with 49 men, a length of 136.8 m/449 ft).

Singapore Maritime Showcase

This museum on the waterfront facing Sentosa Island is due to open during 1992. This museum, like the Science Centre (*see* page 179), is founded on the principle that learning should be entertainment: all exhibits are to be very interactive, with computer games mimicking the likely career opportunities within Singapore's highly successful port.

The museum will contain replicas of the Tanjong Pagar Terminals and the Brani Terminal, with floating ships and all the various port facilities and activities shown. Nearby computer terminals will enable visitors to load and unload ships, operating the container handling equipment. In the **Shipbridge** overlooking the **Terminal Replicas** there will be navigational control simulators to guide ships into and out of port.

Within the 14 m (46 ft) globe-shaped **Technodrome** will be audio-visual shows projected all around the audience, while the exterior of the dome will show Singapore's position as a centre of the world's shipping lanes. On either side of the large replicas will be moving containers from which to view 3-D dioramas of Singapore's port's history, from Temasek to developments planned for the 21st century.

For businessmen, as well as a **Marine Information Centre** providing the latest data on ports, the maritime industry and shipping matters, there will also be a **business centre** for hire for social or business occasions.

Haw Par Villa

262 Pasir Panjang Road, Singapore 0511
Telephone: 774 0300
Opening Hours: 9 a.m.–6 p.m. Mondays–Fridays, 9 a.m.–9 p.m. Saturdays, Sundays and public holidays
To Get There: SBS Bus 10, 30, 51 and 143 to Pasir Panjang Road; MRT to Buona Vista then SBS bus 200

This recently renovated and enlarged Chinese mythological theme park, now stretching over 95 hectares (235 acres) replaces the Tiger Balm Gardens with more of the same. It was originally built with money from the uniquely successful cure-all Tiger Balm lotion devised in the early 1900s by the herbal doctor Aw Chu Kin and marketed all over South-East Asia and China by his two sons Aw Boon Haw and Aw Boon Par, though today's theme park is owned and managed by International Theme Parks, a joint venture between Fraser & Neave and Times Publishing.

The basic tenet of the original and the expanded gardens is that the tableaux and attractions are highly moralistic. Whether you are watching a pageant in the South China Sea Amphitheatre, or taking the Tales of China Boat Ride through the belly of the 60-m (197-ft) dragon you see from Pasir Panjang Road as you enter, you learn that evil doers meet horrible ends, while goodness always ultimately reaps its own reward. The painted concrete and wire sculptures are highly grotesque, yet somehow often horribly fascinating. The scenes of the Ten Courts of Hell now located within the dragon's belly display a truly morbid

Scene from the Ten Courts of Hell. Moral—don't be wicked.

fascination with torture and suffering: sinners are fried to death, chopped into pieces, and so on, while their tormentors look on cheerfully.

For the fairly high admission fee ($16 for adults and $10 for children in 1991), you can see a variety of Chinese pageants and theatrical events, on-screen attractions, a puppet theatre, performing lions, and listen to tales of Chinese legends, history and heroes. The tone of all these presentations (in English) is geared to children, so may grate slightly to adults. The highlight of the trip for most adults as well as children is undoubtedly a ride on the Wrath of the Water Gods Flume—though the length of the queue dampens the enthusiasm somewhat, and a second ride may well involve an hour's wait on a busy day. (Also arousing some critical comment from early visitors are the long queues, sometimes as

long as one hour, at the different food outlets within the park at lunch time—so, to avoid frustration, bring a snack with you if you have hungry children in tow.)

Highly popular and well-frequented, most people who visit Haw Par Villa do thoroughly enjoy themselves, taking photographs of one another next to grotesque figures and sampling some small taste of Chinese legends in an easily assimilable form.

West Coast Park

Pasir Panjang Road/West Coast Highway, Singapore 0511
To Get There: Buses 30, 51, 143 and 184

Further west along the West Coast highway from Haw Par Villa is a pleasantly landscaped park with co-conut trees leading down to the sea. No tourist spot this, just a place for a picnic or a quiet sit by a small lake or watching the sea and the bumboats and fishing boats going about their daily business.

Lee Kong Chian Art Museum

Block AS6 (5th floor), National University of Singapore, 10 Kent Ridge Crescent, Singapore 0511
Telephone: 775 6666 (main NUS switchboard)
Opening Hours: Monday–Friday 9 a.m.–12.30 p.m., 2 p.m.–4.30 p.m. (closed between 1 p.m. and 2 p.m.); Saturday 9 a.m.–12.30 p.m.
To Get There: Bus 96 or 216 from Clementi Interchange

The legacy of a rubber tycoon and philanthropist, this collection of over 3,000 pieces of ceramics, bronze, archaic jade and Chinese paintings spans 6,000 years of Chinese culture. The Lee Foundation gives sums annually to charities, social and medical causes, as well as continuing to enable this museum to purchase new items.

Once you have found the block AS6 (no mean feat, but try heading for the Law Faculty and turning left at the cul-de-sac), you come firstly to a large Painting Gallery. This is semi-divided into five different rooms, respectively containing 16th–18th-century scrolls, calligraphy and scenes; 17th–19th-century stylist clerical scripts and scrolls; 19th–mid-20th century scrolls, with display cases of ink sticks and slabs; and 20th-century seal scripts which look strangely Egyptian; and contemporary South-East Asian paintings and scrolls as well as two cement sculptures. Quite well captioned in English and Mandarin, some of the calligraphy is fascinating to look at, with highly contrasting stylized forms. The scroll paintings vary from the traditional bamboo, landscape, and stylized

horses to more modern brushwork, with the more use of colour as you progress through the centuries.

In the Display Gallery of bronze and jade artefacts are archaic bronzes dating as far back as 1600 BC, cooking vessels, spears, bells, wash basins, mirrors, pendants and plaques. Also on display are jade carvings and plaques, often in grey or white rather than the more familiar green colour. Some modern sculptures and stone sculptures from Bali are also displayed.

The Ceramics Gallery contains over 1,000 pieces, and again is arranged clearly and chronologically. Starting with terracotta-coloured neolithic painted pottery, and pottery models of watch-towers, granaries and houses dating from the Han period (222 BC–AD 206), the display progresses to terracotta horses, and gradually to the blue and white Ming, the later red and green colours also used in Ming and Ching styles and continues with examples of styles up until the present day.

Well worth a visit for anyone interested in Chinese art and artefacts, the collection is set to expand, particularly its ceramics and jade sections.

Ming Village

32 Pandan Road, Singapore 2260
Telephone: 265 7711
Opening Hours: 9 a.m.–5.30 p.m. daily
To Get There: Bus 245 from Jurong Interchange

A large industrial site near the **Sungei Pandan** in Jurong houses a collection of reproduction Qing and Ming porcelainware. You can visit the moulding, hand turning and painting areas, and explanations from the guide clarify that porcelain shrinks by about 15 per cent during firing and other such details. Recently under new ownership, the Ming Village now runs pottery and antique valuation courses, and collectors can take pieces there for valuation.

It's worth a quick stop if you're in the area, though don't go specially or miss another site if short of time. They expect tours rather than individual tourists, but are happy for you to look around, ask questions and not too pushy at talking you into purchasing from the galleries (which I didn't find all that competitively priced compared, say, with the Holland Village stores or with the Thow Kwang pottery.

Craftsman at work on a reproduction jug at the Ming village.

Jurong BirdPark

Jurong Hill, Jalan Ahmad Ibrahim, Singapore 2262
Telephone: 265 0022
Opening Hours: 9 a.m.–6 p.m. daily
To Get There: MRT to Lakeside, then bus 240 or 188 to Jurong Interchange; alternatively bus 10 or 30 from Clifford Pier or 198 from Supreme House, Penang Road also all go to Jurong Interchange. From the Interchange, buses 250, 251 or 253 to the BirdPark

The BirdPark is well worth a visit: allow at least 2–3 hours and wear comfortable shoes if you plan to walk round the whole park. Alternatively, if you are short of time or less mobile, there is a new monorail system called a "Panorail". A total of over 5,000 birds of 450 different species from all over the world are to be seen in this 20-hectare (49-acre) site near Jurong Hill.

Immediately after the entrance are colourful cages of macaws, complete with a carefully painted mural of their natural environment, followed by the newly opened Penguin Parade of 100 Humboldt, Macaroni, Rockhopper and Fairy penguins. This air-conditioned and carefully monitored exhibit has an underwater viewing gallery so that you can watch the penguins swimming, while a grand mural behind the exhibit shows the ice flows and icebergs of the region. The whole exhibit is cleverly enlarged with the aid of two side mirrors.

Next door is an exhibit of over 50 northern seabirds, including Atlantic puffins donated by Iceland. Feeding times at the Penguin Parade are at 10.30 a.m. and 3.30 p.m.

A **World of Darkness** exhibition of night birds (sadly these seem rather squashed in their small areas) is next on your left, with owls, night herons and kiwis, before the open-air enclosures of cockatoos, flamingoes and the swan lake area inhabited by pelicans, swans and sacred ibises amongst others, bordered by the songbird terrace where you can breakfast with the birds, and by the waterfront cafe which will serve welcome drinks and meals. More flamingoes and cranes are seen on the way to the **Fuji Hawk Centre** which runs regular shows of hawk

*F*lamingoes *at Jurong BirdPark. Wherever possible bird's enclosures are not fenced in, giving a feeling of freedom.*

and birds of prey, well worth seeing. Colourful species of flightless birds, a wide-ranging selection of birds of prey, the recently completed and carefully landscaped toucans and hornbills exhibition, birds of paradise and smaller woodpeckers and shorebirds line the route back to the entrance, where the inevitable souvenir shops and burger outlet can be found. Here too you can be photographed with parrots and cockatoos adorning your shoulders if you so wish.

There are a number of shows daily: as well as the songbird breakfast, regular displays of hawks and parrots are staged, subject to weather, and audiovisual shows are given at the theatrette. Check with the BirdPark for times and details of these before or during your visit.

A number of improvements are currently under way to improve the BirdPark for its birds and to increase visitor numbers. These include substituting the traditional chain-mail mesh of cages with a rectangular-shaped mesh that is more likely to disappear visually. Careful planting schemes within the birds' cages are designed to simulate their traditional habitats, providing areas of shade and privacy while not impeding their flight paths.

The **Pools Amphitheatre**, opened in early 1992, stages bird shows of trained flamingoes, macaws, cockatoos, and ostriches as well as birds of prey, against a backdrop of fibreglass rocks and plants to a seated audience of up to 2,000 people sheltered from the heat or rain by a translucent roof. The shows include a 20-minute free-flight display as well as a shorter circus act.

The new monorail has a station in the new Waterfall Walk-in Aviary as part of its 1.7-km (1-mile) journey.

A new walk-in aviary for South-East Asian birds, to be completed by the end of August 1992, will house 3,000 birds of 250 South-East Asian species, with separate enclosures for the rarer or more territorial species but a general free-flying area. The main walk-in aviary to be known as the Waterfall Aviary is scheduled for completion in December 1992. It will contain birds from Africa, the Amazon and the rest of Asia, in a free area of 1.6 hectares (4 acres), with tall trees and shrubs, a waterfall and pools. A new suspension bridge and better facilities for the handicapped are also being prepared.

The flamingo enclosure at the entrance to the park is to be increased to 144 m² (172 yd²) and given a new pool in order to reduce surface detritus. This renewed area will contain the Greater and Chilean Flamingoes, separated from one another by a rock barrier, and from the public by a low plant barrier.

The BirdPark also houses a Breeding and Research Centre for rare and endangered birds. These include the Scarlet Ibis, the Hawk-headed Parrot, the Mollucan Cockatoo and Pink Pigeons. Eggs are incubated and occasionally even hatched by machine (what else would you expect in high-tech Singapore); birds are encouraged to lay two clutches of eggs when the first is removed for incubation; some birds are even hand-reared if rejected by their parents. Research into breeding and rearing birds is constantly being undertaken, with 111 species bred successfully between 1980 and 1988.

The Breeding and Research Centre is not open to the public.

Jurong Crocodile Paradise

Jurong Hill, Jalan Ahmad Ibrahim, Singapore 2262
Telephone: 261 8866
Opening Hours: 9 a.m.–6 p.m. daily
To Get There: The Crocodile Paradise is just next door to the BirdPark, so as above. Some people try to see both on the same trip, which is possible on a cool day, but you'll enjoy each more if you see them separately.

Well, it's really just crocodiles—obviously—two and a half thousand of them, lazing in the sun in an area of 2 hectares (5 acres), which also includes a restaurant, fast-food outlet, souvenir and products shop. There is a Thrilling Wrestling Show at 11.30 a.m. and 3 p.m. daily (4.30 p.m. on Sundays and public holidays), if an overfed crocodile seemingly wrestling with a man is to your taste, and regular feeding times are 10.30 a.m., 1.30 and 4.30 p.m. if you prefer to watch the crocs devouring crates of fresh fish. You can also purchase chicken wings suspended on wires above a crocodile enclosure, and jiggle them out of the way just as a hungry crocodile attempts to reach them. Look out for the extremely entertaining cautionary notices—and take note!

Garden of Fame

Jurong Hill Top, Singapore 2262
To Get There: short taxi ride or walk

from the BirdPark or Jurong Crocodile Paradise

On the hill above the BirdPark and the Crocodile Paradise is a small well-tended garden, with trees planted by former celebrities and world leaders. You can just wander through the garden to read of fallen heroes and world leaders, or you can climb up the lookout tower to view the industrial port of Jurong and the busy shipping lanes beyond. On a clear day you can see **Bukit Timah** hill and the central city district towers to the east, the hills of mainland Malaysia to the north, a selection of the oil-refining and other Singaporean and Indonesian islands to the south.

The Mint Coin Gallery

249 Jalan Boon Lay, Singapore 2261
Telephone: 261 4749
Opening Hours: 9.00 a.m.–4.30 p.m. Mondays–Fridays, closed weekends and public holidays
To Get There: MRT to Boon Lay; buses 99, 188, 192, 199, 206, 240, 248

Housed in a room overlooking part of the Mint's shop floor, a persistent pounding noise adds interest, though you can't actually see that much despite a labelled floor plan by the window. This small museum houses a limited display of coins, medals and medallions from around the world, or rather from those countries which have used the Singapore Mint to coin commemorative coins for them. Corporate souvenirs, medals, civilian decorations are all made here and displayed in rather sleepy surroundings—not all display cases are lit or labelled. A

souvenir counter offers replicas and the real things for sale, as well as a publication of all the coins minted in Singapore—clearly only for the really serious collector.

Thow Kwang Industry (Pte) Ltd

85 Lorong Tawas, Singapore 2261
Telephone: 265 5808
Opening Hours: 8.30 a.m.–5.00 p.m. Mondays–Saturdays, 9.00 a.m.–3.00 p.m. Sundays

Those particularly interested in buying china may like to visit one of the remaining dragon kiln potteries in Singapore along Lorong Tawas, in Jurong. Hidden down a small track off Jalan Boon Lay, the Thow Kwang Industry imports much produce from China, as well as making a selection of plant pots, china elephants and the like itself. Wander at will through the packed storehouses and see if anything takes your fancy—though do take cash, rather than credit cards, with you.

Tang Dynasty City

2 Yuan Ching Road, Singapore 2261
Opening Hours: 9.00 a.m.–10.00 p.m. daily

This $70 million theme park opened in part in January 1992, run by the same organization that runs the Sung Dynasty theme park in Hong Kong. It is based on the original Chang-an (Xian) city in China, the cultural and commercial hub of the Tang dynasty from AD 618–906 Visitors have a chance to step back into by-gone days in China, walking through an imposing entrance gate to an open courtyard graced by two statues and two model chariots. An arched bridge leads over a small moat, lined on the gateway side with stone lanterns, with a few resident white ducks and just submerged bamboo platforms whose purpose becomes obvious during one of the many cultural shows. You can gain an overview of the village by climbing on to the wall, seeing the whole complex beneath you including the second part to be opened in mid-1992, and beyond it the striking structure of Jurong Town Hall.

The **Silk Road Open City**, a collection of replica Tang-style houses, as well as enticing carts of goodies, is a fascinating area to wander through. Each shop displays different wares, often with a craftsman working or at least a helpful assistant ready to explain the items to you: everywhere you can and should wander upstairs, through back passageways unless it's clearly marked that you should not. Products typical of the Tang period are featured in shops on the main street just across the bridge: tricoloured pottery, ornate jade carvings, glazed wooden sculptures of horses, camels and warriors, traditional and modern-style jewellery, a highly ornate ivory carving of Chinese heaven, bamboo carvings, Chinese traditional rice wines, medicinal halls, a bank to change your dollars into Tang-style coins for purchases at the shops, and a tea house.

Back and side streets to the south (BirdPark) side of the main road across the bridge reveal embroidered tableware, lanterns, kites, porcelain and flour pottery, incense and joss sticks, a temple dedicated to Guan Yin, who is guarded by a ferocious-looking warrior statue, a gambling den where you can learn, play (and buy) Chinese chess, a fruit shop and the House of Li Bai a famous poet of the Tang dynasty contains scroll paintings.

The main road culminates at a woodcarver's shop where songbirds are suspended in cages. Turning left (northwards) a court-house on the left displays instruments of torture and regular displays are held to show how trials took place; upstairs are two rooms furnished in rosewood inlaid with mother-of-pearl, with desks and writing utensils in the first room, opium beds and sofas in the second. Next to the courthouse is the **House of 1,000 Pleasures**, where consorts dressed in finery can explain the history of the Tang dynasty and the silk road. (When I was there a bridal couple were having photos taken in one of the chambers!) Then come two shops, the first selling model terracotta warriors, the second bonsai or penjing trees. On the opposite side of the road is a shop where a craftsman is painting on pottery, then comes a school-house, furnished with lectern-style desks and kneeling blocks, and a couple of fun-fair exhibits, archery and a lucky draw. At the end of this street a sanded enclosed area is sometimes inhabited by a camel and two ponies, with whom visitors can be photographed.

The remaining shops which are open on the left (north) side of the main street include stalls of woodblock printing, chop carving, parasols and bamboo hats, Chinese scrolls, carpets,

Beautiful twin pagodas at Jurong's Chinese Garden. During some of the Chinese celebrations, the garden is decorated with lights and lanterns

Indonesian and other souvenirs, Indian brassware and papier mâché goods, jade carvings, and a silk house complete with loom and selling a variety of musical instruments. Several shops are still undergoing the final touches, with nothing for the shopper or visitor as yet.

Three daily shows are given in the movie studio, and press releases had suggested that one would be able to see filming in progress at these. Sadly not: the show is mainly a film show, though a couple of times the fighting sequence on the film cuts to the same characters fighting in front of the screen for two or three minutes, with slick timing so that they disappear behind the screen in time for the film to continue.

Regularly advertised and announced displays, parades and dances are given: a celebration parade of dragon dance, parasol carriers, javelin throwers and masked dancers followed by several characters in elaborate costumes. Another show, the journey to the west, entails a fighting display along bamboo duckboards in the moat, spectacular fighting suspended on a cable 10 m (10 yd) above the ground.

Virtually all the food outlets are in the same place, a large building on the left (as you enter) perimeter wall.

Banquets and live performances are given daily for lunch, tea and dinner at the **Tai He Lou Theatre Restaurant** on the first floor; beneath it a food court sells mainly Chinese dishes; on the second floor the **Tang Palace** is a straightforward Chinese restaurant, while the **Sanga Japanese Restaurant** is on the third floor. Adjacent to this building is the **Chang 'An Food Court**, virtually uninhabited save for a couple of drinks vendors during my visit.

Still to be opened late July 1992 are the **Heng Yang Pagoda** and **Underground Palace**, which will house models of the terracotta warriors; opening at a later date are the **Imperial Palace**; the **Hua Ching Pool**; the **stables**; the **Lodging house**; and some countryside.

Further shopping opportunities await you as you leave the park, with assorted retail outlets offering a selection of mainstream souvenirs to either side of the main gateway.

Chinese Garden and Japanese Garden

Yuan Ching Road, Singapore 2261
Telephone: 264 3455
Opening Hours: weekdays 9.00 a.m.–7.00 p.m., Sundays and Public Holidays 8.30 a.m.–7.00 p.m. (last admission at 6.00 p.m.)
To Get There: MRT to Chinese Garden (W10) then a 5-minute walk takes

you to the Chinese Garden, thence to the Japanese Garden. Buses 10 and 30 from Clifford Pier go to Jurong Interchange; then take 240, 242 or 406 to the gardens; bus 7 from Orchard Road goes to Jurong East Interchange; then a 98 takes you to the gardens.

These two gardens in Jurong are linked by a 65-m (203-ft)-long footbridge, and it's possible to visit both on the same trip—the entrance ticket covers admission to both venues.

The **Chinese Garden (Yu-Hwa-Yuan)** comprises an assortment of theme gardens, from herb and bonsai gardens, to a lotus pond and a garden of fragrance. The main building, which you reach as you cross the bridge from the main entrance by the car park, is modelled on the Peking Summer Palace and displays the architectural style of the Sung Dynasty (AD 960–1279).

A stone lantern in the Japanese Garden. Much less popular with visitors than the Chinese Garden, the Japanese Garden is refreshingly tranquil.

Colourfully tiled gate houses, tea houses and twin pagodas abound in the 13.5-hectare (33-acre) grounds, together with a statue of Confucius, a stone boat which houses a tourist boutique and a refreshment area. Set on an island on Jurong Lake, itself surrounded by HDB apartment blocks and the raised MRT line, the mirage of tranquillity is never quite complete as you see the environs from the top of the pagodas, or from any hill in the grounds. At Chinese New Year and the Mid-Autumn Lantern Festival, this garden is alive with celebrations.

The **Japanese Garden (Seiwaen)**, claimed to be the largest outside Japan, is contrastingly minimalist, and styled in the Muromachi (AD 1392–1568) manner, though planted with tropical plants, trees and shrubs. Respect for nature, and a balancing of space and scenery in harmony are the principles on which this graceful 13-hectare (32-acre) site is built. Stone lanterns, imported from Japan, are strategically placed, while the various streams and lakes boast waterfalls, carp and play host to occasional kingfishers. *Keiseien*, the Garden of Zen, in front of the main entrance, comprises a careful balance of rocks, plants and lanterns, and this principle of uncluttered harmony is present throughout the garden. You can feed the carp in the pond in front of the Guest House Blessed with Buddha's Mercy (*Tenkyokaku*).

Refreshments are available at both gardens, and soft drinks are generally much needed after a stroll in the sun. The food, available in the Chinese Garden, is microwaved and bland—don't plan to eat there, though it would do for an emergency.

Plans are afoot to upgrade and expand the Chinese Garden right up to the Chinese Garden MRT station on Commonwealth Road. Inspired by a 1991 trip to Suzhou in China as part of a delegation led by Brigadier General (Res) Lee Hsien Loong, the Jurong Town Corporation chairman Mr Yeo Seng Teck plans to fill the additional 5,800 m^2 (6,937 yd^2) area with about 2,000 *penjing* (bonsai) from different countries, including 400 or so created locally. The garden will have a new pavilion-style entrance, itself guarded by two lion-shaped *penjing*, and with a ceramic wall screen of legendary dragons, and a huge bridge modelled on the oldest bridge of the Sui Dynasty is also planned.

Even more ambitiously, an underground Chinese museum, in a way an extension of the Empress Place Exhibition Hall (*see* page 127) for which Mr Yeo is also responsible, is planned beneath the Garden. This will initially feature pieces loaned from Hong Kong private collections, until the museum is able to purchase and keep its own collection of works of art.

Just off the Japanese Garden Road is the **CN-West Leisure Park**, 9 Japanese Garden Road, Telephone: 261 4771. Opening Hours: 12 p.m.–6 p.m. Mondays–Fridays; 9.30 a.m.–6.00 p.m. weekends and public holidays. This is little more than a rather sleepy public swimming pool with a few extra amenities that may or may not be operational if you visit—a whirlpool, a water slide, some sideshows and funfair rides.

Singapore Science Centre

Science Centre Road, Off Jurong Town Hall Road, Singapore 2260
Telephone: 560 3316
Opening Hours: Tuesdays–Sundays 10 a.m.–6 p.m. and all public holidays including Mondays/Omni-Theatre Tuesdays–Sundays 10 a.m.–8 p.m.
To Get There: MRT to Jurong East, then bus no 336 or a 10-minute walk to the Science Centre. Bus 196 from Shenton Way to Boon Lay Interchange, then TIBS 178 or SBS 97. SBS

bus 7 from Orchard Road to Jurong East Station, then bus 336. SBS buses 51, 66, 78, 97 and 336, and TIBS buses 178 or 852.

The Singapore Science Centre, was opened in 1977, designed by Raymond Woo, the local winner of an architectural competition for its construction. It is acclaimed one of the top ten science centres in the world and attracts over 1 million visitors a year. About 10 per cent of the exhibits are changed and updated every year. It contains four galleries positioned around a hexagonal atrium gallery of temporary exhibits, with a total floor area of 7,400 m^2 (8,850 yd^2). It boasts a very appealing "hands-on" treatment of science, which is largely due to the creative approach of its director from 1982–91, Dr Leo Tan, whose approach also managed to excite numerous commercial sponsors for the exhibits. No exhibit, whether of a computer, or of a general physical principle such as electric impulses, is complete without at least a button for the viewer to press (though, sadly, not all those I pressed were working). A large proportion of its visitors are schoolchildren, either in groups in buses from school, or with their families during holidays and weekends. Captions to the 650 or more exhibits are generally clear, and these are backed up with special talks and programmes for schools to heighten the educational value of a visit.

The Centre rightly points out that it is impossible to visit all the exhibits meaningfully: if you take 5 minutes at each exhibit, it will take you 7 days to visit them all, so be selective in what you view—or return another time. Mini theatres show 15-minute long programmes on evolution and aviation, plus shorter films on birth, population and so forth.

To the right of the entrance hall is the Physical Sciences Gallery. Its electronics section contains examples of anodes and cathodes, microelectronics, explanations of ATM (Automatic Transfer of Money) machines and barcode readers, simple and increasingly sophisticated binary and computer systems, communications systems from morse code to SBC infotel systems, fibre optics, different applications of electronics in medicine, security, industry and entertainment. The omni-technology section contained an exhibition of ergonomics and productivity during my visit, though this may change over time. The mathematics section is filled with geometric designs and brain-teasers, well staged and intriguing; while the dynamic domain section explains the different sources and uses of energy throughout the world.

Returning to the central atrium, next on the right in an anticlockwise direction is the Aviation Theatre, largely sponsored by the prestigious Singapore Airlines. The early history of flight and avionics, from hot-air balloons to the Wright brothers is well-captioned and presented, before a range of exhibits which demonstrate the principles of flight and the workings of engine models. A variety of engines and motors are displayed, together with a model cockpit engine where you can play with the control buttons—if they are working and switched on! An explanation of gyroscopes and navigational techniques, principles and applications completes the gallery. There is also an audio-visual show four times daily to explain the history and principles of flight.

Next to the Aviation Theatre is the Discovery Centre. This gallery is designed for young children, to encourage them to explore and enjoy basic scientific ideas, so all the buttons and eye-holes are positioned at child's height. Dinosaurs, mirrors, space travel, the senses of sight, smell and sound—all are imaginatively staged to allow the child to discover, touch and question.

Finally, completing the anticlockwise tour, is the Life Sciences Gallery, recently renovated and reopened in May 1992.

On the upper level of the Science Centre are administrative offices, a small souvenir shop and an adequate, though somewhat tatty, canteen which serves drinks, snacks and meals. The Science Centre also boasts further educational facilities which can be used, by prior arrangement, by students and schoolchildren. These include a library collection of over 12,000 books and periodicals, a computer centre with 15 networked microcomputers, a weather station, a primary science room, a brain-teaser room, an Ecolab and Ecogarden Reference Centre, a Herbal and Spice Garden and a mini Rubber Plantation.

With your entry ticket to the Science Centre you can also visit the 50 or so exhibits of the Information Technology galleries at the next-door Omni-Theatre (where there is also a Burger King restaurant, if that appeals more than the Science Centre Canteen). Here are telephone systems, numerous computers, video-conferencing booths, tele-screens, visual phones and pagers, all of which you can play with and all loaned and sponsored by Singapore Telecom.

You can also see the projection room for the Omni-Theatre, for which you can buy tickets in the foyer, at C.K. Tangs Department Store or at Parkway Parade. The 180° curved projection on to a 23-m (75-ft) domed screen tilted at 30 degrees to the horizontal is impressive and does seem to include the audience in the action. A 6-channel, 20,000-watt sound system provides high-quality sound. Films shown are generally a rather servile pro-Singapore historical survey, together with a subject to show off the powers of the cinematographic technique—whether fibre optics within the human body, sporting prowess, scenic beauty and discovery—all generally sponsored by private business.

Upstairs there is a further Hall of Science, with exhibits on space, the planets, the sun and the moon. Singapore's first Public Observatory, opposite the Omni-Theatre, houses a 40-cm (16-in) Cassegrainian telescope within its 5.5-m (18-ft) dome but which is not generally open to the public.

Jurong Town Hall

Jurong Town Hall Road, Singapore 2260

You can see the tower of this bizarre building from the Japanese Garden, as well as from other local viewpoints. Built in 1979 as a result of an architectural competition, the building looks nautical and comprises restaurants, a conference hall and various offices.

Monkeys, Memorials and Much More

In the north and centre of the island there are a number of sites to visit. Singapore's Open Zoo, beautifully landscaped along the shores of the Seletar Reservoir, is a delight for animal-lovers; the Mandai Orchid Garden and the Botanic Gardens are well worth visiting for an overview of the natural flora; elaborate Buddhist temples in Toa Payoh and Bishan house religious communities and welcome interested visitors; numerous reservoir and nature parks allow you to view natural vegetation and some of the fauna— including the macaque monkeys.

Singapore Botanic Gardens

Cluny Road, Singapore 1025
Telephone: 470 9900
Opening Hours: 5 a.m.–11 p.m. weekdays, 5 a.m.–12 midnight Saturdays, Sundays and public holidays; Orchid Enclosure 7 a.m.–6.30 p.m., Bonsai House 8 a.m.–6 p.m., Plant House Annexe 7.30 a.m.–2 p.m.
To Get There: SBS Nos 7, 14, 75, 105, 106, 174, 390 and CSS No 2 along Napier Road; SBS Nos 153, 154, 170, 171, 172, 173, 175, 179, 180, 182, 190 along Bukit Timah Road

The Botanic Gardens of Singapore have a long history. Sir Stamford Raffles, the "founder" of Singapore, was himself a keen botanist, and set up Singapore's first Botanic Garden on Government Hill (now Fort Canning Hill) in 1822. The present 47-hectare (116-acre) Botanic Gardens were founded in 1859 by an Agri-Horticultural Society, and were, as their predecessor, used for researching and distributing useful crop plants for the region. They were taken over by the government in 1874 and opened to the public in the same year. One of the milestones in local botanical history was the introduction of Para Rubber trees (*Hevea braziliensis*) from

*E*vening light falls on the fountain and pagoda at the landscaped MacRitchie Reservoir Park.

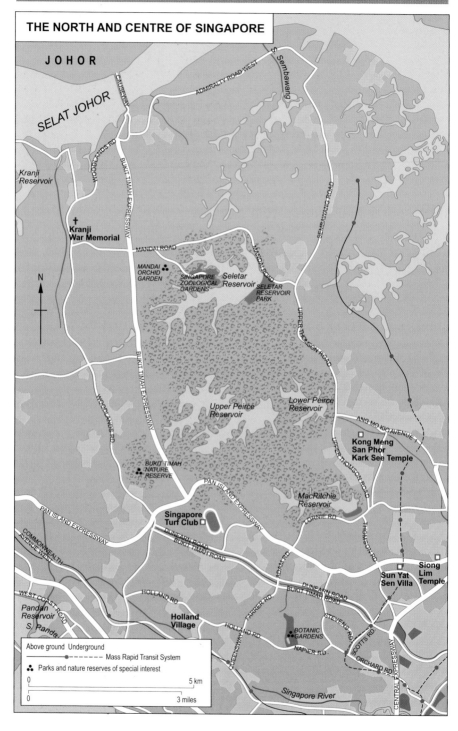

THE NORTH AND CENTRE OF SINGAPORE

JOHOR

SELAT JOHOR

CAUSEWAY

ADMIRALTY ROAD WEST

S. Sembawang

Kranji
Reservoir

WOODLANDS RD.

BUKIT TIMAH EXPRESSWAY

SEMBAWANG ROAD

✝ Kranji
War Memorial

MANDAI ROAD

N

MANDAI
ORCHID
GARDEN

SINGAPORE
ZOOLOGICAL
GARDENS

Seletar
Reservoir

SELETAR
RESERVOIR
PARK

MANDAI ROAD

UPPER THOMSON ROAD

Upper Peirce
Reservoir

Lower Peirce
Reservoir

ANG MO KIO AVENUE 1

Kong Meng
San Phor
Kark See Temple

UPPER THOMSON ROAD

WOODLANDS RD.

BUKIT TIMAH EXPRESSWAY

BUKIT TIMAH
NATURE
RESERVE

PAN ISLAND EXPRESSWAY

MacRitchie
Reservoir

Singapore
Turf Club □

PAN ISLAND EXPRESSWAY

COMMONWEALTH AVENUE WEST

DUNEARN ROAD

BUKIT TIMAH ROAD

LORNIE RD.

THOMSON RD.

ADAM RD.

□
Siong
Lim
Temple

□
Sun Yat
Sen Villa

WEST COAST ROAD

Pandan
Reservoir

S. Pandan

HOLLAND RD.

Holland
Village

HOLLAND RD.

FARRER RD.

DUNEARN ROAD

BUKIT TIMAH ROAD

STEVENS RD.

QUEENSWAY

BOTANIC
GARDENS

NAPIER RD.

SCOTTS RD.

ORCHARD RD.

CENTRAL EXPRESSWAY

Above ground Underground

●------●------ Mass Rapid Transit System

⁂ Parks and nature reserves of special interest

0   5 km

0   3 miles

Singapore River

London's Kew Gardens to Singapore in 1877 by "mad" H. N. Ridley, then director of the Gardens, who persuaded reluctant coffee planters to try the new crop on their estates in mainland Malaya, with far-reaching economic results still in evidence to this day. Since then the Botanic Gardens have spearheaded Singapore's orchid-growing programme, and supplied over 6,000 saplings to its Garden City Programme, the benefits of which we see all over the island today. Horticultural research and breeding programmes continue at the Horticultural School, and the Gardens retain a central role in the island's development into a tropical city of excellence.

There are over 3,000 species of tree in the Gardens today. The main entrance to the Gardens is at the junction of Holland and Cluny Roads, a convenient starting point for a tour. (Also a convenient finishing point, if you need sustenance, since the Taman Serasi food centre is just across the road, serving delicious *satay*, *rojak*, *nasi padang* and other Malay-style foods, together with welcome drinks.)

Walking along the **Main Gate Road** from this entrance, you come firstly to a **Marsh Garden**, then to the **First Lake** which boasts tremendous examples of the towering Nibung Palm, as well as entertaining notices forbidding, amongst other things, the release of turtles (the lake is stocked with

M ap of the northern and central areas of Singapore, including Holland Village.

Flower Power

Singapore's National Flower, the Vanda Miss Joaquim, was discovered by one Miss Agnes Joaquim in 1893. It is a hybrid of two orchids, the Vanda hookerana and a Vanda teres, and its bright purple colour was chosen as the national flower in 1981. Examples can be seen in both the Botanic Gardens and the Mandai Orchid Gardens, and cut flowers are readily available throughout the island—even at the airport. The motif now graces Singapore NTUC taxi drivers' shirts, as well as a whole host of tourist memorabilia.

Japanese carp and various terrapins already!). There was a recent scare when snakehead fish (*toman*) were released into this lake and ate three cygnets as well as damaging several carp: anglers were called in to rid the lake of this menace! You may catch a fleeting glimpse of a kingfisher flying low over the water here, as well as the graceful and sedate black swans who reside here.

Beyond the First Lake is a wrought-iron bandstand, constructed in 1860, which in turn overlooks the formal **Sundial garden**, **Rose garden**, a rather bizarre topiary area, and a small **Japanese** and **Sculpture Garden**. Turning back towards Cluny Road and walking up the hill you will find a rubber tree near the Garden offices; the herbarium is in the offices, and is open to botanists and students. Beside Cluny Road you can see the **Plant House**. Look out for the **Swiss Granite gall Fountain**, an intriguing gift from Switzerland to the Gardens in 1991 to mark the 700th anniversary of the Swiss Federation. An 80-cm (32-in) diameter granite ball weighing

720 kg (1,588 lb) floats on a thin layer of moving water powered by an underground pump.

A charming Victorian cast-iron gazebo stands next to the souvenir kiosk beside the orchid enclosure, where examples of the Gardens' successful hybridization programme are exhibited, and species shown include Singapore's National Flower, the Vanda Miss Joaquim. You may have to dodge around wedding parties here: the Botanic Gardens is a prime spot for wedding photographs!

Palm Valley leads downhill from the orchid enclosure towards the **Second Lake**—which has a rubber monument beside it. There are a series of free evening concerts given by the Singapore Symphony Orchestra here every summer (check the local press for details) and it is a pleasant way to enjoy the different Travellers', Nibung, Sealing Wax and other types of palm. Adjacent to Palm Valley is the 4-hectare (10-acre) stretch of primary tropical rainforest, with species dating from the first establishment of the Botanic Gardens on this site. This is, in fact, the largest stretch of rainforest left on Singapore, and an opportunity to see just how complicated and parasitical the various life-forms within the canopy are.

The **Bukit Timah Extension Zone**, reached by a tunnel near the Second Lake going beneath Cluny Road, is receiving the main thrust of the Botanic Gardens' improvement plans, due for completion by 1995. These will turn the existing 1.4-hectare (3.5-acre) concrete-lined lake, originally used to contain flood water, into an "eco-lake" with a more natural lining, various water and shore plants, together with a flock of water fowl, and species which have already settled here—the lesser tree duck, herons, kingfishers and some of Singapore's rich selection of butterflies. Adjoining the lake will be a new spice and cash crops garden on a newly elevated plot of land. Crops will include bamboo, jute, cotton, coffee, cacao, and medicinal herbs, as well as fruit and root crops. Nearby the two-storey black and white Corner House on Cluny Road, originally the residence of the Assistant Director E. J. H. Corner, is currently in a despondent state of disrepair, but has been offered for tender for restoration as a British colonial-style restaurant. Inspired by the Alkaff Mansion, the Singapore Tourist Promotion Board hopes that it will start serving tourists with teas and *stengahs*—half whiskies—in keeping with its British colonial past.

Other improvements to the Gardens include quadrupling the size of the orchid enclosure, in order to enable visitors to see how orchid hybrids are created in the laboratory, and the improved 4.3-km (2.7-mile) walkway, currently just another construction site, linking the Gardens with Tanglin and Orchard Roads.

For a detailed guide to plants within the extensive grounds of the Botanic Gardens, buy a copy of the *Pictorial Guide to the Singapore Botanic Gardens*, available at the souvenir kiosk. Most trees and plants are labelled so that you can identify favourites such as the Cannon Ball Tree (*Couroupita guianensis*), the Bodh Tree (Ficus religiosa) or the Nibong Palm (*Oncosperma tigrilarium*).

Nature and Wildlife in Singapore

For all its modern urban feel, Singapore still boasts about 2,000 different plant species and a vibrant range of wildlife, some of which you have to struggle to see, some of which is easily viewable.

Trees

Singapore has a number of fine palm trees, from the Traveller's or Fan Palm, to the Red Stemmed Sealing Wax Palm, the Oil Palm and the towering Nibong Palm and the Areca Palm. Bamboos and rattan palms are also common. You will probably see examples of the Malayan Banyan tree with its wide trunk

Traveller's or Chinese Fan Palm at sunset. This is one of the many species of palm tree that you can readily see in Singapore.

and drooping aerial roots, the Tembusu tree with scented cream flowers and then red berries on its hanging twigs, and the high flat canopy of the Rain Tree, planted along highways such as the East Coast Parkway. Banana trees, generally so shabby you wonder how restaurants can obtain the square mats you eat curries off, are dotted here and there, and the occasional Cannon Ball Tree, originally native to South America, with its drooping "balls" hanging loosely by its side is also seen.

Flowering trees include the Flame of the Forest with its bright red flowers, the Poison Apple with white flowers and green mango-sized poisonous fruits, and different cassias and sweet-smelling frangipanis. At muddy coastal areas mangrove trees, their roots exposed to the air at low tide and submerged at high tide, are readily seen; further inland on sand dunes and reclaimed soil are casuarinas, fir-tree-like trees.

A heliconia plant, photographed at Heliconia Valley near the entrance to Singapore Zoo.

Shrubs

Singapore's many shrubs include the Common Seashore Screwpine, with its edible fruit, the Oleander with pink, red or white flowers, the Pinwheel Flower with dark green shiny leaves and fragrant white flowers, the Adenium or Japanese Frangipani, also known as a Prosperity Tree, different Hibiscus and Gardenias, and the myriad colours of the Bougainvillea, now planted along walkways, footbridges and in road divisions.

Ferns and Epiphytes

The Antler or Staghorn Fern, nestling in the branches of larger trees is a fairly common sight, as are the Climbing and Rabbit's Foot Fern. Several orchid species grow naturally, including the Pigeon Orchid and the Bulbophyllum.

Fruits, Vegetables and Herbs

Rambutans, durians, pineapples, papayas, mangos and breadfruit all can grow in Singapore, though the bulk are imported due to lack of space. So too Lady's Finger, Aubergine and Long bean grow here, as well as Water Convolvulus and the Chinese cabbage Choy Sum, and the spices ginger, pepper, nutmeg and asam, the latter used in flavouring curries and Malay dishes.

Birds

Singapore has about 300 species of bird. Everywhere you will see and hear the different species of Mynah bird, with black or brown feathers and yellow patches around its eyes. Tree Sparrows and pigeons are also common. You may catch sight of the Black-naped Oriole, a bright yellow bird the size of a magpie, and the White-throated Kingfisher, larger than its European cousin, is fairly commonly seen near water. Sea Eagles with white bellies soar over Singapore's seas, as do Brahminy Kites and other birds of prey, as well as vast black crows. Different types of tern can be seen, some visiting only during the northern hemisphere's winter. Purple and Grey Herons and Bitterns are seen in certain areas—Kranji Reservoir for example, where efforts are being made to preserve their habitat, and White-breasted Waterhens survive in the decreasing wetland habitat.

It is hard to see, though easy to hear, the variety of birds inhabiting the forest of Bukit Timah, which include drongos, bulbuls and even parakeets.

Animals and Reptiles

As well as the common macaque monkeys, easily seen at the reservoir parks, native species to Singapore include squirrels, bats, mouse deer and civet cats. There are 40 different types of snake, and the monitor lizard, freshwater turtles, the occasional crocodile and varying sizes of lizard including the household gecko all occur here.

Insects

A huge variety of butterflies, some of which are larger than sparrows, can be found on the island, while cicadas and crickets make a constant noise particularly in the early evenings. Less pleasant creatures, such as cockroaches, mosquitoes and ants are kept at bay by pest control companies.

Fish

There are coral reefs near Sentosa Island, and between it and Buran Darut, as well as near the Southern Islands, and at the time of writing a scheme to relocate corals from islands scheduled for industrial use to the unspoilt south-west coast of Sentosa Island is under way. These support a variety of fish, though it is far harder to see them than in Malaysian or Indonesian waters, since the water is fairly polluted, reducing visibility for scuba-divers.

Where to See Singapore's Natural Heritage

Many different tree and shrub species can be seen as you travel within the urban areas of Singapore, as part of the government's Green City plan. The central part of the island, comprising the Zoo, the Mandai Orchid Garden, Bukit Timah Nature Reserve and the MacRitchie, Upper and Lower Peirce and Seletar Reservoirs, remains a rich habitat for a number of plant, mammal and bird species despite the Ministry of Defence's nearby shooting ranges. Some off-the-beaten-track wildlife sites,

A wild macaque monkey scavenging near the car-park at Seletar Reservoir Park. You are not encouraged to feed the monkeys.

which the Malayan Nature Society is keen to preserve as such, include Sungei Seletar Reservoir, Khatib Bongsu, Cho Chu Kang, Marina East and Jalan Kedai, as well as St John's Island. Sentosa's Butterfly Park has a large number of species, both in display cases and more agreeably flying in the butterfly garden.

Specialist nature and bird-watching tours are arranged by the STPB fairly regularly: check with them or in the listings section of *The Straits Times* for activities of interest. The Botanic Gardens has recently started running short courses for the public, generally for a couple of hours on Saturday mornings: again, check with the STPB, the listings section, or phone the Botanic Gardens. For more details *see* page 183.

Holland Village

Holland Road, Singapore 1027
To Get There: Buses 2, 32, 103, 145, 202, 216

A popular shopping and eating venue for expatriates and tourists in search of bargains and unusual items, Holland Village has a rich variety of shops, restaurants, galleries, a wet market and several other services. Porcelain and China items, as well as basketry and antiques and local handicrafts are reaily available. Its general vivacity and real "village" feel make it a model for architects to emulate as they construct new "town centres" for Singapore's new towns.

Bukit Turf Club

Turf Club Road, Bukit Timah Road, Singapore 1228
Telephone: 469 3611

There are flat race meetings at the Turf Club approximately 15 weekends a year, as part of the Malayan Racing Association's annual fixtures. Bustling and fun occasions, though not without fairly apparent undercurrents of occasional race fixing and tardy starting from a favourite or two, it is highly recommendable for horse-racing enthusiasts or those who want to see something slightly off the traditional tourist track. Betting, apart from through the government-backed tote, is strictly illegal, so there are no bookmakers, but large wads of cash are placed on the tote and the odds can change drastically a couple of minutes before races start, clearly due to tips and the like. The spectators, who are predominantly Chinese, prove an enthusiastic crowd, and the atmosphere in the stand is electric as races thunder towards the finish. Even if you don't win, keep your tote tickets for a couple of days: they are all entered into a draw, the results of which are printed in *The Straits Times*, and you may be lucky enough to win a few hundred or several thousand dollars. If you are after more style, you could try to book a box, though you will need to give advance notice, particularly for highly popular events such as the Singapore Gold Cup or the Singapore Derby.

The Turf Club is open to the public on days when there is no racing: indeed the Rasa Singapura food centre is located in part of the grandstand, from where you can see the track. In the early mornings, around 7.30 a.m., the horses train on the inner track of the course, which members of the public can watch provided they do not wear shorts, singlets or slippers or take photographs.

Singapore's first racecourse was on what is now Farrer Park, just north of Serangoon Road—which explains the popular road of South Indian eating houses named Race Course Road. The racecourse was moved to its present location in 1935. A previous owner of the Turf Club, Runme Shaw, installed the large video screens, which replay all races a couple of minutes after they finish. They also show the racing in Penang, Ipoh and Kuala Lumpur—the other three venues for the Malayan Racing Club's fixtures—live, and you are also allowed to bet on these races using the computerized totalizator. These screens are also used for occasional outdoor film showings.

Bukit Timah Nature Reserve

Hindhede Road, Upper Bukit Timah Road, Singapore 2158
To Get There: buses 171, 173, 179 or 182 from Orchard Boulevard or Scotts Road

A spot of virtually unspoilt jungle lies just to the north of the Bukit Timah/Clementi Road interchange, up an unpromising track shared with a nearby limestone quarry. Here you can follow a well-signed choice of four paths through 75 hectares (185 acres) of primary forest up to the highest point on the island, approximately 162.5 m (533 ft) above sea level. Remember to take insect repellent—the mosquitoes there are vicious—and something to drink, since there are no tourist kiosks or cafes here, and the walking is at times quite energetic.

You are very likely to see and hear the Long-tailed Macaques, often in evidence near the car-park. You may also hear a variety of birds, though you are unlikely to be able to identify any species. Cicadas add to the noise, and grasshoppers, stick insects, beetles and spiders are easily seen, along with geckos and small lizards. The flora is more easily identifiable, and the Nature Reserves Board, as well as publishing a helpful guide to the reserve with a map of footpaths, has also placed labels next to various different trees including the seraya and Diptercarpaceae trees. You will notice a variety of climbers, such as the Rattan Palm; as well as the large number of epiphytes, plants growing parasitically on other plants, like the spectacular Staghorn fern, or even a wild orchid.

Ivan Polunin, in *Plants and Flowers of Singapore*, identifies five different levels of trees in this example of tropical forest. At the top level are the seraya trees, as much as 50 m (160 ft) high, reaching into full sunlight and experiencing the greatest temperature variation of the forest flora; below these the canopy is a continuous level of growth, broken only with the occasional fallen tree; a third level of shaded trees, generally with spindly trunks, follows; then two levels of treelets, herbaceous plants, seedlings and the detritus forming the forest floor, which only receives 2 per cent of sunlight, and experiences a comparatively cool and even temperature—this floor stays damp for days after rainfall.

To the right of the entrance to the Reserve you will see the **Taban Valley**—*taban* is the Malay word for gutta-percha, and there was an old plantation on this site: you can identify the trees by the diagonal cuts on their trunks where the latex was drawn from.

If you do want to "get away from it all", Bukit Timah Nature Reserve is one of the more peaceful spots to do so. That said, the adjoining Hindhede Quarry is still worked, so lorries use the private road in the reserve. The top of the hill, as the highest point on the island, does have a high detector pylon on it, and while you can look out to the east to admire the seeming expanse of countryside around the various reservoirs (*see* below), hidden from view are two main expressways—the PIE and the BKE—and you may find your peace interrupted by firing from one of the military areas or from low-flying military aircraft.

Kranji War Memorial and Cemetery

Woodlands Road, Singapore 2573
To Get There: bus 182 from Orchard Boulevard or Scotts Road, buses 170, 178, 180, 181 and 925

This peaceful cemetery on a slope overlooking the Straits of Johor is a memorial to those Allied military personnel who lost their lives during the Second World War. The War Cemetery contains the graves of 4,000 allied servicemen, and is beautifully maintained with planted flowers and trimmed grass. The Singapore State Cemetery lists the names of 20,000 further forces personnel who have no known graves in its walls.

Kranji War Memorial and cemetery. A peaceful and sobering memorial to Allied Military personnel.

Kranji Reservoir

Kranji dam, to the west of the Woodlands Checkpoint, is reached through the industrial backstreets of Woodlands and well off the beaten tourist track. The car-parks near the dam do give a spectacular view across the Strait of Johor to the Abu Bakar Mosque (*see* page 230), while sleepy looking fishermen work the fertile waters nearer home.

The reservoir itself, which you can walk alongside from Car Park B, or reach from the Kranji Pumping Station, is home to the decreasing Singapore population of herons, and hence a bird-spotter's delight. The nature protection lobby has ensured that Kranji will be left as it is to keep the mangrove nesting sites, and the drive along to the pumping station gives a rare glimpse into the former *kampong* (village) lifestyle, which has now almost totally disappeared.

The North Coast

Running parallel to the Straits of Johor, from Woodlands New Town to Sembawang, is Admiralty Road. This road is now crowded with military bases, (as are so many peaceful-looking roads to the north-west and west of the island), but between these you can catch sight of some good examples of black and white houses, built for the British naval personnel in the 1920s. These houses are generally built with raised floors in Malay or *kelong* style to keep out snakes and the like, as well as to encourage cooling breezes, and they also mainly have shutters and verandahs—evocative of those *stengahs* (small whiskies) consumed by the colonials. The former Admiralty House on Old Nelson Road was designed by Sir Edwin Lutyens, and is mainly on two storeys, with an additional single-storey wing. Having served various naval and administrative functions

View across the Johor Strait from Kranji dam to the Abu Bakar Mosque.

over the years, it is now part of the Yishun golf club, with a restaurant open to the public.

Mandai Orchid Gardens

Mandai Lake Road, Singapore 2572
Telephone: 269 1036
Opening Hours: 9.00 a.m.–5.30 p.m. daily
To Get There: Mandai Orchid Gardens are on the same road as the Singapore Zoo, so as below

An opportunity for the amateur or the enthusiast to look at a wide range of orchids, not all of which, sadly, are clearly labelled. This garden was started in 1950, and is situated on an

Zebras at Singapore's Open Zoo. Most animal enclosures have ditches rather than high fences, which creates a less caged environment than zoos.

east-facing slope just north of the northern end of the Seletar Reservoir, where the zoo is, and you can see rows and rows of various shades and breeds of orchid. To the right of the entrance is a well-laid-out water garden, displaying a variety of tropical plants and wooden bridges.

Plants are available for sale, or for ordering for special occasions, and can be sent abroad to various European and antipodean countries as well as to Japan. Do check with your home country customs before leaving if you are intending to import or have plants sent, since there can be quite rigid controls on such goods.

Singapore Zoological Gardens

80 Mandai Lake Road, Singapore 2572
Telephone: 269 3411
Opening Hours: 8.30 a.m.–6.30 p.m. Mondays–Saturdays, 8.00 a.m. 6.30 p.m. Sundays and public holidays
To Get There: Zoo Express bus from major hotels (telephone: 235 3111); SBS Bus No 171 from Queen Street, Orchard Boulevard and Bukit Timah Road; MRT to Toa Payoh, then Bus No 137; MRT to Yishun then SBS No 171; TIBS No 926 from Woodlands on Sundays and public holidays

Singapore is rightly proud of its 28-hectare (69-acre) Open Zoo, beautifully landscaped on the north shore of Seletar Reservoir. Ditches and natural barriers are used rather than cages to separate over 170 species from each other and from the public, and spacious enclosures, whenever possible, make it a photographer's heaven.

Many of the animal exhibits are sponsored by private concerns or public companies, whose names are prominently displayed by the enclosures. There is a tram service, complete with taped documentary, around the zoo for those short of time or energy, though you do see the animals better if you walk around on your own, and refreshments are available at a selection of kiosks on your route.

Check with your hotel or the local paper or as you enter the zoo if you want to time your visit to coincide with an animal show: breakfast with an orang-utang (Ah-Meng, the nation's heart-throb) remains popular, while there are generally shows of snakes, elephants, sea lions, orang-utangs and polar bears. Feeding times are also displayed as you enter the zoo, and seeing an animal fed is generally a hit with children. You can also have pony or elephant rides.

The enclosures are well captioned, with maps showing the animals' original habitat, together with descriptions of reproduction, lifestyle and life expectancy, etc. A high proportion of the species on display originally come from the Malayan Peninsula or Indonesia. There is also a large zone of eight different enclosures of African animals, including the kudu, oryx, nayak, lechwe and waterbuck, and some continuing favourites include the Polar Bear living nearest the equator and the penguins. Also of interest is the tropical crops plantation, a chance to identify those pineapples, rubber trees and spices that you always hoped to see in the Far East!

A newly opened 1-hectare (2.4-acre) Primate Kingdom houses primates from three continents on well-landscaped islands divided by waterways filled with over 1,000 Japanese carp donated by a Japanese trading company. Though they are at some distance from the public, it is refreshing to see the animals moving and living almost naturally in such habitats. The species there include Patas monkeys with moustaches, reddish jackets and grey bodies from Africa; Colubus leaf monkeys with their spectacular white trim around their heads; lion-tailed macaques from India; Capuchin monkeys from South America with rich brown colouring and hood-like tufts; silver leaf langur from Malaysia and Sumatra, silver grey in colour; De Brazas monkeys from Africa with orange headbands and blond moustaches and beards and black stippled fur; and various lemurs, tamarins and so forth. Telescopes are to be installed, but do take binoculars or a long camera lens if you want to watch them closely.

At the furthest point from the entrance is the newly opened Children's Zoo, still marked as under construction on the zoo map but actually in operation. Here you can see miniature horses, llamas, dromedaries, sheep, goats, ponies, donkeys, chickens and other poultry, pigs, cows and small pets—rabbits, mice and guinea pigs. Milking displays and sheep-herding displays are given in central pens. At the reservoir end of the main Children's Zoo is a curious steam area, where jets of water swiftly turn into cooling steam whatever the outside temperature; next to this is a play area containing a netting space walk for adventurous climbing children. Various pools for paddling and sailing boats are in the middle of the zoo, which also contains a small walk-through aviary. Two miniature steam trains link the main Children's Zoo to the nearby playground and eating area: the train ride allows a view of most animals in the children's section, as well as a view across the reservoir to Seletar Reservoir Park on the opposite side.

Like the BirdPark in Jurong, the Singapore Zoo has an extensive research and breeding programme in operation, and its most notable success is in breeding orang-utangs.

Seletar Reservoir Park

If you have not seen enough of this reservoir from visiting the zoo, you can gain access to a tranquil section from Upper Thomson Road or Mandai Road. Wild monkeys are often seen around the car-park litter bins, and some keep-fit facilities and public paddle-boats are available.

Upper Peirce and Lower Peirce Reservoirs

A drive or taxi ride along to one of the Peirce reservoirs is good for a picnic or walk. Upper Peirce has a small landscaped picnic park at the reservoir dam, together with public toilets, but then you can walk as you wish along the reservoir side or down to Lower Peirce Reservoir, though you fairly rapidly come up against the private golf-course land of the exclusive Singapore Island Country Club.

Kong Meng San Phor Kark See Temple

Bright Hill Drive, Singapore 2057
To Get There: MRT to Bishan then bus 57, bus 130

Built in 1981, this is the largest religious complex in Singapore, stretching over an area of 12 hectares (30 acres). It is in many ways the centre of Singapore's Buddhist religion: the installation of a new abbot there in 1991 was a national spectacle, and the procession there each Vesak Day (*see* page 92) is attended by thousands from the whole island.

The many buildings are constructed according to *feng shui* principles, and include a single-storey crematorium with a Thai-built roof; two halls—the Hall of Great Virtue, and the Hall of Great Compassion—each with Taiwanese-built roofs. It also comprises a liberation garden, with a turtle-filled lake, an old people's home, and numerous prayer halls. Visitors are welcome to wander around this tranquil area, and may even be lucky enough to find a monk willing to explain the buildings or the Buddhist religion to them in more detail.

Roof detail at Kong Meng San Phor Kark See Temple near Bishan New Town.

MacRitchie Reservoir

Lornie Road, Singapore 1129
To Get There: buses 104, 132 and 167 from Orchard Boulevard or Scotts Road

This park is named after James MacRitchie, the government surveyor who suggested increasing this water catchment area to approximately the size it is today. You can visit this park and walk right along the reservoir to the Singapore Island Country Club golf-course at Sime Road, following either the main forest track, also used for joggers and keep-fit training, with exercise areas placed along the route to encourage you to do sit-ups or bench presses, according to your workout schedule. Alternatively, you can take the smaller reservoir side path which hugs the inlets and coast of the lake. You may see monkeys, the occasional turtle, and hear noises of birds while a dense network of trees masks the traffic noise from the nearby Lornie Road, so you really get a feeling of space and peacefulness. There's a landscaped park, complete with ornamental bridges, a fountain and a cafeteria, at the car-park entrance, but if you walk further you see little except for other walkers and joggers, and the scenery.

Sun Yat-Sen Villa

12 Tai Gin Road, Singapore 1232
Telephone: 256 2080 (Mandarin speaker only: try the Singapore Chinese Chamber of Commerce if necessary on 337 8381)
Opening Hours: 9.00 a.m.–4.30 p.m. daily

To Get There: bus numbers 4, 122, 123, 124, 125, 126, 130, 139, or 145 to Balestier Road, then walk up Ah Hood Road

This excellent example of a Victorian villa, with open verandahs and a covered entrance porch, is hidden behind Balestier Road, squeezed in between HDB flats and the PIE but still somehow retains its peaceful quality. The site was originally an (unsuccessful) sugar plantation owned by the first American Consul to Singapore, Joseph Balestier. The house was built some time during the 1880s by a wealthy Cantonese businessman Boey Chuan Poh for his mistress, and was subsequently bought by Teo Eng Hock for his mother.

It now commemorates the leading Chinese revolutionary Dr Sun Yat-Sen, who briefly became the first provisional president of the Republic of China in 1912 (for one month), and who visited Singapore on several occasions in the early years of this century. He stayed in this villa on three occasions between 1906 and 1908, setting up a Singapore headquarters for the T'ung Meng Hui organization which was plotting to overthrow the 267-year-old Manchu Dynasty in mainland China. Money raised through the Singapore branch funded three abortive uprisings in the Middle Kingdom during this period (the Huang-kang Uprising in May 1907; the Chen-nan-kuan Uprising in December 1907; and the Hokow Uprising in April 1908), but could take no credit for the successful revolution on 10 October 1911, since Dr Sun Yat-Sen was in America fund- and consciousness-raising at the time.

His statue stands in front of the villa, erected in 1966 by the Singapore Chinese Chamber of Commerce, who also now run the building for the general public.

Rather a sleepy place, but nonetheless interesting for this, the ground floor of the bungalow contains exhibits and photographs from Dr Sun Yat-Sen's life and those of other revolutionary leaders of the time. Upstairs is a Chinese library, together with a display of photographs of Chinese citizens from the Occupation years and some rather moving objects left by some of those who died during this period.

Next door to the Villa is a new Burmese Buddhist centre and temple.

Siong Lim Temple

Jalan Toa Payoh, Singapore 1231
To Get There: buses 26, 142, 149 and 154

This very moving and well-frequented temple and monastery now looks directly out over the Pan Island Expressway, one of the island's busiest thoroughfares. It has several inner and outer temples and courtyards, a small Chinese Suzhou-style rock garden, a bonsai collection, monks' quarters and some extremely ornate bronze Buddha statues. Parts of the temple date from 1898, and it is the largest Buddhist temple in Singapore. Termite infestation was discovered in late 1991 and at the time of writing all but the building shown below were closed for repairs.

Its full name is Lian Shan Shiong Lime Shan Si, which in Fujian means Lotus Hill Twin Groves. There are several impressive statues, including the Four Kings of Heaven, the Goddess of Mercy Guan Yin, various Siamese marble Buddhas, as well as ancestor tablets, including one to the founder Low Kim Pong.

*T*he main hall of Siong Lim Temple in Toa Payoh. The whole temple complex is the largest in Singapore.

Prisons, Planes, Playgrounds and Picnics

Singapore's Changi Airport is itself an attraction and achievement; beneath the flight paths of aircraft lie the East Coast beaches, Changi Beach and the Singapore Crocodilarium; out at Changi village are the Republic of Singapore Air Force Museum, the Changi Prison Museum of wartime POW mementoes, and the murals painted by POW Stanley Warren; the Malay quarter of Geylang is also in the east of the city, as is the sports and entertainment centre of Kallang.

Changi Prison Chapel and Changi Prison Museum

Upper Changi Road, Singapore 1750
Telephone: 543 0893
Museum Opening Hours: Mondays–Saturdays 9.30 a.m.–4.30 p.m., Sundays 3.30 p.m.–5.30 p.m., closed public holidays; Chapel open to visitors daily, Sunday Service 5.30 p.m.–6.30 p.m.

Changi Prison Memorial Chapel, built in 1987 as a replica of the chapel built by Allied POWs during World War II.

To Get There: SBS bus No 13 from Orchard Road to Victoria Street, transfer to SBS bus No 1 or 2 to Changi Prison

This small memorial to the allied POWs interned during the Japanese Occupation is situated within the grounds of the main Changi Prison, on the left as you go through the main prison entrance before the security checkpoint. The prison complex itself dates from the 1930s, an example of the municipal work carried out by the then surveyor, Frank Dorrington Ward, and was used shortly after its completion to house European prisoners of war. A replica chapel, typical of those built in Singapore and on the notorious Burma Railway by Allied prisoners of war, with a simple

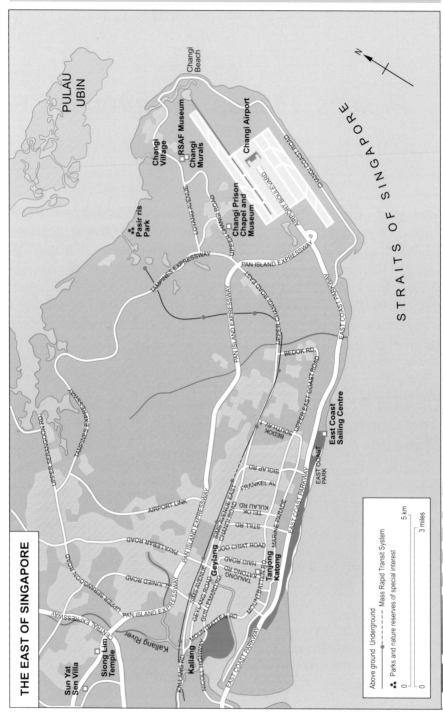

THE EAST OF SINGAPORE

PULAU UBIN

Changi Beach

Changi Village

RSAF Museum

Changi Murals

Changi Airport

Changi Prison Chapel and Museum

Pasir ris Park

CHANGI COAST ROAD

AIRPORT BOULEVARD

LOYANG AVENUE

UPPER CHANGI ROAD

TAMPINES EXPRESSWAY

PAN ISLAND EXPRESSWAY

PAN ISLAND EXPRESSWAY

UPPER CHANGI ROAD EAST

BEDOK RD.

EAST COAST PARKWAY

STRAITS OF SINGAPORE

TAMPINES EXPRESSWAY

UPPER SERANGOON RD.

TAMPINES EXPRESSWAY

AIRPORT LINK

PAYA LEBAR ROAD

PAN ISLAND EXPRESSWAY

UPPER SERANGOON ROAD

ALJUNIED ROAD

CENTRAL EXPRESSWAY

Sun Yat Sen Villa

Siong Lim Temple

Kallang River

Kallang

KALLANG RD.

NICOLL HIGHWAY

MOUNTBATTEN RD.

GEYLANG ROAD

GUILLEMARD

SIMS AVENUE

SIMS AVENUE EAST

CHANGI ROAD

HAIG ROAD

JOO CHIAT ROAD

MOUNTBATTEN RD.

TANJONG KATONG RD.

Geylang

Tanjong Katong

MARINE PARADE

STILL RD.

FRANKEL AV.

KILLAU RD.

TELOK

SISLGAP RD.

UPPER EAST COAST ROAD

BEDOK
SOUTH AV. 1

EAST COAST PARKWAY

EAST COAST PARKWAY

EAST COAST PARK

East Coast Sailing Centre

Above ground Underground
—•—•— Mass Rapid Transit System
❖ Parks and nature reserves of special interest

0   5 km
0   3 miles

thatched roof and open-air wooden bench seating, was constructed by prisoners under the direction of the Singapore Tourist Promotion Board and the Singapore Prison Service in 1987. It sits peacefully within a small garden of bougainvilleas, with open-air benches and visitors are welcome to pick the flowers in remembrance of those who died in this region during the Second World War.

The museum itself, housed in a small prefabricated building, contains displays of drawings, sketches and photographs by different prisoners of war, including watercolours by the late Traffic Police Superintendent W. R. M. Haxworth and photographs by the Australian soldier George Aspinall. These pictures include images from the Thai—Burma railway, responsible for so many POW deaths. (For the full horror of life on this railway, visit the museum constructed at Kanchanaburi along the railway line itself in Thailand—it's about 3 hours' journey from Bangkok.) Together with memorabilia from the various regiments involved and examples of the currency in use in Singapore under the Japanese, the exhibition is an intensely moving look at the day-to-day conditions in Changi and other POW camps during the Second World War.

A small shop sells books about Singapore's war experiences, together with the usual range of souvenirs, and a visitors' book contains numerous entries from mainly Caucasian visitors.

M ap of the eastern parts of Singapore.

Perhaps because the museum and chapel are on a site so near to where the 85,000 soldiers and civilians were held captive during the war, and perhaps because the displays are sympathetically housed in this quiet building, the experience of visiting is quite different from the theme park treatment shown at Sentosa's Fort Siloso, and very worth the visit.

For those tourists particularly interested in recent war history, there is a new tour (*see* page 243). Alternatively, visit this museum and Kranji cemetery in the north of the island (*see* page 192) on your own without the rest of a tour group.

Air Force Museum

Block 78, Cranwell Road, Singapore 1750
Telephone: 540 1515
Opening Hours: Tuesdays–Sundays 9 a.m.–4.30 p.m., closed Mondays and public holidays
To Get There: Bus numbers 2, 9 and 29

The Republic of Singapore Air Force opened a small museum in September 1991 within the military camp area around Changi. It details the history of the air force from colonial and Malaysian days through to the Republic's fleet in the early 1990s. The bulk of the displays are set out in the three halls, though outside the museum are displayed various engines and planes.

Hall One contains a display of photographs, newspaper articles and defence speeches on the milestones of the development of the Republic's air

203

force. Mannequins model historic uniforms, and side cabinets contain memorabilia, medals, insignia and ceremonial swords as well as old licences and forms. In the middle of the hall are small models of aeroplanes used by the RSAF over the years, some of which are still in operation today.

Hall Two is a display of the history of the air force and its bases, with photos of various air force "firsts" achieved by former heroes. Equipment displayed includes the tacan avionic set, sewing machines used to sew leather and parachutes, an oscilloscope, various wind dials, analogue clocks and avionic sets. Instrument panels and control sticks of a Jet Provost and a T33 are also shown. A model office from the 1970s shows a sparsely furnished manpower officer's room. The history of Singapore's different air bases at Tengah, Payar Lebar, Changi, Sembawang and Seletar is expounded, with a papier-mâché model of Tengah airbase in the centre of the hall. Records of practice bombings and various achievements are displayed, as well as lists of disbanded squadrons, and a latest additions panel which includes the F16 Fighting Falcon, the E2C Hawkeye and a re-engined Skyhawk.

Hall Three has a small display on the history of the museum itself on the ground floor, before you reach the main exhibition rooms upstairs. On the right-hand side of the staircase are models of the Bloodhound Mark II anti-aircraft system, a history of the 35 mm anti-aircraft guns and the Bloodhound system, photographs of exercises and training in the United Kingdom, Sweden, the USA and Australia, and a display of the RSAF's different logos over the years. A missile launcher is displayed in cutaway fashion for easy viewing, and a Hawk missile tailcone and a Rapier missile are shown. A pilot attack instruction room and a procedural trainer with a mock-up of a map-reader's pilot are displayed, along with an explanation of the history of helicopter training.

Across the landing in Hall Three you come firstly to a rather disappointing model of the rescue efforts after the 1983 Singapore Cable Car Disaster, before reaching the display of the history of air-traffic control for Tengah, Sembawang, Seletar and Changi. Entering the room triggers a voice-over explanation. There is a radar model of Seletar airfield approach and a triangulation board. The mock-up of the radar unit in a darkened room seems realistic. The history of pioneers of radar is also explained.

Outside the different halls are a number of pieces of equipment, all with nearby recorded information for you to call up: Rolls Royce engines; a Bloodhound Mark II missile cutaway so that the engine is visible; an air-raid siren and fork-lift truck to handle a missile launcher; an airfield identification beacon and a radar scanner. Behind Halls One and Two are several planes: an A4S Skyhawk, a subsonic jet attack bomber; a UH-1B helicopter, a light tactical transport helicopter; a F74 Hunter, a subsonic jet aircraft; a BAC 167 Strikemaster; a Cessna 172K; and T-33A Shooting Star.

It's really a place to visit only for those truly interested in aeronautical history and Singapore's own history, more an example of military glasnost than designed as a public museum. Security remains tight—I was grilled for a while for taking notes when I was visiting—and photography inside the halls is prohibited. Unlike the Science Centre, it is not a place where children can clamber about and play with machinery or control panels and gain inspiration from their explorations. A 15-minute walk up Cranwell Road away from Loyang Avenue will lead you to Martlesham Road. Within Block 151 of the military camp there is **St Luke's Chapel**, used as such by allied POWs held in the dysentery ward here during the Second World War. On the walls are five murals painted on his apparent deathbed by the British Bombadier Stanley Warren in 1942. These comprise the Nativity, the Ascension, the Last Supper, the Crucifixion, and St Luke in Prison, and were all painted at the behest of the then padre G. F. Chambers. Warren did, in fact, recover, and has twice revisited Singapore to restore four of the five murals, which had been covered over with distemper when the dysentery ward was moved by the Japanese.

The chapel is open to the public during normal office hours, and fairly regularly visited. You present yourself at the Martlesham Road sentry office, where a guide will be allocated to you. The chapel block is about 200 m (200 yd) back from the road, along fairly rough ground used for some fitness training, by no means ideal terrain for disabled visitors. The experience is quite moving, with today's daily military routine almost adding to the original makeshift nature of the place.

Changi Village

To Get There: bus No 2, 14, 29

Changi Village is something of a misnomer if you expected a few attap huts, a couple of goats and not much else: a few HDB blocks sit opposite the Changi Medidien Hotel, with access through their car parks to the ferry departure point to Pulau Ubin and the small lagoon, while the road in turn leads past the colonial-style hospital to a military complex.

There are 38 further photographs by the Australian POW George Aspinall on permanent display on the fifth floor of Le Meridien Changi Hotel on Netheravon Road. These include the infamous Selarang Square Incident, when 15,000 Allies POWs were left for 3 days on a parade ground until they agreed to sign a promise not to escape, and a variety of POW shots including some from April 1943 when Aspinall joined F force to work on the Burma railway.

Continuing along Nicholl Drive from the village, the road curves and a bridge dissects two small lagoons where fishing boats are moored. From here you can cross a footbridge to the ferry departure point for Pulau Ubin.

Changi Beach

Nicholl Drive
To Get There: Bus numbers 9 and 29

This is a small 8-hectare (20-acre) park along the sea front by Changi Point, on what was mangrove swamp, planted with Wild Cinnamon and Sea Almond trees as well as numerous bougainvilleas. Here you can swim, and watch the aeroplanes taking off and landing at Changi Airport next door. If you wanted to have a barbecue without the correct licence (*see* page 23) or pitch a tent, you would be breaking the numerous regulations posted beside the park, and may even risk a fine, but if you simply want a swim or somewhere with a sea view, Changi Beach is an option if you're in the area. You can also rent canoes here.

No description of Changi is possible without mentioning its highly successful international airport, now sometimes marketed as Airtropolis. Largely built on reclaimed land of what used to be coconut plantations and steep cliffs in the 1920s, this site became a British air-force base and naval base in 1926. The present runway was prepared by Japanese POWS after the Second World War and the airports expansion is expected to increase over the next few decades.

Changi Airport became the island's international airport in 1982, with an additional terminal completed in 1991. The airport is popular as a studying place for exams, and as a meeting place for old people, as well as its highly efficient airport role.

Pasir Ris Park

To Get There: Bus numbers 12, 19, 350

To the north-west of Changi, you can visit the Pasir Ris Park, also opposite Pulau Ubin, divided by Sungei Tampines and a newly designed public park. A clean and fairly inviting beach, together with three different playgrounds graded by children's age, mid-week this is a good site for a family picnic, though it is busy at weekends and public holidays.

East Coast Park

East Coast Service Road
To Get There: Bus 401 on Sundays and public holidays, otherwise taxi

The reclaimed land to the south of the East Coast Parkway has been left as parkland, with coconut trees, rough grass and several bird sanctuary areas of closely planted bushes and trees. Again, as at Changi Beach, you need a licence to use one of the numbered barbecue pits, but if you just want a walk or jog alongside the coast, with a view out through the Eastern Anchorage of ships stretching towards the Indonesian islands of Batam and Bintan, then the east coast park is ideal.

Drivers on the East Coast Parkway can simply turn off left at a number of car parks and entrances and taxis can obviously do likewise.

East Coast Sailing Centre

East Coast Park Swimming Lagoon, 1210 East Coast Parkway
Telephone: 449 5118

The East Coast Sailing Centre, a sailing club for windsurfers and sailors, runs courses for laser dinghy sailing and windsurfing. If you are not on a course, you do have to be a member or a guest of the Centre to enjoy their Saturday and Wednesday night barbecues.

The **Food Centre** next door is highly popular, especially at weekends—and rightly so, as its variety of fresh seafood in particular is staggering. You will find dishes such as turtle soup along with Satay, Chilli Crab and Sweet and Sour Mussels. I have found the food as good at the Food Centre, as at the **UDMC Seafood Centre** close by, just the other side of the Sailing Lagoon, where a number of restaurants are grouped together, offering a mainly Chinese menu of seafood at coffee shop or restaurant prices.

Along the East Coast Service Road are a number of fast food outlets, as well as a golf driving range and the Big Splash water chute (for addresses, *see* Sport, pages 252–253).

Singapore Crocodilarium

730 East Coast Parkway
Telephone: 447 3722 Opening Hours: 9 a.m.–5.30 p.m. daily
To Get There: taxi

One of the many attractions on view at the Singapore Crocodilarium.

There are over 900 crocodiles of fresh- and seawater species being bred at the Singapore Crocodilarium. You can see the tiny (20 cm/8 in long), virtually motionless babies, only a couple of months old, in one pen and adjoining them adults in their prime of 60 years or more, stretching to over 2 m (6 ft). The place is horribly smelly, and vaguely alarming when a large croc makes a sudden move towards you, even though the cages are quite secure.

There are wrestling shows twice daily, subject to weather, and feeding times every second day. Check the exact times before your visit to avoid disappointment. There is also a gift shop, where a variety of crocodile skin goods are on sale, together with designer handbags and accessories not made of the crocodile produce. Do check your home country's customs regulations before you buy any such goods.

Geylang

To Get There: MRT to Payar Lebar, Bus numbers 2, 3, 4, 7, 9, 12, 13, 24, 26, 28, 30, 32, 33, 40, 41, 50, 51, 62, 71, 84, 100, 152, 155, 853

The original Malays or *orang laut*—sea people—were moved from the centre of Singapore to the area now known as Geylang in the 1840s, soon to be joined by Javanese and Boyanese immigrants in the 1860s, as well as by Arab traders. The area was originally a fishing and farming centre, with coconut, rubber and tapioca plantations, and the famous *serai*—lemon grass—grown by the Alsagoff (Arab) family as a medicinal herb, well before its culinary use as practised today.

There are some stunning examples of shophouses and unspoilt shops in the area—and, refreshingly very little

A *night market stall selling embroidered goods and fabrics in Geylang Road during Ramadan.*

evidence of the renovation work so visible in other areas with shophouses— as well as raised bungalow-style houses sitting within their own grounds: just explore a couple of the lorongs off Geylang Road and discover your own favourites, sometimes showing a Chinese baroque style of decoration, sometimes colourful ceramic tiles, sometimes a curved verandah with shutters matching the fading plasterwork of the house. (You may also see some of the less salubrious side of Singapore, as brothels are still in evidence down some Geylang backstreets!)

During the mid-1960s there was much fear amongst the Malay community here that the mainly Chinese government planned to resettle everybody in high-rise apartments—as they have indeed done with many families in the nearby new town of Bedok—but their fear that this would erode the nature and charm of Geylang was misplaced. Visit its market, watch Malays and others buying foodstuffs, herbs, batiks and clothes, and if you are in

White Elephant?

One as yet unsuccessful attempt to encourage visitors to Geylang has been the creation of the Malay Cultural Village on Geylang Serai, a charming Malay-style architectural display of stalls and shops which bustles with activity during the Hari Raya (end of Ramadan) festivities, but at the time of writing remains tenantless. This is probably because the Malay Cultural Association, Mendaki, has stipulated that only Malay-race stallholders and shopkeepers may trade here, and only *halal* food may be served—in order to retain the very Malayness it was built to promote. A quick glance at the majority of shopkeepers even within Geylang, let alone on mainland West Malaysia, shows what a high proportion of shopkeepers within Malay areas tend to be the industrious, money-minded Chinese.

Kallang

To Get There: MRT to Kallang, then a 15-minute walk; SBS buses 14, 31, City Shuttle No 8 all go along Stadium Road; SBS 7, 10, 16, 30 and 70 travel along Nicholl Highway

Kallang, once the site of the island's airport as it was ideally situated for early seaplanes, now houses a range of sporting and leisure facilities. There is a **Tennis Centre**, the **National Stadium**, used for football matches in the Malaysian and domestic leagues as well as for rallies on National Day, Labour Day and such like, while opposite are the **Kallang Theatre** and the **Indoor Stadium**. The Kallang Basin itself has been cleared and cleaned and beaches have been created artificially in order to make a pleasant watersports and leisure area, with a view across to the tower blocks of the city district.

Within the National Stadium, reached through the Singapore Sports Council's Offices beneath the West Entrance, is the **Singapore Sports Museum**. Its six small galleries, or rather rooms, boast Singapore's sporting history and achievements from its colonial past through to the present day. It is open from 9.30 a.m. to 4.00 p.m., though closed between 12.30 p.m. and 2.00 p.m. for lunch, and since it is rather out of the way it is best to telephone—340 9652—if a group is considering visiting.

The first gallery displays photographs of swimming contests between Europeans and Chinese, tennis teams for the Malayan Lawn Tennis Championship, swimming medals and cups for various sports. An engraved

town during Ramadan, visit this area once darkness has fallen: it is a blaze of lights and activities, as the day's fasting is over, prayers are said, and an array of colourful night market stalls overflow from the pavements grabbing your attention.

A road well worth wandering slowly down if you have the time is Joo Chiat Road, leading south-east from Geylang Road just opposite the Malay Cultural Village. Here are 5-ft ways with goods pouring out on to the pavement as they do along Arab Street, though unlike that street you can simply look at the variety of household wares, fabrics or fruits without the shopkeepers pestering you to buy. This street ultimately leads down towards the Peranakan area of Tanjong Katong and East Coast Road, and examples of Peranakan architecture and eating habits abound.

wooden notice lists the milestones in Singapore's sporting history: cricket was first played on the Esplanade in 1837 and horse racing first took place in 1843 for example. The second gallery contains exhibits—photographs and items—of indigenous games, including *sepak takraw*, the woven rattan ball kicked or headed over a net, in a cross between volleyball and football. Other games include *conkak* and *capten*, and Malay tops—*gasing*. The history of various sporting clubs, including the Singapore Swimming Club, is documented, and a dragon boat from Penang also graces this gallery. The third gallery shows the government's investment and involvement in sport, with models of the whole Kallang development as well as photographs of the Singapore Grand Prix held between 1966 and 1973. Early photographs of school sports are also shown here. The fourth gallery is the Hall of Fame, where display cases contain swimming trunks, shirts and other memorabilia belonging to former sporting stars. These include Henry Tan, the first Singaporean bowler to gain international recognition with a score of 298 in London in 1975; Ng Liang Chiang the hurdler; Tan Howe Liang, the Olympic medallist weightlifter; and Wong Peng Soon, All-England Badminton Champion in 1950, 1951, 1952 and 1955. Gallery five is dedicated to the South-East Asian and the Asian Games and Singapore's achievements within these events—Singapore hosted the South-East Asian games in 1973 and 1983 (this museum was founded in the latter year). The sixth gallery shows photographs and posters of the Olympic Games: a large

sum of money is on offer for Singapore's first gold medal from a commercial sponsor. The last, seventh, gallery is the Roll of Honour, changed every year with photographs of sports persons of the year mounted on wooden replicas of the trophies they receive as well as recognition of their coaches.

Between the Kallang area and the start of Geylang Road is all that's left of Gay World, now a tatty car-park and small hawker centre, but in its prime in the 1930s one of the three entertainment parks of the island, with tea dances, live shows, rollercoasters, fun fairs and even stripteases. The other two "worlds"—referred to in fiction and faction written in the 30s until their demise—were closed down during the 1960s.

Following Mountbatten Road, which becomes East Coast Road, you can see seaside-style bungalows now over 1 km (½ mile) from the shore—all the intervening land, including the East Coast Parkway expressway, was reclaimed. The Tanjong Katong (Turtle Point) area this road passes along is a charming hotchpotch of colonial architectural styles, with expensive bungalows now mainly inhabited by successful Peranakan families cheek by jowl with variously decorated shophouses. Unlike Tanjong Pagar to the west of Chinatown, this area has so far escaped any mention of conservation, so remains authentic to itself—to my mind, a much more pleasing place to visit. There are several tasty eating places, and this remains a Peranakan area of town today, with furniture shops and Nonya speciality stores offering tempting fare.

Architecture and Conservation

Singapore's architecture is a fascinating mixture of the old and new, the massive and the small scale, with traces of the colonial era mixed in with examples of state-of-the-art construction.

The Colonial Heart

Much still remains of the grandiose municipal buildings built in the late 19th and early 20th centuries by Singapore's colonial administrators. The cluster of buildings which surround the Padang— the City Hall, the Supreme Court, the Parliament Building, the Empress Place Building, the Victoria Memorial Hall and Theatre—all date from Singapore's days as the governing centre for British Malaya. (They look particularly fine when floodlit on Fridays, Saturdays and Public Holidays.) The cast-iron Fullerton Bridge over the Singapore River leads to the heavily colonnaded General Post Office in the Fullerton Building which again echoes the grand aspirations of colonial richness, while the National Museum and the *Istana* (formerly Government House) display a certain civic pride and majesty of former times. The Raffles Hotel again fits into this era, recently having been renovated to its state in the 1920s.

The shophouses, rows of two- or three-storey buildings with shops or workshops at ground level and living quarters above, and covered 5-ft ways sheltering pedestrians and shop owners from tropical sun and rain, date from Raffles' earliest plans. He had come across the design in Batavia on Java, and similar constructions were familiar to immigrants from mainland China.

Shophouses are readily seen in Chinatown and Little India, (where many are undergoing extensive renovation); other examples remain in Arab Street and in parts of Geylang area.

Also from the colonial settlers came the black and white bungalows (from

Parliament House, originally designed as a private house for a wealthy merchant by G.D. Coleman.

211

the Hindi word *bangla*—a single-storey house), seen along Scotts Road as well as further afield in Sembawang and Changi. These were constructed from the early 1820s onwards by expatriates, who brought the design from India. In Singapore, bungalows incorporated Malay stilts or European brick arches, and subsequently followed the Georgetown, Penang, two-storey design. Traditionally such bungalows had open first storeys, with staircases and bathrooms in the four corners, and then on the upper floor a central dining room, with bedrooms and a verandah-style living room, usually above the entrance leading off it. Kitchens and servants' quarters were traditionally in detached buildings.

As well as a legacy of individual buildings, Singapore's early town planning by Sir Stamford Raffles and the then government architect G. D. Coleman remains in evidence today. The European settlers and traders were encouraged to build their homes north of the river, around today's Padang area, while the land to the south of the Singapore River was reclaimed and

Pastel shades grace the newly restored shophouses on Tanjong Pagar road.

drained, and the business district located there. Today's Raffles Place in the city was formerly Commercial Place, the hub of the colonial business district, where the prestigious Robinson's department store and nearby John Little were patronized by colonial shoppers.

Modern Singapore
After the Second World War came the task of reconstruction. The Asia Insurance Building on Finlayson Green, completed in the mid-1950s by local architect Ng Keng Siang, was the tallest building not only in Singapore but in South-East Asia during the 1950s. The challenge of rehousing the island's population was creatively taken up by the subsequent PAP government. New towns provided new outlets for home-grown architectural talent and new identities for the new areas (*see* page 214).

Today Singapore's skyline contains staggering examples of modern architecture, from I. M. Pei's OCBC Centre (known as the pocket calculator building, with Henry Moore's largest ever sculpture placed outside it) and Raffles City complex, designed in the 1970s, to his recently opened and still controversial Gateway Building—its two triangular towers forming an opening to the city and possibly pointing towards his even more controversial Bank of China building in Hong Kong. (The Gateway does have good *feng shui*—see page 79.) Kenzo Tange's OUB tower in Raffles Place (known as The Pinnacle), and his rival UOB tower, rising opposite it on Chulia Street to reach exactly the same height, now dominate the city skyline, while his indoor stadium at Kallang is a striking outline on that waterfront.

The Tropical Garden City is kept in mind and planned for in the future. Marina City Park and Pasir Ris Park combine modern art and sculpture with nature to merge unified landscapes. Increasing use is being made of waterways, whether monsoon drains, streams or rivers, with Little Guilin in Bukit Gombak using an exhausted quarry, and revitalizing landscaping programmes are under way for rivers in Pasir Ris and Tampines to turn unsightly streams and canals into focal points of recreative landscape.

Conservation Matters

Along with innovative tower blocks and skyscrapers, today in Singapore there is increasing interest in conservation of old, historically or architecturally interesting buildings. Twenty-three buildings are currently gazetted by the Preservation of Monuments Board, which was set up in 1971, and a further 60 are recommended to join these. Guidelines are issued on maintenance and renovation, systems are put in place for fining owners for lack of maintenance and restoration, and for the government to acquire unmaintained buildings, and each building is separately funded for its upkeep. Beside the Singapore River, the Empress Place restoration is a good example of the success of government-backed schemes, with floodlit buildings now providing a cultural focal point to the city.

The well-publicized renovation of shophouses in the Tanjong Pagar area (*see* page 150) has largely been successful, though some commercial outfits are finding the rents too high for this out-of-centre location. Renovation projects for Telok Ayer Market and Bugis Street are likely to be successful since they are closely linked to the profitable tourist industry, though plans for improving the Istana Kampong Glam and surrounding area near Arab Street may not prove so successful—particularly with the future of the nearby Malay Village along Geylang Serai, an innovative attempt to promote Malay culture, arts and crafts in a traditional-style environment, still in doubt and making a loss daily. Further residential areas are earmarked for conservation plans—such as Blair Road and Joo Chiat Road—following successful renovation programmes in Emerald Hill, just off Orchard Road, where renovated shophouses have been sold off to private individuals. At the time of writing, the shophouses along much of Little India's Serangoon Road are being restored, as are many shophouses in Chinatown's back streets while those shophouses along Boat Quay to the south of the Singapore River are almost all undergoing radical reconstruction.

Housing

Singapore has been extraordinarily successful in housing its citizens adequately and providing all modern amenities, which was one of the main goals of the first PAP's manifesto back in the late 1950s. The colonial Singapore Improvement Trust, in existence from 1927 to 1958, built a total of 23,000 dwelling units. The town population of 250,000 in 1907 was housed in 20,000 buildings; by 1931 the population had increased to 570,000 and the number of buildings to 37,000; and by 1947 the population of 938,000 was squeezed into 38,500 buildings in an area of 80 sq km (31 sq miles).

By contrast the HDB—Housing and Development Board—built 147,000 units in the first 10 years of its existence, from 1960 to 1970. Of these 80,000 were built to relieve overcrowding, and the remainder to relieve the natural population increase. When the disastrous Bukit Ho Swee fire made 16,000 people homeless on 21 May 1961, 6,000 were rehoused within one week—a staggering achievement. Simultaneously the newly formed Jurong Town Corporation built a further 24,000 units between 1963 and 1979, starting the trend easily seen in Singapore today of housing much of the population away from the central area. The new towns around the periphery of the island are increasingly self-sufficient, with 90 per cent of residents purchasing food and domestic goods locally rather than in the centre. The new towns all strive to maintain their own identities, and local services and amenities are increasingly organized at the local level, by town councils representing the local people. The HDB built 11,793 flats in 1989, and a total of 653,836 flats from 1960 to 1989 inclusive.

As well as constructing new flats, the HDB is also involved in modernizing blocks constructed in the 1960s and 70s, improving their facilities and giving them a more modern look, often as requested by residents. By far the majority of recently constructed flats are three- or four-room flats. More than 87 per cent of the population live in HDB new towns and estates.

The remainder of housing is constructed and provided by private consortiums, prime locations often selling at extremely high prices and offering swimming pools and other sporting facilities, arranged in blocks or condominiums sharing these facilities. Also available, in ever decreasing amounts, are the old black and white colonial-style bungalows and restored shophouses in the Tanjong Pagar and Emerald Hill areas particularly: though rather more individual than private apartments, both of these options are less comfortable to live in, with limited air-conditioning and fewer on-site facilities being the main drawbacks.

An extraordinarily large proportion of Singaporeans own or are in the process of paying off loans to own their own homes. The 1990 Census showed that 90 per cent of Singaporeans own their own homes, of whom the Malay race are the most numerous, with 94 per cent owning their own homes. Home ownership is strongly encouraged by the government, and is one of the main reasons for the CPF—Central Provident Fund—contributions from each worker and employee every month, with 25% and 17.5 per cent of salary respectively paid into a savings fund. Money from this is used to pay monthly instalments on flats over a maximum of 25 years, and can also be used for the initial down payment.

There is now a new booking system for allocating HDB flats to prospective owners, with 12-monthly building programmes announced to the public quarterly, so that interested residents can submit applications to book flats for about 2½ years ahead. Allocations are decided by ballot, within the Ethnic

Integration Policy guidelines, whereby a maximum of 22 per cent of any neighbourhood may be Malay, 84 per cent Chinese and 10 per cent Indian and others (the allowed percentages per individual block are 3 per cent higher for all groups), an attempt to avoid creating racial ghettoes and to make residential areas reflect the ethnic mix of the population. In order to qualify to buy or rent an HDB flat applicants should have monthly incomes below the fixed ceiling—currently $5,000—and should be family groups or married couples. It is quite common practice for young couples to become legally married at the Registry of Marriages in order to apply for an HDB flat, and then to complete the marriage ceremony in the traditional manner (*see* pages 66, 69 and 70) once a flat is available for them. Young unmarried people virtually always live at home with their family or relatives—Western-style shared flats among friends, or the permissive system of unmarried couples "living together" are uncommon, and not allowed within the HDB guidelines—nor are homosexual

Bishan, one of Singapore's new towns, designed in almost play-school style.

couples. Singapore permanent residents (those expatriates who have gained residence status in Singapore) are now allowed to purchase HDB flats, though from the resale market rather than directly from the HDB.

Although some of the HDB blocks may look like Lego in the different architects' attempts to create new town identities, the housing quality provided is generally good. Most Singaporean families enjoy clean and bright apartments, accessed by walkways, stairs and lifts, which are mainly clean, usually work, and—importantly—are generally safe from muggers, a stark comparison with some blocks in the West. Within, the same basic shapes are uniformly finished by the HDB, but the individual residents add their own touches. If you happen to be invited to any Singaporean home, do remove your shoes before entering, so as not to bring outside dust into the flat.

Beaches, Butterflies, Boats and Bicycles

Singapore's nearest island, Sentosa, is a holiday "fun" island, with several attractions still under construction, and numerous others linked by a monorail system and buses. It boasts a number of museums, a walk-through aquarium, a butterfly park, some sandy beaches and a variety of food and shopping outlets. Several of Singapore's other islands can be visited (*see* map on page 8), though many more are used either for industrial or military purposes. A cruise around Singapore's islands (*see* pages 271–272) is an ideal way to see these islands.

A map of the offshore islands, whose number changes periodically as islands or reefs are reclaimed and joined together, may lead you to believe that a host of unspoilt tropical islands sit at your doorstep. Other than those described below, virtually all the islands are used either for military purposes or for industrial and petrochemical sites—the time when they were all uninhabited, peaceful, tropical islands has long since gone. Ferry times and details of cruises are given on pages 271–272.

Pulau Seking, the one remaining unspoilt Malay-style island.

Sentosa Island

Formerly known as Pulau Blakang Mati, Sentosa—island of tranquillity— was developed as a tourist resort in 1968. Its 376 hectares (928 acres), just a 3-minute ferry ride from the World Trade Centre on Telok Blangah Road, or a 1.8-km (1.1-mile) cable-car ride from Mount Faber, or from the midway station at Cable Towers next to the World Trade Centre, are packed with family entertainment. You pay your initial entry fee to the island ($3.50 per adult, $2.00 per child in 1991), and then all rides on the monorail and on any buses are free of charge, as is access to beaches and swimming lagoons, though you do pay extra to enter the individual sites. It's certainly not everybody's cup of tea—particularly not for those who enjoy silence, since recorded voices speak to you the whole time from the monorail (itself due for an extensive upgrading process to be completed by 1992/3), buses and in a majority of the museums and sights, speaking in an easy Americanese in bite-sized chunks. And of course there's shopping and eating, since this is after all Singapore—though again bargain hunters and gourmet connoisseurs will do better on the mainland, where you can pay less for better fare. **Rasa Sentosa** is a fairly ordinary, slightly overpriced hawker centre; **Cafe Edelweiss** in the ferry terminal somewhat bland and mediocre.

A ride around the monorail in 1991 shows a vast swathe of construction going on, as work continues on expanding hotel facilities, improving existing sites and developing two forthcoming attractions. These are the **Asian Cultural and Entertainment Village**, to be completed by 1992 in the area between **Underwater World** (*see* below page 223) and the ferry terminal, beneath the cable car; and the **Fantasy Island Theme Park**, between the ferry terminal and the **Maritime Museum**. The Fantasy Island Theme Park, a water theme park, is due to open in 1993–94. Modelled on Disney's Typhoon Lagoon in Florida, its 34 attractions will include simulated submarine and rollercoaster rides shown through high-speed film projectors, dinghy rides through artificially created river rapids, boat trips through tunnels and imaginary jungle, and a giant geyser throwing water 20 m (66 ft) high into the air.

In addition to all this work, the lagoon is being upgraded, with all public swimming and boating facilities relocated to the sandy Siloso beach.

Sentosa's Ferry Terminal building, the main entrance to the island.

Hotel development continues: (telephone: 275 0031) the 214-room Beaufort hotel is now open and the 450-room Rasa Sentosa Beach Resort on Siloso Beach and another 354-room hotel also scheduled for the early 1990s.

You can also walk along the beaches at the south of the island, looking out towards Indonesia and the busy shipping lanes, and towards the oil refinery island Pulau Bukom. As well as the official Nature Walk (see below page 222), you can just walk around the island, and it's peaceful when you can escape the buzz of the monorail, the occasional bus and the persistent building work you can't fail to spot all over. There are two golf-courses, a roller-skating rink, a bicycle hire outlet, a plant nursery and Singapore's satellite earth station, and increasing night-time attractions at the musical fountain near the ferry terminal—concerts, variety and fashion shows have proved very popular. It's possible to stay there by prior arrangement, at the various new hotels, the youth hostel, or the camping site (see page 24 for details).

Sentosa is becoming such a tourist success that a new road link to the mainland is under construction. A 330-m (1,080-ft) causeway is to link Keppel near the World Trade Centre with Pulau Brani, currently a naval dockyard but destined to become a new container terminal. From Pulau Brani a 380-m (1,247-ft) bridge, consisting of a covered pedestrian walkway, balconies and tree-lined areas, a cycling track and a projected "elevated people-moving system", will lead to Sentosa Island. There will be a two-way road, a pedestrian walkway, balconies with views of the city and the island, a bicycle track and an elevated track for the train system, and, when it opens in late 1992, the whole structure will be able to transport 5,000 people an hour, or 13,000 people daily. This new link will doubtless ease the congestion as people flock to the islands on weekends and during school holidays in particular.

It would take a fairly full day to see all the attractions, and more are being planned at the time of writing—so it's best to select just a few and take them slowly. For further information on all the sites, contact the Sentosa Development Corporation, 1 Garden Avenue, Sentosa, Singapore 0409, telephone: 275 0388.

Fort Siloso

Opening Hours: 9 a.m.–7 p.m. daily

This fort at the western end of the island was built to guard the western entrance to Keppel Harbour in the 1880s, and is a wonderful network of underground tunnels, exhibits of guns, ammunition, oil storage and engine rooms, observation posts and the like which you can explore at will. As you explore the 4-hectare (10-acre) site you will trigger the multifarious noises of the Sounds of Siloso—gunfire, shouting, footsteps—an attempt by the Sentosa Development Corporation to add life and excitement to the attraction. The arrival of the monorail train also triggers the sound effects.

A brilliant venue for children to play hide-and-seek, the museum traces the fort's history from the 19th century through the war years until independence. The massive 6-inch guns here

Siloso Beach, Sentosa Island, viewed from Fort Siloso.

were designed to prevent attack by sea and amphibious landing, and hence contributed little to Singapore's defence in 1942, though they were turned landwards towards the approaching Japanese army and inflicted some damage before being destroyed by the British immediately after the surrender.

During the Second World War the fort was used as a POW camp, and hence a small diorama exhibition of Behind Bars Life as a POW is staged here. Two cell scenes are shown, complete with wax figures, bedding and other accoutrements, with the inevitable 5-minute video show providing constant noise. When this exhibition was first staged in October 1990, war veterans complained that the wax figures were too healthy and the portrayal was unrealistic. As a result of this criticism, further wax figures, this time looking very Caucasian, have been installed in replacement, looking as thin and haggard as some of those who survived did. Reproductions of drawings by W. H. Haxworth depicting daily camp life are displayed, together with other photographs and

sketches, though the constant sound of the video and the general theme park treatment reduce the impact of these, many of which are also displayed more sombrely and in my view more meaningfully at Changi Prison Museum.

Maritime Museum
Opening Hours: 10 a.m.–7 p.m.

Most of this museum is housed in three large Malay-style corrugated-iron wharves, and the whole attraction was put together by and explains the history and achievements of the Port of Singapore Authority (PSA). So don't expect a display of impressive large ships: there are some small dugout canoes—*jongkongs* and *jaluis*—some small keeled boats—*kolehs, sampans*—and unkeeled boats, but most of the display consists of models, charts, maps and photographs. Old fire engines, plus some dragon boats and a Vietnamese refugee boat, together with a model of a *kelong* (fishing house) sit side-by-side with panels illustrating the increasing tonnage of cargo passing through Singapore, the crucial historic role of the dock workers' unions (whose 1950s legal representative, Lee Kuan Yew went on to better things), and the increasing computerization and technology used to built Singapore's greatness.

As well as the inevitable souvenir shop, a temporary exhibition room houses differing items—a tea clipper display during my visit in 1991—and there is also a permanent display of navigation signals, lighthouses and systems. Entry to the museum involves a ticket machine, often supervised by a guide carrying change, but do visit with coins to spare.

Pioneers of Singapore and Surrender Chambers
Opening Hours: 9 a.m.–9 p.m.

A couple of large maps start off the description of Singapore's past, but the first diorama waxwork display is of Sir Stamford Raffles signing the historic treaty and "discovering" the island. Each of the 12 or so diorama scenes is explained by a tape-recorded voice-over and is captioned. Scenes from daily life along the river, the harbour, in Commercial Square (subsequently Raffles Place) together with the momentous discovery of rubber take us through the colonial past and also give us a glimpse at the immigrant Chinese and Indian and the local Malay lifestyles.

These cosy scenes end with (yet another) video on the build-up of defences and Singapore's airfields on the eve of the Second World War. The **Surrender Chambers** follow on, with maps and panels of newspaper cuttings, headlines and explanations of Japan's expansion into Manchuria in the 1930s and the gradual advance through South-East Asia. Malaya and Singapore's initial profits from the high demand for rubber and tin during the war is explained, together with the muddled chain of command of defence forces, and sound effects, (yes, more voice-overs), explain the initial bombing on 8 December 1941 when the street lights were all on, the fall of Singapore, the imprisonment of allied soldiers, the gruesome Operation "Sweep Up" when suspect Chinese were rounded up and many thousands disappeared, and daily life under Japanese Occupation. A waxwork diorama of the British surrender is staged upstairs, whilst downstairs the panels and videos show the allied re-offensive and subsequent victory, with another diorama of the Japanese Surrender.

Despite—or even because of—the noise of the sound effects—the display here is effective, though it does treat the war rather like a theme park, sanitized as much as possible for the wide variety of visiting tourists presumably. If exhausted, there's a tearoom just outside the Chambers—though don't get too excited about the cappuccino, which is only Cona coffee with cream whirled on top!

Butterfly Park and World Insectarium

Opening Hours: 9.30 a.m.–5.30 p.m. Monday–Friday, 9.30 a.m.–6.30 p.m. weekends and public holidays

There are two parts to this attraction: the first part is a natural history

One of the residents in the Butterfly Park on Sentosa Island.

museum treatment of pinned out butterflies and other rather gruesome stag beetles, stick insects, scorpions and other insects; then comes the second part which comprises a butterfly garden where you can walk around and spot the various types of butterfly as they fly past. The display cases are clearly useful in identifying butterfly types, though I found the walk-through garden a lot more enjoyable. In the garden are 2,500 butterflies of 50 species: the largest is Papilio Isworth (Great Helen), at 15 cm (6 in); the smallest is Eurema Sari at 2.5 cm (1 in). The down-side is that to leave the park you have to run the gauntlet of a huge souvenir shop.

Nature Walk

This rather tame and mainly flat path through secondary jungle enables you to escape from the bustle of the rest of the island, and most of the trees are clearly labelled for identification. If you wish, climb up to the old sentry post of Mount Imiah—though the view of Pulau Bukom is hardly worth the climb. Apart from the ubiquitous cicadas and general jungle noise, there's little apart from trees to see here.

Coralarium

Opening Hours: 9 a.m.–7 p.m.

At the easternmost side of the island is the coralarium, which houses a display of different corals, tropical fish and over 2,500 shells from all over the world as well as a display on the history of diving. After visiting this display, wander on along the nature ramble to glimpse the turtle pools, kites and other attractions—or just to visit the quiet beach. A good time to visit is during the monkeys' feeding time (3 p.m.), when the keepers ring a bell and you can give small bananas to the tens of small monkeys who come dashing out of the trees to eat.

Rare Stone Museum

Opening Hours: 9 a.m.–7 p.m.

A collection brought from Taiwan in 1985 of, believe it or not, over 4,000 weird and wonderful stones of various shapes and sizes, housed in a two-storey building at the far end of the formal garden and fountain network from the ferry terminal building. Only 1,000 stones are on display at any one time. Some rubies, jades and other precious stones are displayed on carved and glazed wooden stands to show off their colours and tones. Some large unlabelled stones, shaped as orbs and titled planets, are then displayed. Most of these stones have been collected from China and show shapes of nature, Chinese characters and horoscopes, legends—and even Mount Fuji. I'm not sure who this museum is aimed at: the serious geologist would find it frustrating that so few stones are geologically labelled; the amateur/general interest person could just as easily see the shapes "revealed" in the stones as different shapes, or as the work of a very fertile imagination.

Fossils of mammals and shells are displayed in the upper storey, together with more scenes, shapes, etc., though the captioning does not run to the stone type in the majority of cases.

Sentosa Art Centre

Situated next to the Rare Stone Museum, this contains 80 pieces of work by 40 or so local artists: oil, batik and silk paintings, and ceramics. Rather than a museum or gallery, it is more reminiscent of a souvenir shop: virtually all items are indeed for sale, though not perhaps the most tasteful or original creations.

Underwater World

Telephone: 275 0030
Opening Hours: 9 a.m.–9 p.m.

Modelled on a highly successful formula tried and tested in Australia, Underwater World's walk-through aquarium is currently Asia's largest tropical fish oceanarium. Its comparatively high entrance fee ($9 for adults; $6 for teenagers and senior citizens—over 55; and $3.50 for children between 3 and 12) gives considerable entertainment and value for money. It is still a comparatively new attraction, so there can be enormous queues, especially at weekends.

While you are queuing to buy a ticket, look at the **Turtle Pool**, with its large green and hawksbill turtles. Inside, a **Touch Pool** is the first attraction, full of starfish, sea cucumbers, baby turtles, hermit crabs, anenomes and corals—all of which you can safely touch if you wish or dare. You then continue past two exhibits: one of sharks' jaws; the other tank containing inhabitants of reef flats in tidal zones including corals, anenomes, spider conches, hermit crabs and clown fish. Next comes the 150-seat theatrette, where a short film on marine life and conservation is shown, explaining how dependent on corals certain types of fish are, and what is required for corals to survive in today's polluted and developing world.

After the film show, you pass further traditional exhibition tanks. One contains dangerous marine creatures: sea urchins, stingrays, crown of thorns starfish, pufferfish, moray eels, stonefish and lionfish. The tubular fish tank at the main entrance which descends to the lower floor contains schooling fish. A **Living Reef** tank contains fairly placid fish, then come the different habitats for invertebrate fish before reaching the main attraction.

The underwater aquaria are home to over 2,300 marine species from the South China Sea, Indonesia and the Maldives. The tanks are divided, with the smaller fish of the coral reef community in the first tank you walk through in the 80-m (260-ft) acrylic tunnel. Then comes a small cave-dwelling habitat before the tank containing the black, blotched stingray, the light brown, spotted leopard shark, giant groupers, the white-tip shark, barramundi cod and shovelnose ray. You can step off the moving walkway at any time to have a closer look at those fish swimming overhead—though do watch out for photography groups (not using flash, which is not allowed in the underwater tunnel) and people walking in the opposite direction. Feeding times are at 11 a.m. and 3 p.m. daily, when a diver enters the aquarium.

Other Islands to the South of Singapore

You can visit several other islands by cruise from Clifford Pier, or take a ferry from the World Trade Centre. (For details and times of cruises and ferries, see page 271.)

Legend has it that two sailors, a Chinese and a Malay, were in difficulties in the South China Sea, and then a giant tortoise appeared and turned into **Kusu Island**, saving them from certain death by drowning. There is a Malay shrine or *kremat* up 140 steps on the top of the hill, in fact three different shrines, with a hotch-potch mixture of Malay and Chinese offerings and inscriptions. This is generally thought to be a shrine to Haji Syed Abdul Rahman and his family who disappeared in the 19th century, and the place is believed to be inhabited by spirits. There is also a Chinese temple on the island, regularly visited from the mainland, particularly during

September/October on the ninth day of the ninth lunar month, when a pilgrimage of Taoist, Buddhist and Confucian Chinese flock there to worship their ancestors and to pray to the God of Plenty, Tua Peh Kong, for good health, prosperity and children. In front of the Chinese Temple is a Turtle Lagoon and Pavilion; there is also a tortoise sanctuary on the island. At other times of year, Singaporeans and tourists come to Kusu for its view of Singapore Island and to swim off its reclaimed man-made swimming beaches which date from the 1970s. Do be careful when swimming on any of the offshore islands of Singapore: there are very strong currents and undertows, especially within the channels between islands, and a seemingly trivial distance may prove beyond the capacity of even a well-seasoned swimmer.

Nearby are **St John's Island, Lazarus Island** and the **Sisters Islands**, peaceful uninhabited spots where sailing and fishing boats can stop provided they have the correct licence. Further south still is **Seking Island**, the only island off Singapore which is still inhabited by Malay village fishing people, who live in traditional *kampung*-style with no mains electricity, water or sewage facilities. Each of the *kelong*-style houses has its own generator for electricity; water is brought daily from the nearby oil refining island Pulau Bukom, where several of the menfolk work; and the island's children catch a daily ferry to the mainland for schooling, now that the only school has closed down. Goats and chickens freely roam the tiny island, removing any grass and threatening any unfenced bougainvillea bushes—or rather trees, they are so large here—so all that remains is dusty scrub and coconut palms.

This time-warp island is quite unlike anything else in Singapore, where traditional agricultural lifestyles have had to adjust to the increasingly urban economy. On Pulau Seking too there is already some change to traditional patterns: some houses are now only occupied at weekends by families rehoused on the mainland, and it is a question of time before the whole community—numbering only 20 or so families—is either transferred and rehoused or simply dies out.

Pulau Ubin

Pulau Ubin, to the north-west of the island, is reached by bumboat ferry from Changi Point. There are no precise ferry times, you just wait on the jetty until about 10 people are ready to go and a boat is available, which should generally take less than ½ hour. Like Pulau Seking to the south, it has no mains electricity, water supply or sewerage system, nor does it have a school. Although increasingly the young people are moving to the mainland to find work, 166 households still remain in traditional *kampung*-style houses. Several *kelong*-type seafood restaurants are situated along the waterfront facing Singapore island, and are popular with Singaporean tourists.

The island is as yet largely unspoilt, with large areas of jungle, wild enough to have enticed a wild elephant from Johor to swim over in early 1991. Overgrown rubber plantations and mangrove swamps are vibrant with wildlife, and coconut groves abound, together with disused and still operational granite quarries. Granite is still supplied to the mainland construction industry from Pulau Ubin: occasional blasting mars the otherwise tranquil atmosphere.

An outward bound school is situated on the north side of the island, and it is possible to camp on the island if you are keen to return to nature, though you should register with the island's police on arrival. Travel on the island is either by taxi—the models here escape the stringent motor vehicle checks of the mainland, so are generally antiquated—by foot, or by hired mountain bike—you will see frequent rental signs in the main village as you leave the ferry, and will have to leave a passport or something of value as a deposit until your return. The island's roads vary from tarmac to gravel tracks, and an hour or so's cycle ride can reveal palm and banana trees, quarries, and farming areas, as well as fairly frequent passing taxis stirring up clouds of dust, enough to have a refreshing "rural" break from the main island of Singapore.

More development is planned in the long term, if Singapore's population increases as projected in the early years of next century, with an extension of the MRT line to join Pulau Ubin to the next-door Pulau Tekong (currently used exclusively by the military), and the island divided into industrial, residential and recreational areas. Until then, though, it is worth a visit for those looking for nature and an escape from the ever-encroaching urban development.

225

Beaches, Batiks and Beautiful Buildings

Singapore is ideally situated as a base for exploring the region. Comparisons between Singapore and her neighbours really show the progress achieved in Singapore—infrastructure, housing conditions and facilities for example—and also such comparisons give an insight into what Singapore would have been like in former, less educated, but also less regulated, days. Day-trips or longer excursions into Malaysia and Indonesia can be planned and arranged with ease.

The average length of stay in Singapore is 3½ days, but this is often because tourists take the opportunity to visit Singapore's neighbours, West Malaysia and Indonesia. Trips to both can be easily organized through travel agents in Singapore as package tours, or you can travel independently, using buses, trains, ferries and taxis as you require. If you plan to stay at one of the more popular resorts over a weekend, or during a holiday period, it would be wise to book in advance from your home country.

The colonial Sultan Abdul Samad Building on the Padang in the centre of Kuala Lumpur.

Addresses of tourist offices are given on page 277. Visitors to both countries need a passport valid for at least 6 months beyond their projected date of arrival. Visas are not required for visitors of Commonwealth countries (except India) and the United States wanting to visit Malaysia, nor for Indonesia. Check with the Malaysia Tourism Promotion Board and the Indonesia Tourist Promotion Office, both located on Collyer Quay, before planning a trip if you are unsure about regulations for your own country's nationals.

Like Singapore, both Malaysia and Indonedia have stringent penalties for drug trafficking; unlike Singapore, you cannot drink the tap water safely—take care!

Mainland Malaysia

Johor Baru

Johor Baru, like Batam in Indonesia, is now part of an economic growth triangle with Singapore, a triangle which gives Singapore investment opportunities and almost guaranteed co-operation with her neighbours for the next 20 years.

Reached by the 1,056-m (1,155-yard) causeway from Woodlands New Town on the north of the island, Singapore's closest neighbour is both strikingly similar to and a great contrast to Singapore itself. Not a particularly flourishing tourist spot, Johor Baru it is not without charm or interest, as well as proving a popular shopping and night-life spot for Singaporeans.

Founded in 1855 by Sultan Abu Bakar on the site of a small fishing village, the city is the capital of Johor state. There are several architectural attractions in the town. These include the brilliant white European-style **Istana Besar**, constructed by Sultan Abu Bakar in 1866. Its North Wing contains the Throne Room, where all state occasions are held, and the Museum, where hunting trophies, weapons, and state regalia are displayed. The 13.3-hectare (33-acre) garden is open to the public every day until 7 p.m.

The Istana Besar, now run as the **Muzium DiRaja Abu Bakar**, is open to the public 6 days a week—all but Fridays—from 9 a.m.–5 p.m.. (The last ticket sales are at 4 p.m., since it takes about an hour to visit.) The palace is closed for certain Johor state occasions, such as the sultan's birthday, as well as for the festival of Hari Raya

The Istana Besar, now the Muzium DiRaja Abu Bakar, Johor Baru.

Puasa at the end of Ramadan, but is otherwise open throughout the year. I do recommend asking for an English-speaking guide' to accompany you around the museum: although the various exhibits are well captioned in English and Malay, the personalized narrative is well worthwhile, and included in the ticket price you pay.

First on the tour is the *Dewan*, or hall, a separate standing building to the north of the main palace, completed in 1866 with an opening ceremony in 1875. This was, and occasionally still is, used for receptions and ceremonial occasions, with a raised central dais area allowing a stately welcome. Chinese *towkays*—rich and successful businessmen or planters—donated various appreciative scrolls in Mandarin calligraphy which are attached to the walls, and throughout the palace the motifs of pepper and gambier on mouldings, carpets and even thrones, pay homage to the early foundations of Johor's wealth. Photographs and mementoes from the Johor Sultanate's history, its transition from *temenggong* to sultan and the sultanate's links with the early Prince Sang Udara, the founder of Singapore, are clearly displayed, along with photographs of the different sultans' wives, cars, medals, etc.

In the main palace, you firstly tour the upstairs part (removing your shoes to do so, which you carry with you in a bag provided). In the different rooms there is a disconcertingly European taste of interior decoration throughout, so that one feels more in an English country house or French château than in South-East Asia. First is the junior library, with miniature chairs for the sultan's children to sit in as they studied or read. Then come a number of bedrooms, dressing rooms and waiting rooms, all full of Anglo-Malay European-style teak wood furniture, before arriving at the large reception room. This contains glass tables and chairs made in France, as well as comfortable seating areas.

A later extension to the palace on the south side of the reception hall contains a large banqueting hall to seat 300 comfortably, which you see from the upper balcony level. Around the balcony area are display cases of porcelain from England, France, Japan and China. Then you come to the Throne Room, where coronations are held: two thrones sit on a raised dais facing the main entrance steps you can see from outside as you approach. Seats fill the main room, and during coronations the parallel aisles are also filled with chairs. Display cases of more porcelain are in both aisles.

The tour continues downstairs to a series of rooms containing impressive displays of silverware, jewellery, materials and fabrics, ceremonial swords and Malay *kris*—dagger-type weapons—and more porcelain cabinets. Outside the palace (you can put on your shoes now) you cross under the main entrance steps to visit the hunting trophy room, where various stuffed tigers, wild buffalo and assorted game are displayed, along with various weapons and statistics.

It is well worth visiting the Istana Besar if you are in Johor Baru, or even making time at the expense of other sights to do so and crossing the causeway specially. Also worthy of note and a visit is the **Sultan Abu Bakar Mosque**

Not for the Faint-hearted

The Singapore press frequently reports road traffic accidents in Malaysia involving Singaporean drivers, and for all my observations on driving in Singapore, driving in Malaysia is much more challenging. Still on the right, virtually all main roads in Malaysia are of varying surfaces, and are heavily used by numerous lorries. It seems to be the style to overtake either when approaching a blind corner, or when approaching a hilltop: then cars will edge slowly forwards, painstakingly gaining on the lorries inch by inch. Should an approaching vehicle appear in its legitimate lane, the style is for the overtaking vehicle to flash its lights: occasionally the approaching vehicle is forced either to brake or to veer on to the fairly common hard shoulder or grass area next to the road; more usually the vehicles just avoid one another.

Drivers generally switch on their right indicators when they have a general intention to overtake or to turn right, and you may follow a vehicle indicating for several kilometres. Generally when a true turning approaches, the driver will also put his right arm out, proving that this time he really will turn.

The north–south highway, a privately constructed expressway, is slowly being completed: on some of the completed sections sudden illegal hawker stalls selling durians or fruits will cause a vehicle to brake and swerve from the fast lane to an abrupt halt.

situated on a hillside overlooking the Straits of Johor in extensive grounds. This was begun in 1892 by Sultan Abu Bakar, and completed in 1900.

Do not bother to visit the Johor State Zoo, particularly if you have seen Singapore's Open Zoo. Situated between the Istana Besar and the Abu Bakar Mosque, this tiny public zoo crams in a lot of primates in small concrete cages, a couple of elephants, some leopards and lions, and even the herons seem rather cramped in their cage.

The current sultan's residence, a rather less spectacular building than the Istana Besar, with green copper roofs and a 350-m (1,150-ft) tower is at Bukit Serene, to the north of the town, and includes a private orchid garden. The Royal Mausoleum in Jalan Mahmoodiah is closed to the public, though you can enter its grounds.

In the centre of town you can't help noticing the 64.2-m (210-ft)-high square brown, almost Florentine-style, tower of the Government Offices Building at Bukit Tinkalan. This is a good spot from which to view the town and the view across the causeway to Singapore—which was exactly what the Japanese Commander Yamashita did before launching his assault on Singapore in 1942. (A friendship visit to Japan in the late 1930s by the Sultan of Johor ensured the preservation of the sultan's palace and treasure during the Japanese occupation.) Two monuments, each built in 1955, complete the list of "sights". One, on the seafront opposite the court-house, is to Sultan Abu Bakar, the architect of much of today's city; the other is to his father *Temenggong* Daeng Ibrahim. A tower from which you can admire the Strait of Johor and Singapore across it and the lido completes the sights, other than the shopping malls.

More a gateway to the rest of Malaysia rather than a tourist magnet itself, Johor Baru is refreshingly free of

tourists: this means you can wander the backstreets and shopping centres and hardly see another Westerner, and may well be approached and welcomed by local people keen to practise their English, or to include you in their photographs.

Kukup

At 80 km (50 miles), roughly two hours' drive, from Johor Baru, is a formerly sleepy fishing village. Most houses are built on stilts (*kelong*-style) over the sea, to facilitate fishing and mooring boats, since much of the village's livelihood is sea-based. The freshly caught and cooked seafood is therefore the village's speciality—if you take a tour, your restaurant will obviously be prearranged; if you travel independently, just wander along the main road until something takes your fancy.

The journey to and from Kukup passes plantations of oil palms, rubber

Kukup fishing village, Malaysia, is a popular spot for Chinese-style seafood and copy watch souvenirs.

trees and pineapples, as well as some coffee and cocoa: coach tours often include a tour around a plantation on this trip. About 7 km (4 miles) from Kukup clearance and construction work is under way for the Kukup Golf Resort—an eyesore at present, though clearly a future money-spinner.

Kukup itself remains a predominantly Chinese fishing village: if you wander off the main road and along the wooden planks which serve as streets for pedestrians, bicycles and pushcarts, you see drying fish, squid and prawns outside many houses. At low tide it is less picturesque as you can see small fish writhing about in the shallows beneath the houses while other inhabitants tend to hurl their rubbish out of their houses so that the next tide will remove it. Copy watches, teeshirts, and souvenirs are all available along the main street of Kukup; the High King's Restaurant also runs boat tours, mainly for its coach parties, which tour the further reaches of the village and stop to look at the nearby fish farms.

Malacca

It might not look all that far on the map, but Malacca can be as much 5 hours' drive from Singapore, or even longer if you're particularly unlucky with the Causeway traffic. Malacca's colonial past has been rather chequered: after Sultan Iskandar Shah fled from Singapore and set up here in 1398 (*see* page 41), it was colonized firstly by the Portuguese, then captured by the Dutch. They in turn swapped it with the British for various Sumatran territories, so it became one of the East India Company's Straits Settlements towns (*see* page 43). It narrowly survived Sir Stamford Raffles' rather unfair plan to destroy it since it was providing too much competition for Penang, and is today a pleasant, slightly sleepy place rich in history, well worth a visit for a (long) day-trip, or preferably a one-night stay.

In the heart of the town is the colonial-style town square, bordered by the famous **Christ Church**, built in the 1750s by the Dutch; the **Stadthuys**, dating from about a century earlier and the **Tan Bee Swee Clock Tower** from the 1880s. There's also a Victoria Jubilee Fountain from the same period. You can generally enter the deep red Protestant church, which has a northern European feel in spite of its

Christ Church Square, deep red Dutch-style colours in the heart of Malacca.

tropical setting. The Stadthuys houses two museums. On the ground floor is the museum of ethnography and upstairs is the history museum which illustrates episodes of Malacca's history from the 14th century to the present.

Behind the Stadthuys you can climb up **Bukit St Paul** (avoiding the fiercely guarded military observation post on the way), and visit the ruined Church of St Paul, built by the Portuguese in 1521. There are several large tombstones, and views through the open doorways of the town and the coast, as well as a view of the Sultanate's Palace to the south. It's worth walking down the southern side of Bukit St Paul, to see the **Porta de Santiago**—the remains of the Portuguese fort destroyed by the Dutch—and thence on the **Malaccan Sultanates' Palace**, which now houses the museum. Here are displayed numerous Malay costumes, crafts, instruments and artefacts in a reconstructed *istana*, beautifully finished in teak wood. The entrance fee is fairly small, and you have to remove your shoes as you enter the building. A Dutch cemetery, dating from the 17th century, lies on Jalan Gereja behind Christ Church.

Over the Malacca river is **Malacca's Chinatown**, an intriguing area of antique shops—particularly on Jonkers Street—selling *nonya* and other Chinese furnishings and wares. For a true feel for the Nonya or Peranakan lifestyle, take a tour of the **Baba Nonya Heritage House** at 50 Tun Tan Cheng Lock. On Jalan Tokong is the oldest Chinese temple in Malaysia, **Cheng Hoon Teng Temple**, dating from 1645 and built in the southern Chinese style with an elaborate and highly decorated roof. Also worth a look is the **Kampung Keling Mosque**, built in 1868 in the square-shaped Sumatran style.

Tourists often flock to and eat at the **Portuguese Settlement**, 3 km (1½ miles) to the south of Malacca, where the street names and the architectural style are distinctly Portuguese. While it is "colonial" architecturally, and some of those running the restaurants are clearly of Portuguese stock, the whole set-up is really run exclusively for the tourists, the food is nothing out of the ordinary, during our visit there were several rats around as we ate, and we were asked to pay protection money so that our car was safe (the implication being that if we didn't it wouldn't be). If you want an out-of-town meal with a difference, I would recommend the **Restoran Peranakan**, at 317 Klebang Besar to the north of town. There you can sit in a secluded courtyard of a traditional *nonya* home overlooking the Straits of Malacca and savour Malay/*Nonya* dishes in an ambient atmosphere.

There are various levels of accommodation available—check with the tourist office (06 225 895) for further details and prices.

Kuala Lumpur

The capital city of Malaysia is only a 50-minute flight from Singapore, so well worth a stopover *en route* to Singapore, or including in a trip of some kind. Whilst at rush hours the dense slow-moving traffic can resemble Bangkok, once you are in the centre the city is surprisingly small, and it is possible to visit most of the main sights on foot or with the help of a short taxi ride.

233

A convenient starting point is the **Padang**, fronted on one side by the **Sultan Abdul Samad Building**, the former Secretariat building built in the 1890s with a 41-m (135-ft) clock tower, and on the other by the exclusive Tudor-style **Selangor Club**. At the southern end of the Padang is the paved **Merdeka (Independence) Square** with its 100-m (33-ft) flagpole and a renovated 90-year-old water fountain, beneath which lies a modern car-park. Opposite the fountain, on the same side of the road as the Sultan Abdul Samad Building, is the Information Centre on Malaysian Handicrafts, in a building completed in 1909.

A short walk across the river brings you to the **Jame Mosque**, situated at the confluence of the Klang and Gombak rivers where the city was first founded. Built in 1909, the domes and minarets peep out between coconut palms: it is best viewed from across either river, though visitors can walk around the outside of the mosque, and sarongs are on hand if you are unsuitably dressed to do this.

The winding streets of Kuala Lumpur's **Chinatown** lead south from the Jame Mosque: Jalan Bandar, Jalan Sultan and Jalan Petaling contain colourful two-tier shophouses, flourishing wayside hawker stalls and street markets, and the occasional Chinese or Hindu temple for good measure. The nearby **Central Market** shopping centre is a happy hunting ground for batiks, basketware, teeshirts and other souvenirs.

You can either walk or take a cab ride to the **Kuala Lumpur Railway Station** with its Arabic-style minarets and expansive arches. It was designed in

*K*uala Lumpur's ornate railway station, an elaborate Arabian Nights flight of fancy.

1911, and initially the design was disapproved by the British colonial office as it failed to meet one important specification for all railways—the ability of the roof to withstand 1 m (3 ft) of snow! Opposite the railway station is the railway administration building, and behind that the impressive **National Mosque** with its 73-m (240-ft) minaret. It is usually possible to visit this, and *sarongs* can be borrowed to cover any bare flesh, though be prepared to miss it if there is a special religious occasion. Over the road from the mosque is the **Islamic Cultural Centre**, host to different temporary exhibitions on Islam.

A must-see is the **National Museum**, past the Railway Station on the way out of town to the south along Jalan Travers. Housed in a Malay-style building completed in 1963, you can view steam engines, the original Penang Hill carriage, rickshaws and trishaws, culminating in the current pride of Malaysia, the Proton Saga car. Also to be seen outside the building is a traditional small-scale but immaculately furnished Malay Palace, and stone and wooden carvings.

Inside the museum on your right (if you enter from the back where the trains are) is a full exhibition of traditional Malaysian costumes, including sultans' headware, marriage garments, everyday and special occasion dress for men and women of the different states. Also included are exhibits of minority groups—the Peranakan or Nonya Chinese and the Indian communities, with costume and furnishings displayed to full advantage. Here too are a variety of musical instruments, and a selection of *wayang* shadow puppets from Malaysia, Indonesia and China. Temporary exhibitions are displayed in the opposite gallery on this level—I saw a fascinating display of skulls and hunting apparatus from islands in the region including Borneo (parts of which, Sabah and Sarawak, are part of Malaysia). Upstairs, above the costume gallery, is a well-staged display of stuffed birds and animals—ideal for identifying those kingfishers and hawks you may have seen on your travels, with scenes of likely habitat included with the displays. Opposite, above the temporary exhibits gallery, is the sports museum of local heroes and their exploits.

Other sights for a longer stay include the **National Art Gallery**, the **Lake Gardens** and nearby **Parliament House** and monuments and the **Karyaneka Handicraft Centre**. For further information, contact the Tourism Promotion Board.

If you have longer to spend in West Malaysia, or are prepared to travel further, you can visit the cooler hill stations of **Fraser's Hill** (almost exclusively a golf resort), **Genting Highlands** (Malaysia's casino centre, as well as golf facilities amidst tea plantations), or the **Cameron Highlands** (English-style mock Tudor architecture, even cream teas made with locally grown tea, and a number of sign posted walks in the surrounding forest). **Penang**, the last of the Straits Settlements towns, is just over an hour's flight from Singapore: here you can stay in 5-star comfort on Batu Ferringhi, the resort on the north side of the island, or in the rather endearing decaying grandeur of the E & O Hotel in Georgetown (formerly owned by the Sarkies brothers who also owned Singapore's Raffles Hotel). The sights and flavours of Penang Island are rich and many, but if still adventurous you could press on to the more remote **Langkawi Islands**, or travel northwards into Thailand.

Kota Tinggi

Kota Tinggi literally means High Fort, and is a sleepy town located at a busy road junction on the road north-east from Johor Baru towards Mersing. About 10 km (6 miles) from the town are the Kota Tinggi Waterfalls, where the Johor River dives 34 m (112 ft) down into a pool deep enough for children to swim in. Mainly an attraction

235

for locals from Kota Tinggi, the place is overflowing with knick knack stalls, souvenirs, food hawkers, while the fall itself is rather too enclosed and dark to be as spectacular as it sounds.

A new resort is planned just down the Johor River from Kota Tinggi, at Kampong Teluk Sengat, where chalet-style accommodation and campsites will be reachable by speedboat up the Johor River past Tanjong Surat at the estuary mouth, just opposite Singapore's Pulau Tekong. You can reach the Johor River further downstream by taking a side road off the main road to Desaru, reaching the charming little village of Telok Senang. The original Johor was situated near this spot.

*T*he beach at Desaru, a popular get-away for Malaysians and Singaporeans at week-ends, but usually quiet during the week.

Desaru

This resort on the east coast of West Malaysia is currently undergoing a somewhat acrimonious and delayed process of large-scale development. Desaru International Resorts Sdn Bhd, a three-way partnership, is planning to construct the world's largest theme park there, to include a ski dome where you can throw snowballs! Hotels are under construction, as are a multitude of golf-courses, and it is envisaged that a high-speed catamaran service will operate directly from Singapore's Changi Point to the resort, enabling golf tourists to disembark from Japan or wherever and take the first ferry up to Desaru.

Don't visit Desaru once this development is completed if you are after a peaceful, unspoilt stretch of beach; go to other places listed below. However, if you are keen on pursuing a variety of watersports, visiting a theme park (whenever this emerges from the

*M*ersing harbour.
Access to the east coast islands is by these little boats which seat no more than 12 passengers.

current construction wrangles), and playing golf considerably more cheaply than in Singapore, this could be the resort you are looking for.

At present there are two beach-front hotels: the **Desaru Golf Hotel** and the **Desaru View Hotel**. In the middle is the administration office of Desaru, together with a Chinese restaurant and a small souvenir stall. Access to the beach—reputedly 25 km (15 miles) long—certainly long enough, is free, and the water is clear and inviting (but watch out for the undertow), though you do have to pay to park. A tollgate structure sits at the entrance to Desaru, though you do not need to pay—yet! The Desaru View Hotel has various watersport facilities open to the public on an hourly or ½-hourly basis; golf facilities are being increased visibly, though most of the construction is currently hidden behind palm trees—except for a clearance site about 2 km (1 mile) before Desaru.

> **Weather Warnings**
> When planning your trip, remember that from November to February the north-east monsoon hits the east coast of Malaysia hard. Flooding frequently occurs on low-lying roads, storms and fierce rain are common, and the island resorts are all closed because of dangerous and unpredictable seas. Scuba-divers and snorkellers should ideally wait until late March for the waters to clear fully. (Those planning to visit the islands off the west coast of Malaysia should avoid visiting them during the south-west monsoon of June to September.)

Mersing

A sleepy fishing town about 3½ hours' drive from Singapore on the east coast of Peninsular Malaysia in the state of Johor. Its main claim to fame is its boat service to the idyllic offshore islands of Tioman, Rawa and Babi Besar, and the bustling harbour with its colourful fishing boats which double as passenger ferries is a sight to behold.

Pulau Tioman

The island where the musical *South Pacific* was filmed, and spectacular it is, with nobbly hills covered in palm trees and dense jungle, and sandy beaches stretching along the coast. Access to Tioman Island is by boat from Mersing (*see* above), by catamaran from Singapore, or by air (*see* page 268). There are various resorts to stay at, including the **Tioman Island Resort** which has a golf-course and offers a wide range of activities—all of which may or may not be working at the time you arrive! Wherever you stay, you will experience the tropical island, palm trees and clear sea that is the real essence of the place.

Pulau Babi Besar

Much smaller than Pulau Tioman, this "big pig island" is also off the coast from Mersing and well worth a visit. Not so many creature comforts here: at the Hillside Chalets you will have a beach or hillside chalet, with running cold freshwater shower, and electricity for enough of the time to power your ceiling fan. A central dining area offers a fairly wide and generally excellent range of dishes, plus beers, coffees and other drinks throughout the day. You can flop under a shady umbrella, swim

or sunbathe by the resort or walk for about 10 minutes to the more secluded and more spectacular "Beach of Passionate Love". Few sporting activities are on offer (though scuba-diving equipment, a couple of canoes, and a windsurf board were in evidence on our last visit); this is more of a retreat from it all.

Other islands offering a similar escape from the 20th century just an hour or so off Mersing include **Pulau Rawa** and **Pulau Sibu**. Other islands offer self-catering in basic facilities, or camping—check with the Malaysia Tourism Promotion Board (*see* page 277).

Indonesia

Batam

Just 20 km (12 miles) south of Singapore—½ an hour by air-conditioned catamaran ferry—is the island of Batam. The contrast when you step ashore on Indonesia's nearest island is extreme. Here you are immediately in the Third World, though a fast developing part of it. Naturally rich in bauxite, and a centre for Indonesia's state oil company's oil exploration activities since the late 1960s, since December 1989 Batam has been part of an economic growth triangle with Singapore and Johor. Forest clearance and preparation for construction work now proceeds along virtually the entire north coast of the island. A total of five industrial estates are currently under way, complete with accompanying accommodation, town centres and leisure facilities for the future workers.

In addition, Singapore is funding the infrastructure of laying a water pipeline from Sumatra via Singapore to Batam, with obvious benefits for Singapore's future water demands.

The population of the island is estimated at 126,000 at the time of writing (1991), of whom 59 per cent are Chinese, and the remainder Malay or Bugis race. A smattering of Indonesian or Malay is helpful, though most people know enough English to count and sell you items or food, and can direct you to wherever you want to go.

The main town on the island, **Nagoya**, is a 15-minute drive from Batu Ampat ferry terminal, or a 25-minute drive from Sekupang, the main ferry terminal. The town was built by the Japanese during their occupation of Indonesia, hence the name, and is a grid pattern of bisecting streets, lined with tatty two-storey concrete buildings housing shops, a wet market, offices and small workshops. The moment you walk around, the numerous taxis will start to attract your attention, hoping desperately for business. A couple of shops sell teeshirts and batik items, all imported from Bali, for tourists, though not with any particular gusto, while duty-free liquor shops abound—the whole island has duty-free status, and it's well worth buying liquor there, either in Indonesian rupiah or in Singapore dollars, which are readily accepted. (Don't be tempted to buy duty-free cigarettes—you can no longer import these into Singapore.) New housing construction is proceeding to the north-west of the town centre, where you can also visit a recently constructed Chinese Buddhist temple, the **Tua Pek Kong Temple**. This is built

*B*atu Besar literally "big rock", Batam Island.

on traditional lines, with lion sculptures guarding the main entrance, red lanterns and offerings surrounding the altar table, and colourful sculptures in the encircling grounds.

The main "sight" or attraction is the century-old fig tree in the centre of the island, used by the Chinese as a place of worship before their temple was constructed, and now fronted by a monument to President Suharto. You can walk all round the tree, past the inevitable local men who are just sitting to pass the time, and past the security guard positioned there to stop them fighting—and *voilà*, you've seen the tourist attraction! Other items of

interest pointed out on my trip included the post office, the radio mast,
the hospital, the one set of traffic
lights, the police station and the one
petrol station—complete with 20-car
queue!

The one as yet unspoilt area of
Batam is **Batu Besar** to the east, where
kelongs jut out over the sea or mud flat
(depending on the tide) and where you
can eat a seafood meal overlooking a
peaceful scene as yet unencumbered by
construction sites. The drive to the inlet is on a dirt track through coconut
groves, and traditional *kampong*
houses with a small school continue to
exist as a small relatively unchanged
community—though you will find
other taxis or tourist coaches at the
restaurants when you arrive.

The **Batam Centre**, a vast construction site on an inlet on the north coast,
will comprise tourist hotels including
the Sheraton, government offices and
a financial centre, as well as housing
for those involved in the expected economic miracle in the late 1990s. The
nearby **Hang Nadim airport**, at present
a mainly domestic airport with two
flights a week to Kuala Lumpur and
two to Ho Chi Minh, is also being expanded to cope with expended economic expansion.

There are a number of hotels on the
island, and their number is set to double at least over the next 10 years.
There are several in Nagoya town, and
some in the adjacent Jojod town—similar but smaller. Resort-style hotels do
exist at the north-west tip (Palm Beach
Resort) and the north-east tip facing
across to Bintan island (Turi Beach
Resort and Batam View Hotel), with
sandy beaches at high tide and good
views across to Singapore. The
Batam View Hotel is currently developing a yachting marina, while the
Turi Beach Resort, with its 78 chalets
arranged on terraces overlooking its
white sandy beach, and its swimming
pool, mooring facilities and watersports, is the most authentic attempt to
re-create what Batam once was—an
unspoilt tropical paradise.

Visiting the island, it's hard to work
out why so many new hotels and facilities—a couple more 18-hole golf-
courses to add to the existing Talvas
Golf Course—are considered necessary, as well as two new 18-hole
courses at Tanjong Country Club on
the north-west shore: a day trip is
more than enough time to savour the
flavour of the island and to see all
sights twice. Two or three hours is all
the time you need to visit the "sights"
and the ubiquitous building work de-
stroys any illusion of a peaceful island
resort such as those on the east coast
of west Malaysia. Sadly it seems a
classic case of tourism destroying its
own potential and unchecked, even un-
planned, building plans resulting in
swathes of deforested earth—an eyesore wherever you look. Unless you're
desperate to visit the nearest point of
Indonesia, I'd save your time and go
elsewhere. If you do go, Singapore dollars are widely accepted in this duty-
free island, as are (obviously) rupiah.

Bintan

The largest of the 3,000 islands of Indonesia's Riau Archipelago, Bintan is,
like Batam, now earmarked for economic expansion and consequent construction work. Its capital, **Tanjong
Pinang**, on the south of the island, is

reachable by ferry (2 hours), either direct from Singapore, or via Batam. Check the ferry times at The Singapore Cruise Centre before you leave, and unless you are certain when you wish to return don't buy a return ticket, as the different ferry operators' tickets are not interchangeable so you may lose money.

Tanjong Pinang is a rather sleepy, likeable town. Arriving at the main pier, you walk along it looking out to Pulau Penyegat (*see* below) on one side, and to the old harbour, stilted houses and small boats on the other. The main street—**Jalan Merdeka**—is comprised of slightly tatty shophouses containing everything from auto parts to groceries. There is one money-changer, down a small backstreet behind the police station, and a small tourist information office at the arrivals hall of the ferry terminal will set you up with a map and basic information.

In Indonesian style, tourists will typically be "adopted" by a local guide, and if you can cope with the company and the constant chatter, this will ease your travel in the area, as your "guide" will arrange taxis and boats or stop the correct minibus for wherever you wish to go. If you do accept such a "guide" you should obviously pay him at the end of your visit: no discussion of money is had as such, it's left to your discretion, and whatever you feel is fair is generally about right.

A 15-minute boat trip just across from the pier on Tanjong Pinang will take you to the 2½-km (1½-mile) square **Pulau Penyegat**, a former seat of power of the Riau Sultanate. The island subsequently became a centre of Malay culture and learning in the mid-19th century: well-known poets from here include Raja Ali Haji (1809–70), while an official printing press circulated the island's output amongst scholars in the early 1900s. The Dutch colonials soon felt threatened by the pro-sultan tendencies of this group of scholars, and in 1905 deposed the Riau royalty.

*T*he Royal mausoleum on Pulau Penyegat, off Bintan Island.

On the island today are the remains of the 180-year-old **Kerajaan Melayu Palace** which is currently being restored, two tranquil mausoleums containing graves of the sultan's family, various other ruined buildings including a former hospital, a modern Malay-style library (shut during my visit—no regular opening hours) and the striking yellow mosque you can see from Tanjong Pinang town. Built in 1818, the mosque is reputedly made from eggs, the egg white being used to bind the other building materials. There are no cars on the island, and very few bikes, so the island's 2,000 or so inhabitants and any visitors walk between the *kampong*-style houses, palm and banana trees on well-paved walkways, an extremely peaceful spot—except from the constant stream of "hellos" from the small children.

A couple of kilometres outside the centre of Tanjong Pinang is a small museum, the **Riau Kandil Museum**, housed within a larger administrative Malay-style building. This contains a display of black and white photographs from colonial days, photographs of the sites on Pulau Penyegat, basketry fish traps, model boats, maps, wedding photographs of different tribes from Sumatra, pottery, spinning tops and various cooking vessels and weapons. All the captions are in Bahasa Indonesia, and the collection is somewhat sleepy and eclectic. The ride there, whether by taxi or by minibus, is well worthwhile, along small streets lined with trees and flowers, and a view out to the sea to the south.

Those with more time could cross the harbour by *bompong* (small bumboats, narrower than the ones in Singapore) to visit the mainly Chinese area of **Senggarang**, and its temples. A boat trip up the **Snake River** is another possibility: check with the tourist information counter and agree your price with the boatman first.

There are beach resorts on Bintan island. **Trikora Beach**, 45 km (28 miles) from Tanjong Pinang, has chalet-style accommodation, and snorkelling is reputedly good on its corals, while the recently opened **Segiling Beach Resort** on the north coast offers a variety of watersports. Future plans to market tourist resorts of the Riau Archipelago together with Singapore's and Johor's attractions are proceeding on Bintan: the **Bintan Beach International Resort** on the north of the island is scheduled to take 10–15 years to complete, and will stretch along 18 km (11 mile) of beach. A new ferry service to Telok Sebang on the north coast is planned to service the resort. Also under way is Bintan's first industrial estate at Tanjung Uban, currently under construction and designed for light industries to supply souvenirs, textiles and locally produced consumer goods and food processing for the anticipated tourist increase.

Short Stays and Tours

The shortest stay transit passengers through Changi airport, with a minimum of 4 hours' stay, can take the free city tour arranged by the STPB every morning and afternoon. Follow the signs or ask at the information counter, for a swift look at **Little India**, **Chinatown** and the central **Padang** area.

Those visitors with limited time will obviously have their own priorities and interests: some may prefer to spend time in a museum, others at the Open Zoo, others shopping in air-conditioned comfort, others exploring unspoilt, backstreets of Chinatown or Little India. The choice is yours: Singapore is so small that you can reach virtually anywhere on the island within ¾ hour by taxi, so pick and choose what you would like to see and plan accordingly. I would recommend spending some time exploring the central areas to the north and south of the river, preferably on foot, and then taking an aerial view to orientate yourself from The Westin Stamford's Compass Rose, or from the OUB's Pinnacle.

Others may find it more fun and relaxing to take one of the many tours available. The main operators, **Holiday Tours, Tour East** and **RMG Tours** run a range of tours, picking up passengers from all the major hotels. Their programmes are similar, though the details vary: all offer city tours in the mornings, afternoons and evenings; tours of the Zoo and the BirdPark, of Haw Par Villa, and of the east coast. They also run day tours across the causeway to Johor Baru, Kukup and Malacca, and arrange tours of Batam island in the Indonesian Riau Archipelago.

Specialist tours are also available which trace the **Second World War combat sites**, including Changi Prison, the Ford Factory on Bukit Timah Road, the Kranji War Memorial, the underground bunkers at Fort Canning, and the Sultan Ibrahim Tower in Johor. These are run by Malaysia and Singapore Travel Centre, and will shortly be run by Singapore Sightseeing, which also runs racing tours of the **Bukit Turf Club** on race weekends, subject to demand. Details of all tours are also available through the STPB.

For an overview, try **Singapore Aerospace's half-hour helicopter tour** recently offered from Seletar Airport at midday daily, which skirts MacRitchie Reservoir, overflies Bukit Timah Nature Reserve and swoops south across Jurong to fly over the harbour to the south of the city and of Sentosa island, before returning to Seletar north over the Kallang Basin. The tour costs $150 for adults and $75 for children and is sold by Safe Travel.

Holiday Tours and Travel
300 Orchard Road #07-05
The Promenade, Singapore 0923
Telephone: 738 2622 Fax: 733 3226

Malaysia and Singapore Travel
    Centre
Tanglin Shopping Centre #06-01
Telephone: 235 4411 Fax: 235 3033

RMG Tours Pte Ltd
#01-02 Allson Hotel
101 Victoria Street, Singapore 0718
Telephone: 337 3377 Fax: 339 5657.

Safe Travel and Enterprises Pte Ltd
3 Lim Teck Kim Road #02-02
Telephone: 220 8866 Fax: 743 4810

Singapore Sightseeing Pte Ltd
2 Dempsey Road
Telephone: 473 6900 Fax: 473 0929

Tour East, Unit 8, Equatorial Hotel
429 Bukit Timah Road
Singapore 1025
Telephone: 235 5703 Fax: 235 0175.

Night-Life and Entertainment

Most of the hotels have some kind of disco or nightclub as well as bars and lounges which are open to the public (*see* hotels section, page 278). Fashions and trends for night-life in particular are notoriously subject to change, but some of the hot spots at the time of writing are listed below. Other types of entertainment—cinemas, theatres, concerts, sports and local cultural forms such as Chinese opera—are also often available.

Nightclubs

Anywhere
4th floor, Tanglin Shopping Centre, Tanglin Road
Telephone: 734 8233
Opening Hours: 6 p.m.–1.30 a.m.

A favoured expatriate watering hole, the game here is receiving your change from the highly priced drinks you order—the drinks and nibbles arrive promptly, the change can take 25 minutes, so remember who your waitress is and keep your nerve. A live band,

A Malay drummer rehearsing before the performance.

headed by transvestite Tania is the main attraction, and a certain level of ritual audience humiliation is the entertainment. No dancing, just spectating or participating in the loud show, with luck at a table rather than being pushed aside by rushing waitresses at the bar. Not a place for intimate conversations—but fun with a group prepared to shout!

Chinoiserie
Hyatt Regency Hotel, 10 Scotts Road, Singapore 0922
Telephone: 733 1188
Opening Hours: 9 p.m.–2.30 a.m.

The Chinoiserie is held out to be one of Singapore's top nightspots, and definitely not a place to sport those designer jeans or spotless trainers—the

245

dress code strictly enforced, particularly against non-Caucasians in my experience. Quite tasteful, dark decor, comfy sofas and a decent-sized dance floor, drinks about as overpriced as you'd expect in an exclusive spot and service quite efficent and almost friendly once you manage to get in. The music (disc jockey) is mainstream and you can dance to it, and it's a very central location. I find the place lacks atmosphere to take it out of the ordinary and the class it seems to imply with its admissions policy, but others disagree strongly.

Europa Lounge and Restaurant
Changi Village Road #01-2011
Telephone: 542 5617
Opening Hours: 12 noon–1 a.m. weekdays, 12 noon–2 a.m. Fridays and Saturdays

A small, friendly and atmospheric bar or club with two different live acts you can watch from your table or wherever you can stand. Meals (Western style) and drinks are served, the music's loud rock and roll and old cover versions (lyrics not so strictly censored!), and the acts are somewhat subversive—but popular bands have a habit of moving on, so shows can change. Another branch of the same organization is **Europa Theatre Pub**, 10 Anson Road #02-02, International Plaza, Telephone: 225 3668. This is open Mondays to Saturdays from 11 a.m.–1 a.m.

Fire
Orchard Plaza #04-19
150 Orchard Road
Telephone: 235 0155
Opening Hours: Happy Hour 4 p.m.–

8 p.m., nightclub open 8 p.m.–3 a.m. daily

Located unpromisingly above a shopping centre, which is deserted by the time the club is open, there are two very different levels to this venue. Firstly you come to the seething mass of dancers jiggling to the disco sounds—fairly bland, but contemporary; then if you struggle through the crowds you can climb upstairs to the smaller area where the live band Energy plays rock music cover versions. There's a central bar, and a dance floor near the band, with enough space to dance or to watch, whatever takes your fancy. Karaoke fans can also book a lounge here. No dress code.

Khameleon
Marina Village
Telephone: 221 6500 (office hours only), 227 4510 (when disco is open)
Opening Hours: Thursdays–Saturdays 9 p.m.–3 a.m.

The one part of the Marina Village development which is still operational, this outlet rivals Zouk as a fashionable night spot for Singapore's young trendies at the time of writing.

Subway
Plaza Hotel
Beach Road
Telephone: 298 0011
Opening Hours: 6 p.m.–2 a.m.

A lively band is on stage for much of the time, playing to a static listening teen and very early 20s audience, interspersed by recorded slow numbers when you cannot reach the dance floor for the smooching couples. More of a dive than anything else, you could probably do better.

Yesterdays

United Square #B1-01
Thomson Road
Telephone: 250 8009
Opening Hours: 12 noon–2 a.m. Mondays to Saturdays, 5 p.m.–1 a.m. Sundays

A lively, somewhat downmarket dive off Thomson Road with a live band doing passable cover versions of mainstream American rock. No problems with dress code here, and reasonable drink prices with even a chance of a seat or at least a view of the stage. Go with a group of friends rather than for an intimate evening for two, and join the mainly male Chinese Singaporeans letting their hair down (as far as it will go, anyway!).

Zouk

17/21 Jiak Kim St
Kim Seng Road
Telephone: 738 2988
Opening Hours: disco 9 p.m.–3 a.m., pub and wine bar open 6 p.m.–3 a.m.

The trendy place in town, located in a renovated warehouse near the Singapore River, Zouk has a restaurant, wine bar, disco and bar, and souvenir shop. You can enter the restaurant, wine bar or shop without paying the fairly high entrance fee for main attraction, the disco, where the entertainment consists of watching outrageously dressed people moving vaguely in time to the funk/fusion/house mixture of music which all blends into one. Once tired of the dance floor, or if you want to hold a conversation, take a drink in the upstairs bar which overlooks the dance floor. Dress code: smart-casual, not too strictly enforced but don't be too scruffy.

Other nightspots which I've not visited myself but have heard recommended include the **Music Room**, Hilton Hotel, Telephone: 737 2233; the **Reading Room**, Marina Mandarin, Telephone: 338 3388; **Scandals**, Westin Plaza Hotel, Telephone: 338 8585; and **Xanadu**, Shangri-La Hotel, Telephone: 737 3644. There is also a revue bar, with dance revues including topless girls and strip shows: **Neptune Theatre Restaurant**, #07-00 Overseas Union House, 50 Collyer Quay, Telephone: 224 3922.

Drinking Holes

Alcoholic drinks are not really as large a part of life in Singapore as they are in the West, partly for religious reasons—Muslims and Hindus are forbidden to drink alcohol, and many Buddhists also abstain—but also by custom soft drinks and eating, rather than drinking, is perceived as a valid form of entertainment.

However, both as a response to tourist and expatriate demand and as a hangover from colonial days, there are places where you can sample that Raffles Hotel classic, the Singapore Sling, or down a glass of locally brewed Tiger beer. All hotels have bars and lounges which are open to the public. Those with a "pub crawl" in mind would do well in the Tanjong Pagar Conservation Area, where numerous new hostelries open, seemingly every week.

Brannigans

Hyatt Regency Hotel
10 Scotts Road

Telephone: 733 1188
Opening Hours: 5 p.m.–1 a.m. Sundays to Thursdays, 5 p.m.–2 a.m. Fridays and Saturdays

A very crowded and smoky drinks and recorded jazz spot, popular with male Caucasians prepared to pay the high prices in order to be well placed to meet local beauties.

Compass Rose Bar
Westin Stamford Hotel
Stamford Road
Telephone: 338 8585

Quite a high minimum charge, and definitely no jeans, so you might as well order a cocktail and admire the spectacular skyline, which is well worth doing—particularly once you have visited several of the sights and have a sense of direction.

Raffles Hotel
11 Beach Road
Singapore 0718
Telephone: 339 1886

A Singapore Sling or a Tiger beer in the Bar and Billiard Room, sitting on the verandah overlooking the fountain court or, perhaps, best of all, in the two-storey Long Bar where the crackling of groundnut shells underfoot is extremely disconcerting at first, is certainly an experience to savour amidst the restored colonial splendour. The billiard tables are in constant use by patrons and provide additional entertainment from the joy of people-watching in the new hot spot in town.

Saxophone Bar and Restaurant
Cuppage Terace
Orchard Road
Telephone: 235 8385

Opening Hours: 12 noon–3 p.m., 6 p.m.–2 a.m.

You can eat here too, but many people go just to drink outside in the evening air, listening to the live jazz band playing in incredibly cramped surroundings by the bar.

Somerset's Bar
Westin Plaza Hotel
Stamford Road
Telephone: 338 8585

Live jazz and old colonial prints in a "long bar" style of pub, pricy cocktails and variable musicianship.

Karaoke

Java Jive
Lorong Liput
Holland Village
Telephone: 468 4155
Opening Hours: 6 p.m.–1 a.m. Mondays to Fridays, 6 p.m.–2 a.m. weekends

A mediocre Filipino rock band cedes the stage after 9.00 p.m. or so and a couple of microphones are passed around the assembled crowd so you don't have to go on stage and can perform at your table. There are numerous other Karaoke bars in town.

Cinemas and Theatres

Spectator entertainment is also readily available in Singapore, whether a film to fill a wet or grey afternoon, a theatrical production or a Chinese opera or dance performance. One-off performances are generally listed in *The*

Straits Times, though street performances during certain festivals are more often found simply by chance. Below are some of the main cinemas and theatres where English or European language productions are shown.

Cinemas

Capitol Cinema, North Bridge Road, Tel: 337 9759

Cathay Cinema, Dhoby Ghaut, Tel: 338 3400

Changi 1, 799 New Upper Changi Road, Tel: 442 4417

Changi 2, 4579 New Upper Changi Road, Tel: 444 6459

Jade 1, Shaw Towers, Beach Road, Tel: 293 2581

Jade Classics, Shaw Towers, Beach Road, Tel: 294 2568

Orchard Cinema, Orchard Turn, Tel: 737 6588

Picturehouse, Dhoby Ghaut, Tel: 338 3400

Plaza Cinema, 200 Jalan Sultan #04-24, Tel: 292 0571

Prince 1, Shaw Towers, Beach Road, Tel: 298 4905

Prince 2, Shaw Towers, Beach Road, Tel: 294 2553

Alliance Francaise, 4 Draycott Park, Tel: 737 8422

British Council, 30 Napier Road, Tel: 473 1111

Goethe Institute, Singapore Shopping Centre, Tel: 337 5111

Theatres

National Theatre Trust, Kallang Theatre, Stadium Link, Tel: 345 8488

TheatreWorks, The Black Box, Fort Canning Centre, Tel: 338 4077

Colourful scene from a Chinese opera.

The head of a dancing dragon at one of Singapore's festivals. There are often several relays of dancers during long dances.

The Drama Centre, Fort Canning Rise, Tel: 336 0005

The Substation, Armenian Street, Tel: 337 7800

Singapore Conference Hall, Shenton Way, Tel: 222 9711

Singapore Indoor Stadium, Stadium Link, Tel: 344 2660

Victoria Memorial Hall and Theatre, Empress Place, Tel: 337 7490

Booking Offices for Theatres, Concerts, Sporting Events

Central Booking Office, Tel: 337 7490

Centrepoint, Tel: 235 6629

C. K. Tangs, Tel: 235 7109

Telok Ayer Festival Market

Sports

There are a lot of sporting facilities available in Singapore, catering for most activities. Check with your hotel, travel agent, the Singapore Sports Council (Tel: 345 7111) or your own sporting club for any reciprocal membership arrangements and special requirements, and with the STPB and the local press for spectator events.

Fishing

Fishing remains incredibly popular with Singaporeans, despite their high-tech, high-rise environment—or perhaps because of it. Since the 1977 clean Singapore River campaign there have been fish in the river, and also in the Kallang River, and you may see local people with a rod alongside the river (though not fishing from the bridges where there are notices forbidding it). Kallang Park is a popular area for fishing, another spot is Bedok jetty along the east coast, not far from the East Coast Sailing Centre (see below). Seletar Reservoir and Kranji Reservoir both also have fishing jetties.

It may be possible to charter a fishing boat if you wish to go on a long fishing trip: try inquiring at a small harbour such as Changi Village, or at the Jardine Steps near the WTC.

Football

Singapore takes part in the Malaysian Cup, and home matches in this league, as well as occasional exhibition matches between foreign teams, are played at the National Stadium, Stadium Road. The daily paper will let you know if a match is on, and tickets are available at the door for all but any finals games, when it is worth buying them in advance. There are local football clubs in the various areas of Singapore, which in turn compete in Singapore's national league.

Golf

Golf is extremely popular and hence expensive in Singapore. Much golf is played in private clubs, several of which admit members of the public on weekdays, provided they have handicap certificates. Check any reciprocal membership arrangement in your home country before you leave, and check with your hotel on arrival as they may be able to arrange access to one of the private clubs. Golfers may wish to travel to Desaru or to other resorts in Malaysia, or to Batam in Indonesia for golfing holidays.

Driving Ranges Open to the Public

Admiralty House Golf Driving Range, Telephone: 754 6424

Fairway Country Club, Telephone: 261 1211

Green Fairways, Bukit Turf Club, Telephone: 468 7233

Parkland Driving Range, Telephone: 440 6726

Golf-Courses Open to the Public

Changi Golf Club, Telephone: 545 5133

Jurong Country Club, Telephone: 560 5655

Keppel Club, Telephone: 273 5522

Raffles Country Club, Telephone: 861 7655 (telephone first)

Sentosa Golf Club, Telephone: 275 0022 (open to the public 7 days a week, including public holidays)

Singapore Island Country Club, Telephone: 459 2222

Tanglin Golf Course, Minden Road, Telephone: 473 7236 (7 holes, no handicap required)

Warren Golf Club, Folkestone Road, Telephone: 777 6533

Horse Riding and Racing

Riding lessons are offered to the public by the Saddle Club, part of the Singapore Turf Club on Bukit Timah Road, Telephone: 466 2782, but are proving extremely popular with Singaporeans, so you may find there is a long waiting list. The Polo Club, Thomson Road, Telephone: 256 4530, also offers riding lessons to the public.

Racing can be watched at the Singapore Turf Club on certain weekends, generally once a month or so. Fixtures are part of the Malayan Racing Association's calendar, with other race meetings held in Perak, Selangor and Penang.

Racquet Sports

Many hotels have their own tennis and squash courts for residents. Public courts are also available at Kallang Tennis Centre (Telephone: 348 1291) and Kallang Squash Centre (Telephone: 440 6839), both on Stadium Road; and at Marina South Tennis and Squash Centre, Marina Road, Telephone: 226 1142. For other racquet sports, such as badminton, ask the Singapore Sports Council, Telephone: 345 7111 for details of the facility nearest to you.

Swimming

The man-made beaches along the East Coast Park are open to the public for swimming, though you should not venture too far out because of currents and sudden changes in depth. Changi Beach and Pasir Ris Park also have pleasant sea swimming areas, and Sentosa's Siloso Beach offers an alternative, still spacious venue. (Sentosa's swimming lagoons are currently being renovated, and should reopen in 1992, hopefully with cleaner water than when I swam in them in 1990.)

Most hotels have their own swimming pools, and there are also a number of public swimming pools. The Big Splash on East Coast Parkway (Telephone: 345 1211), has a number of water slides as well as a wave pool and flow pool (Opening hours 12 noon–5.45 p.m. weekdays, 9 a.m.– 5.45 p.m. weekends); nearby the East Coast Park Swimming Lagoon is open daily from 8 a.m.–7.30 p.m. (Telephone: 340 9622). CN Leisure Park, 9 Japanese Garden Road (Telephone: 261 4771) has similar facilities, though it is a somewhat sleepy spot.

Public swimming pools include the River Valley Swimming Complex on River Valley Road (Telephone: 337 6275) and Kallang Basin Swimming Complex on Kallang Bahru Lane (Telephone: 295 4261). Check in the Yellow Pages, in your hotel or with the Singapore Sports Council for further details.

Ten Pin Bowling

An extremely popular sport in Singapore, there are a number of bowling alleys throughout the island. Lanes will generally be booked up a week or so in advance for the evenings, but you should be able to book lanes during the daytime (except during some school or public holidays). Some of the more central alleys are listed below, but check in the Yellow Pages for further details if these are unavailable.

Orchard Bowl, 8 Grange Road, Telephone: 737 4018; **Kim Seng Plaza Bowl**, #04-01 Kim Seng Plaza, Telephone: 734 8388; **Plaza Bowl**, 200 Jalan Sultan, Telephone: 292 4821.

Watersports

The East Coast Sailing Centre, Telephone: 449 5118 is a private club for laser dinghy sailing and windsurfing, but hires out both laser dinghies and windsurf boards to the public at an hourly fee. It also runs beginners' courses for windsurfing and laser sailing. A hive of activity on weekend afternoons, particularly Sundays, you will have little difficulty hiring a boat or a board during the week.

William Water Sports, 35 Punggol 24th Avenue, Telephone: 282 6879 and Seashore Boating Centre, Track 24 Ponggol Road, Telephone: 482 0888

*P*articipants in the annual Dragon Boat Race festival.

will both rent a speedboat, carrying up to six people, plus a driver, skis and lifejackets on an hourly basis. The drivers of both companies will also help beginners master this frustrating sport.

Annual spectator events include the Dragon Boat Festival in June (*see* page 93), and the Formula One Powerboat Grand Prix in November. Both events are held in Marina Bay and are well advertised in the local press.

Things to do With Children

Singapore is a very child-friendly place: children accompany and eat out with their parents comparatively late in the evenings, with none of the disapproving glances experienced in some European countries. Children of all ages can enjoy the ubiquitous and varied selection of electronic games, readily available for sale or hire depending on the outlay, which is Singapore's current fad, and an ideal failsafe in case of sudden rain or as entertainment between activities.

Some specific sites are ideal for children. **Sentosa** island, with no cars, bikes for hire, a monorail and various specific attractions, is a good family day out. Younger children would find the Pioneers of Singapore and Surrender Chambers too slow, but the sound effects and ability to explore the tunnels and lookout points of **Fort Siloso** are ideal for kids. So is **Underwater World**, a particularly good choice if it's raining: who can fail to find sharks and stingrays swimming overhead interesting? And the Coro-

larium, at the east of the island, with its turtle pool and feeding times for the wild monkeys nearby is a popular choice for families.

On Singapore itself, the **Zoo** offers various animal shows and rides, as well as having a special children's section; the **BirdPark** again has displays of various bird species; and **Crocodile Paradise** and indeed the **East Coast Crocodilarium** provide an interesting

spectacle. **Haw Par Villa** has a water flume ride and a range of other attractions, including a boat ride through the centre of a large dragon, though much of the imagery and statuary illustrates ancient Chinese legends and moral tales, and parents may not feel some of the gruesome tableaux are suitable for children. **Tang Dynasty** gives a number of other attractions (*see* page 174).

Kite flying is a very popular pastime among both the Chinese and the Malay communities. These brightly coloured and elaborately designed Chinese-style kites are on sale in Chinatown.

Indoors, the **Science Centre** can supply hours of hands on fun—and education—while young vistors play with computers, video screens and a range of exhibits. It also has a specific **Discovery Centre**, where all exhibits are at a child's height. The **National Museum** also has a children's section, but remember that both this and the Science Centre are closed on Mondays. The **Guiness World of Records** is open 7 days a week for collectors of superlative statistics.

For picnics, try the **East Coast** beaches, or Sentosa's **Siloso Beach**, or try booking a barbecue pit (*see* page 23) at one of the approved sites. Good picnic sites inland are at **MacRitchie Reservoir Park**, at **Upper Peirce Reservoir**, or at **Seletar Reservoir**: at all these sites you may well see wild monkeys keen to pick over your leftovers, though you shouldn't really feed them as it will make them too dependent on people for food.

The best playground I've seen, with four different areas graded by children's age, is at **Pasir Ris Park**, which also has a beach looking east towards Pulau Ubin. Bikes can be hired at the **East Coast Park**, near the Sailing Centre, and for older children mountain bikes can also be hired on **Pulau Ubin** (*see* page 225), which is easily reached by bumboat from Changi.

There are several swimming pools available, or try visiting the **Big Splash** or even the **CN Leisure Park** for a water slide. When it opens, in 1993 perhaps, Sentosa's **Fantasy Island** water theme park will offer much more variety of this kind. For further information on sports in Singapore, *see* page 251–4.

Language Guide

English is the most widely used language in commerce, business and in day-to-day life in Singapore today. Street signs, maps, hotel names, roads—all are in English, and all taxi drivers speak and understand English fairly fluently—unlike those in Hong Kong, for instance. The different races—Chinese, Malay and Tamil—do all have their own languages, with school qualifications and art forms using them, but for communication between Singaporeans of whatever race, and even between those Chinese of different dialect groups, English, or rather "Singlish", is used.

Singlish is a hotchpotch blend of Hokkien and Malay words and grammar styles woven into English, and is at times unfathomable to an outsider: persevere patiently and slowly, and you will eventually understand most of what is being said. Rather than "yes", in Singapore people say "can", (the different grades of emphasis affirm the likelihood of "yes" rather than "maybe"); instead of "no" they say "cannot". A taxi driver will "bring" you to or from the airport; "marketing" is shopping in the market for groceries rather than a global sales strategy; and the expression "is it?" translates into the English "really?"— and would be used in situations such as "I forgot to bring my wallet". "Is it?" "Lah" is frequently added to a sentence or phrase, for emphasis or rather the lack of it: "OK" is marginally more positive and pleased than "OK lah"—the latter means you'll tolerate the situation, the former is more like the English meaning.

Some Useful Phrases

English	Malay	Indonesian (if different)
Good morning	**Selamat Pagi**	
Good afternoon	**Selamat Petang**	**Selamat Siang**
Good evening	**Selamat Malam**	**Selamat Sore**
Hello, welcome	**Selamat Datang**	
Goodbye (to the person leaving)	**Selamat Jalan**	
Goodbye (to the person staying)	**Selamat Tinggal**	
Please	**Sila, silakan**	
May I?	**Boleh?**	
Thank you (to which the reply is)	**Terimah Kasih**	
	Sama-sama or **Kenibali.**	
How are you?	**Apa Khabar?**	
I am well thank you	**Khabar baik**	
Yes	**Ya**	
No	**tidak/bukan**	
Never mind, don't worry	**tidak apa, tak apa**	
left	**kiri**	
right	**kanan**	
straight on	**terus**	
stop here	**berhenti di sini**	

As a tourist you are unlikely to need to understand more than Singlish, adapting your English accordingly. Food terms are described on page 258, or you can just point at what you fancy if you prefer. The government is now encouraging the use of Mandarin as opposed to the individual dialects—Hokkien being the most common, though Teochew and Cantonese are also spoken—but the language is so tonal that a quick phrase guide would be meaningless without a 6-month course—and really not necessary for Singapore. Tamil and Hindu are also spoken in Singapore, but again speakers also use English to conduct their business.

If you are planning excursions out of Singapore, a couple of phrases of Malay or Indonesian would prove helpful. These two languages are broadly similar, and speakers of one can generally understand the other, though the Malay usage, particularly in Singapore, is markedly less formal than that in Indonesia.

If you are planning an extensive tour of either country, it is worth buying a phrase book and learning the numbers so you can bargain and shop. In those spots within a day's travel from Singapore, you will usually find enough English speakers to get by, though more so in mainland Malaysia than in the Indonesian Riau archipelago.

A Quick Guide to Local Food

While much of the food on offer in Singapore will probably be recognizable and familiar, particularly to those who regularly eat in Asian restaurants, several dishes and specialities are unique either to Singapore or to the region, and you should try them. You will have to order them using the local term, whether you are ordering in a hawker centre, wayside coffee shop or even in a full-blown restaurant (though some of the international hotel menus do give instant definitions of dishes, as here).

Main Meals—Savoury Dishes

ayam goreng—Malay deep-fried chicken, coated in breadcrumbs and served on the bone.

bak kut teh—Pork soup with chillies and garlic.

bird's nest soup—An expensive delicacy of boiled swiftlet's nests made into a thick and sweet soup: the birds' saliva on the nests is the gourmet's delight.

biryani—An Indian dish also served by Malay stalls and restaurants, comprising specially prepared and coloured rice and a fairly mild chicken or mutton curry, always served on the bone.

carrot cake—A type of omelette, highly spiced with chillies and garlic, of which the "carrot" is in fact a large white radish or "moolie".

century eggs—A Chinese delicacy, often served in rojak (see below), or as part of mixed appetizers in a Cantonese or Szechuan restaurant, these eggs are preserved for a month or more in ash, lime, clay and tea leaves, so that the egg white turns black. They are also said to be preserved in horse's urine, believe it or not!

char kway teow—A Chinese dish of fried flat noodles, the shape of tagliatelle, with onions, chillies, garlic and the odd prawn, spring onion (scallion) and coriander. A beef *char kway teow* is, fairly obviously, this dish with beef. You can have it dry, or in soup. Generally not too spicy, it is essential to add *sambal* to appreciate the true taste of this dish.

char siew fan—Bright red barbecued pork, served with rice, sliced cucumber and soy sauce.

chicken rice—Originally a Hainanese dish, this is a Singaporean speciality. You will receive a plate of rice cooked in chicken stock; a separate plate of chicken—either hot or cold, with or without skin and bones, depending on the cook's preference, but generally in slices or small pieces; a bowl of clear soup; and, the vital ingredient, a small saucer of chilli and garlic sauce to eat with the rice. The ingredients are simple, and the tastes of the ingredients (apart from the sauce) subtle, so all depends on the skill of the cook, the way the chicken is prepared—and the particular mix of the chilli and garlic sauce ingredients to give it a punchy kick.

chilli crab—A real contender for Singapore's best-known dish, this tasty and colourful dish consists of mud crabs baked or fried and served in a rich, often rather sweet chilli and tomato sauce. Order either rice or bread to dunk in the sauce, and take care to wear clothes you don't mind covering in chilli sauce—it is impossible to savour the flavours of this speciality without using your fingers.

A Singaporean speciality—chilli crab—particularly delicious when you dip chunks of white bread into the rich sauce.

curry mixture hits home.

dian xin—Dim sum, a variety of small, dainty and tasty dishes, often steamed, otherwise deep fried.

fish ball soup—A Chinese thin soup, generally with thick noodles, some spring onions (scallions), garlic, coriander and floating white fish balls.

fish-head curry—Sounds disgusting, but do try this dish of curried red snapper or a similarly large oily fish in a bowl of chilli curry. There's a surprising amount of tasty meat on the head of a large fish, and you don't get too bogged down in extracting bones. The eyes are reputed to be the highest delicacy, though I've not yet ventured that far. You'll need the accompanying rice to digest the sauce.

Fish-head curry served on a banana leaf. This is far more appetizing than it sounds!

gado gado—A cucumber and raw red onion salad served with a peanut sauce and fried prawn crackers as a Malay or Indonesian starter or accompaniment to *satay*.

claypot—A means of baking rice, meat and/or vegetables. Originally a means of cooking for the poor of inland China, the result is interesting and delicate, with a different texture from steamed or boiled produce. Try a bean-curd claypot as an accompanying dish in a hawker centre or coffee shop.

Hokkien prawn mee—A dish of noodles (*mee*), with prawns, garlic, onions and perhaps some squid. As with *char kway teow*, you can have it dry or in soup; the soupy version is generally served in a claypot.

congee—Generally a Teochew dish of rice porridge, rather watery and well-cooked rice with a variety of pork sausage, spring onions and the like served with it.

ikan bilis—Deep-fried dried whitebait or anchovies, served with shelled unsalted peanuts as part of a Malay *nasi lemak* (*see* below), or as an appetizer.

ketupat—A tightly packed rice cake, re-boiled in a woven coconut leaf package and served as an accompaniment to *satay*.

curry puff—A savoury pastry case filled with curried chicken, mutton or vegetables, good as a snack or a light lunch. The best curry puffs should have a fiery aftertaste, as the chilli in the

laksa—A Nonya (Straits-born Chinese) dish of spaghetti-sized noodles in a creamy curried coconut sauce, with fried bean curd, bean sprouts, prawn paste and cockles, prawns or meat depending on what's available. Some *laksas* are very hot (with chillies), some are quite mild.

lontong—A rich Malay speciality of vegetables and rice cakes cooked in a curried coconut milk sauce. Eat this for breakfast and you needn't eat for the rest of the day!

masala dosai—A South Indian vegetarian dish, comprising a fried pancake (*dosai*) filled with curried potato and vegetable stuffing, with accompanying pickles and chutneys.

mee goreng—Originally a Malay dish, this dish of spiced and fried noodles is also prepared by Indian hawker stalls and coffee shops, as well as by some Chinese eating houses. Each culture adds its own particular flavour to the dish, which basically consists of spaghetti-sized noodles, fried chillies, garlic, onions and pieces of chicken, occasionally mutton or prawns.

mee rebus—A Malay dish of noodles with beef, chickens or prawns and bean curd served in a spicy brown gravy sauce.

mee siam—A *nonya* mixture of a sweet and sour soya bean and coconut gravy, prawns and thin vermicelli-type noodles.

murtabak—An Indian dish of a large fried eggy *roti prata* (*see* below) fried with either a chicken or mutton filling and served with a fiery curry sauce.

nasi ayam—The Malay dish of chicken rice. Again, the rice is cooked in stock, but rather than being sliced up, in *nasi ayam* the chicken is generally a whole

A prata and murtabak maker on North Bridge Road.

leg or wing and often deep fried.

nasi goreng—A Malay dish of fried (*goreng*) rice (*nasi*), generally containing pieces of prawn, chicken and some vegetables.

nasi lemak—Literally rich rice, a Malay breakfast combination of rice cooked in coconut milk and turmeric (hence its richness), *ikan bilis* (*see* above), *sambal belacan* (*see* below) and vegetables.

nasi padang—This Indonesian and Malay term comes originally from Padang in Sumatra, and is really nothing more than the term to describe a buffet or selection of dishes. You are served rice (*nasi*) and then select from the various curries, fried and barbecued dishes and vegetables you see before you—the *padang* (literally field).

261

otak-otak—An Indonesian or Malay preparation of minced and spiced fish wrapped in a banana leaf and grilled over a *satay*-style grill.

oyster omelette (or chien)—A Chinese dish of, you've guessed it, oysters cooked in an omelette—though not a particularly milky one, since juice from the oysters is added to the mixture, and it is served with a punchy chilli sauce.

popiah—These are small, light pancakes filled with a mixture of bean sprouts, onions, garlic and spices, occasionally mixed with minced meat and chicken. The dish is a Nonya speciality, bearing no more than a passing resemblance to the pancake roll served in Chinese restaurants in the West.

pow—Chinese steamed buns, somewhat like dumplings and slightly glutinous. These are either filled with pork, chicken or beans, or are served as an accompaniment to sweet pork dishes. Szechuan restaurants sometimes deep

An otak-otak seller at Geylang night market during Ramadan.

fry their *pow*, resulting in a delicate crispy crust and a delicious sweet taste.

rendang—A Malay or Indonesian spiced dish, curry-like, though relying largely on lemon grass and chilli, and often quite dry. The most common type is beef *rendang*, though chicken and fish *rendang* are also served. It is particularly good when eaten together with Malay *roti*, though plain rice is a good alternative.

rojak—A dish of vegetables and assorted bits and pieces served in a peanut sauce. Some stalls allow you to choose your own bean curd, Chinese sausage, fish ball, and potato in the sauce.

roti—The Malay and Indian word for bread, which comes in different types—*see* below.

roti John—No one has yet satisfactorily explained the bizarre name of this pleasant dish to me yet. The dish consists of a piece of French bread (baguette) fried in a mixture of garlic, onions, coriander and possibly mutton, served with cucumber and a chilli sauce.

Malay roti—A stringy, doughy pancake, somewhat glutinous and lacy, this yellowish bread is delicious with *rendang* (*see* above).

roti prata—An Indian or Malay pancake, the basis for *murtabak* (*see* above) or it can be eaten plain.

sambal—A fiery chilli, tomato, garlic and *belacan* (dried shrimp paste) sauce, served with a variety of Singaporean, Malay and Indonesian dishes. Try a small piece on some rice so you can gauge how hot it is before smothering the whole plate with it.

satay—These skewers of barbecued marinated chicken, mutton or beef are becoming increasingly familiar to Western eaters, served with a sweet peanut sauce to dip the meat into. *Satay* in Singapore is traditionally a Malay dish (also spelt *sate* in Malay), though you can also find Chinese *satay* stalls—where they may also serve pork. The marinades and the style of cooking are quite distinct as between the Chinese and Malay styles, and the Indonesian sauce is different again, much smoother and less oily than the usual Singapore variety.

satay bee-hoon—A Chinese dish of thin noodles and vegetables served in a peanuty satay sauce, hence the name.

shark's fin soup—Expensive and glutinous textured soup.

A choice of ingredients at a rojak stall. Just point to whatever takes your fancy and you won't be disappointed.

soto ayam—A Malay or Indonesian clear chicken soup with floating vegetables and chunks of chicken.

steamboat—A Chinese type of fondue, with a pot of boiling stock at your table into which the diner puts skewers of meat, fish balls, fish and vegetables until they are cooked. The steamboat is traditionally eaten on Chinese New Year family reunion dinners (*see* page 89).

tahu goreng—Deep-fried (*goreng*) bean curd served in a peanut sauce.

udang sambal—Grilled or steamed whole prawns served in a piquant chilli sauce.

Desserts

Many of the desserts and sweetmeats are extremely sweet, and some of the very vibrant colours not perhaps the most appetizing, but do try some of the following.

Ais Kachang—This colourful concoction, also known as ice *kachang*, is mainly composed of ice shavings with coloured flavourings, jelly, and condensed milk.

Bubor Chacha—A mixture of sweet potato and tapioca boiled in coconut milk.

Bubor Hitam—Black rice pudding with hot coconut milk.

Chendol—A mixture of coconut milk, palm sugar, beans and green jelly served topped with ice and food colourings—more appetizing than it sounds!

Gula Melaka—A mixture of palm sugar, kidney beans, sweet corn, strands of green jelly, condensed milk and ice—yes, this is very sweet and rich.

Kuah Lapis—Literally sweet cake, these come in a variety of forms, and often in vibrant greens, whites and pinks.

Fruits

There is an immense variety of fruits in Singapore, a country where fresh fruit juice is available for $1 or so virtually wherever you stop. As well as the thirst-quenching lime, lemon and orange juices, do try watermelon juice, honeydew juice, guava and sugar-cane juice. Some fruits which may be unfamiliar to visitors to the region are listed below.

Durian—This spiny fruit the size of a pineapple has a malodorous smell at times stomach-turning. It is prized by both Malays and Chinese, and large quantities of durian are imported from Malaysia and Thailand during the two main seasons, March and November. You cannot fail to notice the smell as you pass a stall selling the fruits, or someone eating one, a smell vaguely lavatorial, pungent and slightly sweet. Try a taste if you dare—some people do like it!—but the taste may linger and recur for several hours afterwards.

Jackfruit—Similar, though no quite so pungent as the durian.

Lychee—Small, soft, white fruits enclosed in pink or brown leathery jackets, increasingly familiar in Western markets. The tinned variety is also familiar. Sweet-tasting, sugary and quite refreshing, an almost scented taste.

Papaya—A luxurious fruit with reddish/orange flesh inside an elongated greenish/yellow skin. Slightly larger than a mango when ripe.

A durian seller showing off his fruits. During the durian seasons, make-shift stalls go up all over town offering the malodorous fruit to mainly Chinese and Malay aficionados.

Pomelo—A vastly oversized grapefruit crossed with an orange, sweeter than a grapefruit but often rather tasteless.

Rambutan—A soft, white fruit within a red, hairy skin (*rambut* in Malay means hair). The taste is similar to the lychee. You can see rambutan trees on the way to Malacca in Malaysia, covered in flower-type fruits.

Sour Sop—A spiny green fruit roughly the size of a mango.

Star Fruit—So-called because you cut cross segments which are star shaped, a yellow fairly tasteless fruit used for its decorative qualities, also increasingly popular in the West.

Water Chestnut—A delicately flavoured and slightly crunchy tasting fruit or nut used in a variety of desserts in combination with sago or tapioca.

Vegetables

Brinjal—Aubergines or eggplants, though the variety available here is longer and thinner than those Westerners are familiar with. Malay dishes of *brinjal* are generally prepared in a tomato and chilli curry sauce, so be sure to order rice and enough to drink.

Chinese Cabbage (kangkong)—Known as water convolvulus, this slightly stringy vegetable is reminiscent of spinach stalks. Malay preparations will again include *sambal* or chilli.

Kailan—Another type of Chinese cabbage. Baby *kailan* look and taste rather more interesting than Brussels sprouts, and are commonly served in a sweet oyster sauce in Chinese restaurants.

Information to Help You Have a Good Trip

Singapore is a rapidly changing place: attractions, restaurants, shops, all can change location, phone number or even disappear seemingly overnight. I strongly recommend telephoning before setting out to a club, restaurant, or even to some of the less well-known sights listed below to avoid possible disappointment and wasting time unnecessarily.

Transport Information

By Air

Changi International Airport (Airtropolis)
Civil Aviation Authority of Singapore: 541 1122
Flight Arrivals and Departures (recorded information—just key in your flight number as asked): 542 4422
Flight Information Terminal 1: 542 1234

T he Goodwood Park Hotel on Scotts Road, designed by the same architect as the Raffles Hotel, its historical rival.

Flight Information Terminal 2: 542 6988
Lost Baggage (at airport): Civil Aviation Authority of Singapore 541 2223
Lost Baggage (during flight/on aeroplane/on reclaim belt): Singapore Airport Terminal Services 541 8553 (Terminal 1); 541 8872 (Terminal 2)

Some Major Airline Reservations and Reconfirmation Numbers
Air New Zealand: 535 8266
Alitalia: 737 3166
American Airlines: 221 6988
British Airways: 253 8444
Cathay Pacific Airways: 533 1333
Garuda Indonesia: 250 2888
Japan Air Lines: 221 0522
KLM Royal Dutch Airlines: 737 7622

Lufthansa: 737 9222
Malaysian Airline System: 336 6777
NorthWest Airlines: 235 7166
Qantas Airways: 737 3744
Royal Brunei Airlines: 235 4672
Singapore Airlines: 223 8888
Thai Airways International: 224 9977
TWA: 298 9911
United Airlines: 220 0711

Flights to Tioman Island
Pelangi Airline: 481 6302
Seletar Airport General Office: 481 3632

Helicopter Sightseeing Trips of Singapore
Safe Travel: 220 8866

By Sea

Cruises
Many of the long-distance cruises which call in on Singapore are operated by foreign companies, with a local handling company or agent only in Singapore. Here are contact numbers for a few of these companies:

Jetset Holidays: 223 3366
5-day return cruises to Jakarta aboard the Cora Princess or Orient Sun; 2-day "cruises to nowhere" aboard the Andaman Princess.

Mansfield Travel Pte Ltd: 224 0000
The Sea Goddess II spends each winter based in Singapore, cruising to Pulau Pangkor, Malacca and other Malaysian ports, up to Phuket in Thailand, as well as to Indonesian destinations, before returning via Bombay to cruise the Mediterranean during the summer.

Seven Seas Cruises Pte Ltd: 227 3310
Catering mainly for a Japanese clientele, the Song of Flower cruises from Singapore to destinations in Thailand, Malaysia and Indonesia.

World Express Travel: 336 3877
The Ocean Pearl cruises to different destinations in Thailand, Malaysia, Brunei, the Philippines, Hong Kong and China.

Ferry Services

To Batam and Bintan Islands
The ferries all depart from The Singapore Cruise Centre at the World Trade Centre; times may change from those advertised by the ferry companies, so check first. Beware of buying a return ticket as you may wish to return with another company: the tickets are not interchangeable. Ferries leave almost hourly for Batam, from 9.00 a.m. to 5.00 p.m.; less-frequent services run to Bintan, some direct, some via Batam.

To Tioman Island
The Tioman Connection catamaran runs 6 days a week (not Wednesdays), departing from The Singapore Cruise Centre at 7.40 a.m., and leaving Tioman Island at 1.30 p.m., generally taking $4\frac{1}{2}$ hours subject to weather. Bookings can be made through:

Tioman Island Resort
11-09 Orchard Towers
400 Orchard Road
Singapore 0923
Telephone: 733 5488, Fax: 733 5487
Telex: RS 33353 TIOMAN
which can also arrange accommoda-

tion; or through Resort Cruises (S) Pte Ltd, Telephone: 278 4677.

To Malaysia and Batam
The Equator Triangle catamaran tours from The Singapore Cruise Centre to Batam and then to Tanjong Belungkor (a 25 minute coach ride from Desaru resort) daily. Contact:

J & N Cruises
1 Maritime Square #@12-04
World Trade Centre (Lobby B)
Singapore 0409
Telephone: 270 7100.

Changi Point Ferry Terminal, currently under construction, is scheduled to be fully operational by September 1992, and will greatly reduce ferry times to destinations in Johor state.

By Land

Long Distance Buses
The long distance bus stop, for destinations in mainland Malaysia, is located on vacant land at the junction of Lavender Street and Kallang Bahru, Telephone: 293 5915

Railway Trains
Keppel Road Railway Station
Passenger Trains Booking and Fare
  Enquiries
Telephone: 222 5165

Long Distance Taxis
Singapore taxis cannot drive in Malaysia. For Malaysian taxis, go to the Ban San Terminal at the corner of Queen and Arab Streets, or use the Kuala Lumpur taxi service (telephone: 223 1889).

Public Transport Within Singapore

Taxi Services
NTUC Comfort 452 5555
Singapore Commuters 474 7707

Taxis surcharge for phone booking, trips to and from Changi International Airport, entering or leaving the CBD during its operational hours, and for late-night commissions.

You can flag down any kind of taxi in most places in Singapore, though some may not stop on very busy thoroughfares or when approaching a taxi stand. When travelling by taxi, don't be alarmed if you hear an uneven jingling bell sound from the dashboard: most cabs in Singapore are fitted with this anti-speeding device, and many drivers ignore it.

MRT (Mass Rapid Transit)
Information Centre: 336 8900
  Lost Property Station Control Room, Orchard Station: 235 5969
The MRT system is easy to use, with maps at every station. Either purchase a single ticket from the machines, or buy a stored value travelcard to allow several journeys on the same ticket. A guide to the MRT is available in all bookshops, giving the nearest stations, connecting buses and locality maps.

Singapore Buses
Singapore Bus Services: 287 2727
You do need to have the exact small change when boarding a bus: drivers do not carry change. Either buy individual tickets or purchase an Explorer ticket for either one or three days

unlimited travel or a Transit Card, valid for both buses and MRT. A useful Bus Guide is published annually, available at all stationers and bookshops, detailing exact routes.

Trishaws

You can flag down a trishaw wherever you see one, but take care to agree the fare before the trip, since these are high for tourists (generally in the region of $30 for a half-hour trip). Alternatively, go on an organized trishaw tour.

Driving

Central Business District (CBD) Licensing Scheme

Operating Hours: Monday–Friday 7.30 a.m.–10.15 a.m., 4.30 p.m.–6.30 p.m.; Saturdays 7.30 a.m.–10.15 a.m. Not operational on public holidays.

You must have a daily or monthly licence in order to drive into the restricted zone during its operational hours; failure to display one results in a hefty fine. Daily licences can be purchased from post offices or area licence booths, sign-posted on approach roads.

Parking Regulations

There are very few places where it is possible to park without paying in Singapore, and traffic wardens and traffic police regularly check compliance. You should not park where there is a double or single yellow line along the side of the road, or where there is a continuous white line in the middle of the road, on a freeway or dual carriageway, or in a taxi or bus stand. There is long-term parking at Changi Airport.

URA Parking Areas

Coupons in denominations of 40 or 80 cents need to be displayed in these areas, validated with the correct date and time of parking for as long as you intend to stay. Coupons can be purchased in garages, roadside booths, select stationery and grocery outlets. URA parking areas within the Central Business District generally charge 80 cents per half hour; those outside it generally charge 40 cents per half hour; parking in these areas is for a minimum of half an hour—you cannot only stay for 15 minutes and pay half the amount.

Car Hire Companies

There are numerous car rental companies in Singapore, which you can easily check and compare by browsing through the Singapore Buying Guide Yellow Pages. Different companies will vary their rates, and their policies on whether you can drive the vehicles in Malaysia, and it generally works out at around 20 per cent cheaper to hire a car in nearby Johor Baru if you are planning a driving holiday across the causeway.

Here is a brief selection of car-hire companies:

Avis Rent-a-Car, Telephone: 737 1668, (Johor Baru office 07 237 971)
Hertz, Telephone: 447 3388, (Johor Baru office 07 237 520)
Thrifty Car Rental, Telephone: 235 5855, (Johor Baru office 07 332 313)

Cable Car Services

From Mount Faber to World Trade Centre and Sentosa Cable Car Station Mondays–Saturdays: 10 a.m.–7 p.m.; Sundays and Public Holidays 9 a.m.–7 p.m.

Singapore River Trips

Eastwind Organization, Clifford Pier
Telephone: 533 3432
One-hour long river cruises at 10 a.m., 12 noon, 2 p.m. and 4 p.m. daily, subject to tides.

Singapore River Cruises, Parliament House Landing Steps, Boat Quay
Telephone: 336 6119
20 minute river cruises daily from 9 a.m.–7 p.m.

A river water taxi service is scheduled to start operations in 1992, run by Singapore River Cruises and Leisure Pte. This will service riverside hotels such as the Hotel New Otani and the River View Hotel.

Ferry Services

To Sentosa Island
Monday–Thursday: Ferries depart World Trade Centre every 15 minutes from 7.30 a.m. to 10.45 p.m.; ferries depart Sentosa ferry terminal every 15 minutes from 7.45 a.m–11 p.m

Fridays–Sundays, eves of public holidays and public holidays: ferries leave World Trade Centre every 15 minutes from 7.30 a.m.–11p.m.; ferries depart Sentosa Ferry Terminal every 15 minutes from 7.45 a.m.–11.15 p.m.; last ferry departs Sentosa midnight. (For further information on Sentosa Ferry

Services, contact the Sentosa Information Office: 270 7888.)

To St John's Island via Kusu Island
Monday–Saturday: Ferries depart World Trade Centre 10.00 a.m. and 1.30 p.m.; ferries depart St John's Island 11.15 a.m. and 2.45 p.m.; ferries depart Kusu Island 11.45 a.m. and 3.15 p.m.;

Sundays and public holidays (except Kusu season) ferries depart World Trade Centre every 1½ hours from 9.10 a.m.–7.40 p.m., returning every 1½ hours from 10.00 a.m.–8.30 p.m. from St John's Island, and from 9.45 a.m.– 8.15 p.m. from Kusu Island.

(Telephone 321 2198 for further information on ferry times, except during Kusu season (October/November) when ferries operate from Clifford Pier.)

To Pulau Ubin
Bumboats leave Changi pier at irregular intervals throughout the day when there are enough passengers—generally every 40 minutes or so.

Singapore Island Cruises

Eastwind Organization, Clifford Pier
Telephone 533 3432
4 cruises a day in an old-fashioned Chinese junk at 10.30 a.m., 3 p.m., 4 p.m. and 6 p.m.

J & N Cruises
1 Maritime Square #12-04
World Trade Centre
Singapore 0409
Telephone: 270 7100

5 cruises daily: 12.30 p.m. (lunch), 3.00 p.m. (high tea), 6.00 p.m. (dinner), 7.00 p.m. (sunset), 10.30 p.m. (disco).

Tai Pan Cruises
2A Clifford Pier, Collyer Quay
Singapore 0104
Telephone 532 4497–6
Cruises in Chinese-style cruise ship (air-conditioned main deck plus open sun deck) at 9.30 a.m., 12.30 p.m. (weekends only), 2.30 p.m., 5.30 p.m., 7.30 p.m. and 10 p.m.

Tour East
Clifford Pier
Telephone 235 5703
Tours of the southern islands by bumboat on Tuesdays, Thursdays and Saturdays, minimum 4 persons.

Watertours Pte Ltd
3-A, 1st Floor, Clifford Pier
Singapore 0104
Telephone: 533 9811
Fax: 535 7743
3 cruises daily—lunch, high tea and dinner—leaving at 12.30 p.m., 3.00 p.m. and 6.30 p.m., in the imperial-style vessel Cheng Ho; also Chinese junk cruises at 10.30 a.m., 3.00 p.m. and 6.00 p.m.

Shopping Guide

Main Shopping Malls
Tanglin Shopping Centre
Tanglin Road
Antiques and handicrafts imported from throughout the region; antique prints; carpets; souvenir shops; tailors and dressmakers.

DFS Tanglin Collections
Tanglin Road
Designer wear, duty-free goods.
Delfi Orchard
Orchard Road
Designer wear and fashion boutiques.
Orchard Parade Hotel
Tanglin Road
Jim Thomson silk—fabrics, clothes and gifts.
Delfi Orchard
Orchard Road
Fashion boutiques.
Palais Renaissance
Orchard Road
Fashion boutiques.
Forum Galleria
Orchard Road
Clothing—international chains (Benetton, Faconnable), Toys 'R Us, Electric City fixed price electrical.
Far East Shopping Centre
Orchard Road
Reptile products, souvenir shops, tailors, cameras, golf equipment.
Liat Towers
Orchard Road
Large branch of Galleries Lafayette.
Orchard Towers
Orchard Road
Bookshop, cameras and audio, tailors, money changers. Food court in basement.
International Plaza
Orchard Road
Fashion boutiques, restaurants.
Shaw Centre
Scotts Road
Antiques, clothing boutiques, discs and records, shoes, sportswear and equipment including equestrian and scuba.
Scotts
Scotts Road
Boutiques and international clothing

chains, Tangs Studio designer fashions, St Michael, Cost Plus fixed price electricals, tourist information; food court and mini supermarket; temporary exhibitions in ground level foyer.

Far East Plaza
Scotts Road
Electrical goods and cameras, restaurants, hairdressers, jeans and teeshirts, leather goods, watches, carpets, Metro department store.

Tangs Department Store
Orchard Road
Batiks and silks, gifts and antiques, household goods, clothing, linen, restaurants, post office, ticket counter.

Lucky Plaza
Orchard Road
Electrical goods, cameras, shoes, watches (including "copy watches" although they are officially outlawed), jewellery. Do be sure to bargain and ask for the "best price". A large branch of Metro department store, restaurants and fast food outlets.

Wisma Atria
Orchard Road
Boutiques, Isetan department store including supermarket, bookstores, sports, hairdressers, antiques and crafts, restaurants.

Promenade
Orchard Road
Clothing boutiques arranged on curious upward spiral—ideal for wheelchairs or skateboards!

Paragon
Orchard Road
Boutiques, international chains and accessory shops like Dunhill, Wedgwood tea rooms, Metro department store.

Orchard Shopping Centre
Orchard Road
Clothing boutiques.

Orchard Midpoint
Orchard Road
Toys, watches, clothes, swimwear, food outlets.

Orchard OG
Orchard Road
Branch of local department store.

Orchard Emerald
Orchard Road
Watches, clothes, cameras, swimwear, small scale handicrafts stalls, food court in basement.

Specialists Centre
Orchard Road
John Little department store, golf and sports shops including bowling accessories, clothing boutiques.

Centrepoint
Orchard Road
Robinsons department store, bookshops, basement supermarket, restaurants, antiques, carpets, furnishings, discs and records, camera and audio, clothing, ticket counter, Marks and Spencer flagship shop.

Cuppage Centre
Cavenagh Road
Market, food centre, shops leading to Centrepoint.

Meridien Shopping Centre
Orchard Road
Fashion boutiques.

Plaza Singapura
Oldham Lane
Yaohan department store, cameras, stereo equipment.

Singapore Shopping Centre
Penang Lane
Restaurants, small scale tailors and dressmakers.

Park Mall
Penang Lane
Restaurants, designer boutiques including maternity and children's.

Raffles City
Stamford Road
Sogo department store, camera and audio outlets, clothing, Marks & Spencer, tourist information, restaurants.

Marina Square
Raffles Boulevard
Metro and Tokyu department stores, gifts, books, clothing, Habitat and Mothercare, posters, antiques.

Peninsula Plaza
North Bridge Road
Cameras and audio equipment, clothing, bookshop, stationery.

Excelsior Shopping Centre
Coleman Street
Indian fabrics, gifts and furniture.

Funan Centre
Coleman Street
Computer software and accessories, bookshop, food court.

OUB Centre
Raffles Place
Restaurants and fast food outlets, computers, printers, books, clothing, cards, clothing and boutiques, tailors, hairdressers.

The Arcade
Raffles Place
Photography, clothing, Marks & Spencer.

Chinatown Point
South Bridge Road
Handicrafts, clothing, gifts and souvenirs.

People's Park Centre
Upper Cross Street
Fabrics, clothing, restaurants, audio and cameras, Oriental Emporium department store.

Liang Court
River Valley Road
Yaohan department store, clothing, restaurants and food outlets.

Sim Lim Square
Rochor Canal Road
Computer hardware and accessories, software, cameras and audio equipment, TV, telephones.

Parkway Parade
Marine Parade Road
Restaurants, clothing, discs and records, books, shoes, Isetan department store.

Other Areas to Shop
Arab Street
Fabrics, especially batiks and silks, scarves, gold and jewellery, basketware.

Little India
Gold and jewellery, fabrics, spices.

Chinatown
Souvenirs, silks, kites, hats, clothing, spices, Chinese medicinal herbs.

Raffles
Designer boutiques, up-market jewellery and watches, merchandising, souvenirs, books, gifts, antiques.

Holland Village
Restaurants, porcelain, clothing, Oriental Emporium department store, antiques, caneware, Cost Plus fixed price electronics.

Tanjong Pagar Restoration Area
Souvenirs, antiques, bric-à-brac, tee-shirts, handicrafts.

Where to Buy Goods
Antiques
Holland Village, Shaw Centre, Tanglin Shopping Centre, Tangs, Tanjong Pagar.

Audio Equipment
Centrepoint, Forum Galleria, Holland Village, Lucky Plaza, Plaza Singapura, Scotts.

Books
Centrepoint, Eu Court, Holland Village, Lucky Plaza, MPH buildings, Orchard Towers, Raffles, Specialists Centre, Wisma Atria.

Cameras
Far East Plaza, Far East Shopping Centre, Forum Galleria, Holland Village, Lucky Plaza, Orchard Towers, Scotts, Sim Lim Plaza.

Chemists
Guardian Pharmacy outlets: Centrepoint, Holland Village, Orchard Towers, Plaza Singapura, Peninsula Plaza, Promenade, Raffles City, Tanglin Shopping Centre, Wisma Atria.

China and Porcelain
Holland Village, Tanglin Shopping Centre, Tangs.

Clothing–Casual
Centrepoint, Chinatown Point, Far East Plaza, Lucky Plaza, Parkway Parade, Tangs, Wisma Atria.

Clothing–Designer Fashions
Delfi/DFS, International Plaza, Le Meridien, Orchard Plaza, Palais Renaissance, Paragon, Park Mall, Promenade, Raffles, Specialists Centre.

Clothing–International Chains
Forum Galleria, "Raffles", Scotts, Shaw Centre, Wisma Atria.

Computers and Accessories
Funan Centre, OUB Centre, Sim Lim Square.

Fabrics
Arab Street, Little India, Orchard Plaza, Jim Thomson Silk at Orchard Parade Hotel and Raffles, People's Park, Tangs.

Gifts
Lucky Plaza, Raffles, Selangor Pewter Museum, Shaw Centre, Tangs.

Handicrafts
Chinatown Point, Orchard Emerald, Tanglin Shopping Centre, Tangs.

Jewellery
Little India, Raffles.

Leather Goods
Far East Shopping Centre.

Opticians
Centrepoint, Lucky Plaza, Orchard Towers.

Post Offices
Chinatown Point, Fullerton Building (Raffles Place), Tanglin (near Marco Polo Hotel), Raffles City, Tangs, World Trade Centre.

Shoes
Lucky Plaza, Orchard Towers.

Souvenirs
Chinatown Point, Far East Shopping Centre, Lucky Plaza, Raffles, Tanglin Shopping Centre.

Sporting Goods
Centrepoint, Far East Shopping Centre, Orchard Shopping Centre, Shaw Towers, Wisma Atria.

Supermarkets
Jasons Supermarket, Orchard Towers; Cold Storage outlets in Centrepoint, Holland Village, Promenade, World Trade Centre.

Tailors and Dressmakers
Lucky Plaza, Orchard Towers, OUB Centre, Tanglin Shopping Centre.

Tourist Information
Raffles City, Scotts.

Watches
Lucky Plaza, Raffles, Shaw Towers.

Singapore Tourist Promotion Board

Australia
8th Floor, St George's Court
16 St George's Terrace
Perth
Western Australia 6000
Australia
Tel: (09) 325 8578/325 8511
Telex: AA 197542
Fax: (09) 221 3864

Suite 1604, Level 16, Westpac
Plaza
60 Margaret Street
Sydney
New South Wales 2000
Australia
Tel: (02) 241 3771/2
Telex: STBSYD AA 127775
Fax: (02) 252 3586

Canada
175 Bloor Street East, Suite 1112
North Tower
Toronto
Ontario M4W 3R8
Canada
Tel: (416) 323 9139
Telex: (06) 217510 SINGA POR
TOR
Fax: (416) 323 3514

Europe
L'Office National du Tourisme
de Singapour
Centre d'Affaires Le Louvre
2 Place du Palais-Royal
75044 Paris Cedex 01
France
Tel: (01) 4297 16 16
Telex: SINGPAR 213593F
Fax: (01) 4297 16 17

Fremdenverkehrburo von
Singapur
Poststrasse 2-4
D-6000 Frankfurt am Main
Germany
Tel: (069) 231 456/7
Telex: STBF D 4189742
Fax: (069) 233 924

Fremdenverkehrburo von
Singapur
Hochstrasse 48
CH-8044 Zurich
Switzerland
Tel: (01) 252 5365
Fax: (01) 252 5303

1st Floor, Carrington House
126-130 Regent Street
London W1R 5FE
United Kingdom
Tel: (071) 437 0033
Telex: STBLON G 893 491
Fax: (071) 734 2191

New Zealand
STPB Representative Office
c/o Walshes World
2nd Floor, Dingwall Building
87 Queen Street
P. O. Box 279
Auckland 1
New Zealand
Tel: (09) 793 708
Telex: WALWOR NZ 21437
Fax: (09) 302 2420

Singapore
Raffles City Tower
250 North Bridge Road #36-04
Singapore 0617
Tel: 339 6622
Telex: STBSIN RS 33375
Fax: 339 9423

United States of America
333 North Michigan Avenue,
Suite 818
Chicago
Illinois 60601
USA
Tel: (312) 220 0099
Telex: SINGPOR TB CGO
798975
Fax: (312) 2200 020

8484 Wilshire Boulevard
Suite 510
Beverly Hills
Los Angeles
California 90211
USA
Tel: (213) 852 1901
Telex: SING-UR 278141
Fax: (213) 852 0129

590 Fifth Avenue, 12th Floor,
New York
NY 10036
USA
Tel: (212) 302 4861
Telex: SING-UR 220843
Fax: (212) 302 4801

Indonesian Tourist Promotion Offices

Australia
Public Relations Agency
Garuda Indonesia Airways Office
4 Bligh Street

P. O. Box 3836
Sydney 200
New South Wales
Australia
Tel: 232 6044
Telex: 22576

Europe
Indonesia Tourist Promotion Office
Wiessenhutten Strasse 17
D-6000 Frankfurt am Main 1
Germany
Tel: (0611) 243 681
Telex: 041 189186 ITIPOD
Cable: INDOTOUR

Japan
Indonesia Tourist Promotion
Office
Asia Trans Co. 2nd Floor
Sankaido Building
1-9-13 Akasaka Minato-ku
Tokyo
Japan
Tel: 585 3588/582 1331 ext. 15-16
Telex: 2422390 ATRANS
Cable: ASTRAJUG TOKYO

Singapore
Indonesia Tourist Promotion Office
10 Collyer Quay
15–17 Ocean Building
Singapore 0104
Tel: 534 2837
Telex: RS 35731
Fax: 533 4287

United States of America
Indonesia Tourist Promotion Office
3457 Wilshire Bldv
Los Angeles
CA 90010
U.S.A.
Tel: (213) 387 2078
Telex: 18292 INDOTOUR LAX

Malaysia Tourism Promotion Board

Australia
Malaysia Tourism Promotion
Board
56 William Street
Perth
Western Australia 6000
Australia
Tel: (09) 481 0400
Telex: AA 197033
Fax: (09) 321 1421

Malaysia Tourism Promotion
Board
65 York Street
Sydney
New South Wales 2000
Australia
Tel: 276 29441/2
Telex: 24675 MTDCAA
Fax: 672 262206

Canada

Malaysia Tourism Promotion
Board
830 Burrard Street
Vancouver
British Columbia
Canada V6Z ZK4
Tel: (1604) 689 8899
Telex: 671 4719 MTICUM
Fax: (1604) 689 8804

Europe

Malaysia Tourism Promotion
Board
29 rue des Pyramides
75001 Paris
France
Tel: (331) 429 4171
Telex: 650 706F
Fax: (02) 535 6650

Malaysia Tourism Promotion
Board
Rossmark 11
6000 Frankfurt Am Main
Germany
Tel: (069) 283 782/ 283 783
Telex: 418 9674 TDCD
Fax: (069) 285 215

Malaysia Tourism Promotion
Board
57 Trafalgar Square
London WC2N 5DU
United Kingdom
Tel: (071) 930 7932
Telex: (51) 299 659 MTDC LOG
Fax: (071) 930 9015

Hong Kong

Malaysia Tourism Promotion
Board
Ground Floor, Malaysia Building
No. 47–50 Gloucester Road
Hong Kong
Tel: (5) 528 5810/11
Telex: 82165 TDCHK HX
Fax: 865 4610

Japan

Malaysia Tourism Promotion
Board
2nd Floor
Nichiginmae
Kyodo Building
3-2-4 Nihombashi-Hongokucho

Chuo-ku
Tokyo 103
Japan
Tel: (03) 279 3081
Telex: (72) 27596 MINJ
Fax: (02) 535 6650

Singapore

Malaysia Tourism Promotion
Board
10 Collyer Quay #01-03
Ocean Building
Singapore 0104
Tel: 532 6351
Telex: 29201 RSTDCMAL
Fax: 535 6650

Taiwan

Malaysia Tourism Promotion
Board
1-2F, 147, Sec. 1
Fu Hsings Road
Taipei
Taiwan
Tel: (02) 7400532-3
Telex: 21899 MAFTEC
Fax: (02) 7400534

Thailand

Malaysia Tourism Promotion
Board
Ground Floor
315 South East Insurance Build-
ing
Silom Road
Bangkok 10500
Thailand
Tel: 236 7606/ 236 2832
Telex: LAYANG 82737
Fax: 236 2832

United States of America

Malaysia Tourism Promotion
Board
818 West 7th Street
Los Angeles
CA 90017
U.S.A.
Tel: (213) 689 9702
Telex: 671 4719
Fax: (213) 689 1530

High Commissions and Embassies in Singapore

American Embassy

30 Hill Street, Singapore 0617
Telephone: 338 0251
Fax: 338 4550

Australian High Commission

25 Napier Road, Singapore 1025
Telephone: 737 9311
Telex: RS 21238 AUSTCOM
Cable: AUSTCOM

British High Commission

Tanglin Road, Singapore 1024
Telephone: 473 9333
Fax: 475 2320
Telex: RS 21218 UKREPSP

Canadian High Commission

80 Anson Road #14-00, Singa-
pore 0207
Telephone: 225 6363
Fax: 225 2450
Telex: RS 21277

French Embassy

5 Gallop Road, Singapore
Telephone: 466 4866

German Embassy

#14-01 Far East Shopping Cen-
tre,
545 Orchard Road, Singapore
0923
Telephone: 737 1355
Telex: RS 21312 AASPUR

Indonesian Embassy

7 Chatsworth Road, Singapore
1024
Telephone: 737 7422

Malaysian High Commission

301 Jervois Road, Singapore
Telephone: 235 0111
Fax: 733 6135

New Zealand High Commission

13 Nassim Road, Singapore 1025
Telephone: 235 9966
Telex: RS 21244
Fax: 733 9924

Thailand Embassy

370 Orchard Road, Singapore
0923
Telephone: 737 2644
Fax: 732 0778
(also contains the Thailand
Tourist Bureau)

The Right Place at the Right Price

Hotels

Facilities and hotels are constantly being built and upgraded in Singapore, so double check this information before arriving. Much of the hotel accommodation is of a reasonably high standard, some is exceptionally good, and there remain the bottom end of the market doss-houses.

Here is a select list of some of the main hotels within all but the cheapest price range. They have been graded into top of the range (∎∎∎); moderately priced (∎∎); and reasonable and fairly comfortable(∎). Prices at any one hotel can vary enormously but you should be able to find a room within the price bracket shown by the grading. However, you can pay much more, particularly in the top of the range hotels. Price ranges are given for a double or twin room and should be used as a guide only.

∎ under $200;
∎∎ $2–400;
∎∎∎ over $400.

Allson Hotel ∎∎
101 Victoria Street
Singapore 0718
Tel: 336 0811; Fax: 339 7019
Telex: RS 21151 ALLSON
460 rooms and suites. Six restaurants. Near to Bugis Street and Arab Street.

Amara Hotel ∎∎
165 Tanjong Pagar Road
Singapore 0208
Tel: 224 4488; Fax: 224 3910
Telex: RS 55887 AMARA
350 rooms and suites. Restaurants: local and Western, sandwich bar, Szechuan, Thai, steamboat, North Indian; bar and lobby. Conveniently located for the Business District, within easy reach of Chinatown. Renowned for choice of restaurants.

Ana Hotel Singapore ∎∎
16 Nassim Hill
Singapore 1025
Tel: 235 6560; Fax: 737 6684
Telex: RS 21817/33545 ANAHSIN
456 rooms and suites. Restaurants: Western, Japanese, cafe, snack bar; pub and disco; cocktail bar. Has been recently upgraded. Despite its off-puttingly drab brown exterior, it is nicely finished inside and has a reputation for a high degree of service, as well as for extremely good value Japanese buffet lunches.

Apollo Hotel ∎∎
405 Havelock Road
Singapore 0316
Tel: 733 2081; Fax: 733 1588
Telex: RS 21077
Cable: APOLLO SINGAPORE
345 rooms. Restaurants: Indonesian, Japanese, Chinese, coffee shop, night club. Reasonably priced hotel near the Singapore River, well placed for the city district.

Hotel Asia ∎
37 Scotts Road
Singapore 0922
Tel: 737 8388; Fax: 733 3563
Telex: RS 24313
146 rooms. Restaurants: Chinese, coffee shop.

Bayview Inn Singapore ∎
30 Bencoolen Street
Singapore 0718
Tel: 337 2882; Fax: 338 2880
Telex: RS 26965 BAYINN
117 rooms. Two Restaurants.

Hotel Bencoolen ∎
47 Bencoolen Street
Singapore 0718
Tel: 336 0822; Fax: 336 4384
Telex: RS 42380 HOTBEN
68 rooms. Coffee shop.

Boulevard Hotel ∎∎
200 Orchard Boulevard
Singapore 1024
Tel: 737 2911; Fax: 737 8449
Telex: BOUTEL RS 21771
512 rooms and suites. Restaurants: Continental, coffee shop, lounge bar. Parallel to Orchard Road. Owned by the Goodwood Park Hotel chain.

Cairnhill Hotel ∎
19 Cairnhill Circle
Singapore 0922
Tel: 734 6622; Fax: 235 5598
Telex: RS 26742
Cable: CANHILL
220 rooms and suites. Restaurants: Chinese, coffee shop. Lounge. A 5-minute taxi ride from the main shopping area.

The Carlton Hotel ∎∎
76 Bras Basah Road
Singapore 0738
Tel: 338 8333; Fax: 339 6866
Telex: RS 42076 CARLHO
400 rooms and 20 suites. Restaurants: Continental, Cantonese and coffee shop. Wine bar and lounge bar. Within walking distance of the Padang and the Raffles Hotel; well placed for Bugis Street and Arab Street.

Cockpit Hotel ▮▮
6–7 Oxley Rise
Singapore 0923
Tel: 737 9111; Fax: 737 3105
Telex: RS 21366
Cable: COCKPIT
176 rooms. Restaurants: Szechuan and Cantonese, local and Continental, seafood barbecue; bar; disco. Has the ex-Raffles Hotel barman, so now offers visitors "the authentic Singapore Sling", and hosts nightly and some morning cultural shows of "Instant Asia".

Concorde Hotel ▮▮
317 Outram Road
Singapore 0316
Tel: 733 0188; Fax: 733 9588
Telex: RS 50141 CHSIN
Cable: CONCORDE
515 rooms and suites. Restaurants: Cantonese, coffee shop; lounge. Recently revamped and tailored for the business traveller; situated close to the Central Business District.

Crown Prince Hotel ▮▮
270 Orchard Road
Singapore 0923
Tel: 732 1111; Fax: 732 7018
Telex: RS 22819 HCROWN
Cable: CROWNHOTEL
288 rooms and 15 suites. Restaurants: Sichuan, Sushi and Sashimi, coffee shop. Centrally placed.

The Duxton ▮▮
83 Duxton Road
Singapore 0208
Tel: 227 7678; Fax: 227 1232
49 rooms and suites. French restaurant; lobby bar. Offers old-world hospitality for those who don't have the budget for the Goodwood or Raffles. Tastefully furnished, it aims to be a "boutique hotel" with a staff/guest ratio of 1:1.

The Dynasty Hotel ▮▮
320 Orchard Road
Singapore 0922
Tel: 235 4188; Fax: 733 5251
Telex: 733 2563
400 rooms. Restaurants: French, Chinese, coffee house. Above the Tangs Department Store.

Hotel Equatorial ▮
429 Bukit Timah Road
Singapore 1025
Tel: 732 0431; Fax: 737 9426
Telex: RS 21578 EQUATOR
228 rooms and suites. Restaurants: Swiss and Continental, Szechuan,

Japanese, coffee house; Chinese tea house; lobby bar. Swimming pool; tours arranged. Popular with both Singaporeans and Malaysian visitors for its various restaurants.*

Furama Hotel ▮▮
60 Eu Tong Sen Street
Singapore 0105
Tel: 533 3888; Fax: 534 1489
Telex: RS 28592 FURAMA
354 rooms. Restaurants: Chinese, Japanese, coffee shop.

Golden Landmark Hotel ▮
390 Victoria Street
Singapore 0718
Tel: 297 2828; Fax: 298 2038
393 rooms. Restaurants: Indonesian, coffee shop.

Goodwood Park Hotel ▮▮▮
22 Scotts Road
Singapore 0922
Tel: 737 7411; Fax: 732 8558
Telex: RS 24377 GOODTEL
Cable: GOODWOOD
235 rooms and suites. Restaurants: Western, Sichuan, Shanghainese, Japanese, Seafood; two coffee shops. Various famous stars have stayed here, enjoying the colonial-style grandeur, the Germanic-style architecture, and courteous 5-star service. One of the sights of Singapore; sample the restored nostalgia by having tea here, or by visiting one of the restaurants or the Highland Bar.

Harbour View Dai-ichi Hotel ▮▮
81 Anson Road
Singapore 0207
Tel: 224 1133; Fax: 222 0749
Telex: RS 40163 DAISIN
Cable: DAISIN
420 rooms. Restaurants: Japanese, Continental, coffee house, centrally placed business hotel.

Hilton International ▮▮▮
581 Orchard Road
Singapore 0923
Tel: 737 2233; Fax: 732 2917
Telex: RS 21491 HILTELS
Cable: HILTELS, SINGAPORE
435 rooms and suites. Restaurants: French, Cantonese, coffee shop, Western/Muslim; tea-room cum disco. Tours from hotel. Spacious and elegant style. The high-class mezzanine shopping arcade often hosts art or photographic exhibitions; plays are staged every few months with a pre-theatre dinner as part of your ticket.

Holiday Inn Park View ▮▮
11 Cavenagh Road
Singapore 0922
Tel: 733 8333; Fax: 734 4593
Telex: RS 55420 HIPV
Cable: HOINPAVIEW
320 rooms and suites. Restaurants: Tandoori, Cantonese, Continental, coffee shop; cocktail lounge, bakeshop. Very conveniently located next to the Istana and directly overlooking the new Central Expressway.

Hyatt Regency ▮▮▮
10–12 Scotts Road
Singapore 0922
Tel: 733 1188; Fax: 732 1696
Telex: RS 24415
317 rooms and 421 suites. Restaurants: American, Italian, Cantonese, coffee shop; disco and two bars. Tours from hotel. A pleasant centrally placed hotel with a new Regency Suite Tower—Singapore's only all-suite tower. When first completed, the front doors were changed and placed at an angle to Scotts Road on a geomancer's advice.

Hotel Imperial Singapore ▮▮
1 Jalan Rumbia
Singapore 0923
Tel: 737 1666; Fax: 737 4761
Telex: RS 21654 IMPHTL
600 rooms. Restaurants: Continental, north Indian, Chinese, coffee shop. Lounge, bar, disco. Well placed for visits to Fort Canning, the Orchard Road shops and all central locations.

The Inn of Sixth Happiness ▮▮
33 Erskine Road
Singapore 0106
Tel: 223 3266; Fax: 223 7951
48 rooms. Restaurants: Chinese tea room, Italian; pub. Running along the top storey of a row of restored shophouses, each room is elegantly furnished, many items being antiques. All mod cons are there too. The staff pride themselves on the friendly service.

Mandarin Hotel ▮▮
333 Orchard Road
Singapore 0923
Tel: 737 4411; Fax: 732 2361
Telex: RS 21528 MANOTEL
1,200 rooms and suites. Restaurants: Western, Continental, coffee shop, Japanese, Beijing, English; two bars and mezzanine lounge; two nightclubs. Central location for shoppers.

Marina Mandarin ▮▮
6 Raffles Boulevard
Marina Square
Singapore 0103
Tel: 338 3388; Fax: 339 4977
Telex: RS 22299 MARINA
575 rooms and suites. Restaurants: Cantonese, Italian, Western and local; pub, two bars; nightclub. Views over the Padang and out over Marina Bay. Well placed for business travellers and tourists alike.

Le Meridien Changi ▮▮
1 Netheravon Road
Singapore 1750
Tel: 542 7700; Fax: 542 5295
Telex: RS 36042 HOMRA
280 rooms and suites. Restaurants: coffee house, brasserie; lounge bar. In Changi village, 10 minutes from airport. Targeted at transit passengers and airline staff. For tourists, it is well situated for visits to Pulau Ubin and to Changi Prison Museum.

Le Meridien Singapore ▮▮▮
100 Orchard Road
Singapore 0923
Tel: 733 8855; Fax: 732 7886
Telex: RS 50163 HOMERI
413 rooms. Restaurants: two French, Indonesian, coffee shop. Patisserie and lounge. Well placed for visiting the National Musuem, the Istana (when open) and has its own upmarket shopping gallery.

Metropolitan YMCA ▮
60 Stevens Road
Singapore 1025
Tel: 737 7755; Fax: 235 5528
90 rooms. Restaurant.

Hotel New Otani ▮▮
177A River Valley Road
Singapore 0617
Tel: 338 3333; Fax: 339 2854
Telex: RS 20299 SINOTA
408 rooms and suites. Restaurants: Chinese, Japanese, American, coffee shop; cocktail lounge; disco. River cruises for guests and other tours. Located up the Singapore River from the Business District. Shares its building with a shopping complex. Its clientele is predominantly Japanese.

New Park Hotel ▮
181 Kitchener Road
Singapore 0820
Tel: 291 5533; Fax: 297 2827
535 rooms and suites. Four restaurants.

Novotel Orchid Inn ▮
214 Dunearn Road
Singapore 1129
Tel: 250 3322; Fax: 250 9292
460 rooms. Restaurants: Hunan, Sichuan, coffee shop; pub. Swimming pool, complimentary bus to town, bicycles, putting green. Quite near to the Botanic Gardens. Offers reasonable value for a slightly out-of-the-way location.

Omni Marco Polo Hotel ▮▮
Tanglin Road
Singapore 1024
Tel: 474 7141; Fax: 471 0521
Telex: RS 21476 OMPS
Cable: OMNIMPS
600 rooms and suites. Restaurants: Continental, French, coffee shop; nightclub. Conveniently located for the Botanic Gardens.

Orchard Hotel ▮▮
442 Orchard Road
Singapore 0923
Tel: 734 7766; Fax: 733 5482
Telex: RS 35228 ORTEL
Cable: ORCHARDTEL
700 rooms. Restaurants: Continental, seafood, Cantonese and Shanghainese. Coffee shop, tea lounge, bar, disco. Well placed for shopping.

The Oriental ▮▮▮
5 Raffles Avenue
Marina Square
Singapore 0103
Tel: 338 0066; Fax: 339 9537
Telex: RS 29117 ORSIN
515 rooms and suites. Restaurants: French/Continental, Szechuan/Hunanese, coffee shop; two lounges; two bars. Jewel of the three Marina Square hotels. Swimming pool on fifth floor gives stunning view of city.

Pan Pacific Hotel ▮▮
Marina Square
7 Raffles Boulevard
Singapore 0103
Tel: 336 8111; Fax: 339 1861
Telex: RS 38821
800 rooms and suites. Restaurants: Cantonese, Japanese, seafood, Western, poolside steamboat, coffee shop; bakery; two lounge bars; disco. Small putting green. Overlooking Marina Bay. Delightful external glass lifts.

Plaza Hotel ▮
7500 Beach Road
Singapore 0719
Tel: 298 0011; Fax: 296 3600
Telex: RS 22150
Cable: HOTEL PLAZA
350 rooms and suites. Restaurants: Cantonese/Thai seafood, coffee shop; karaoke lounge; lounge bar; disco. Business and exhibition facilities and many sports available. Well placed for Arab Street and Little India.

Raffles Hotel ▮▮▮
11 Beach Road
Singapore 0718
Tel: 337 1886; Fax: 339 7650
Telex: RS 20396 RINTL
104 suites. Restaurants: Continental, Tiffin Room, Cantonese, coffee house, outdoor cafe; bakery and self-service delicatessen; five bars plus lobby. Theatre, museum. Became the place of legend among colonials who dropped in hoping to catch sight of the rich or famous. The present hotel is much larger than the original.

The Regent Singapore ▮▮
1 Cuscaden Road
Singapore 1024
Tel: 733 8888; Fax: 732 8838
Telex: RS 37248 REGSIN
441 rooms. Restaurants: Chinese, French, coffee house. Nestled behind Tanglin Road, convenient for the Botanic Gardens and for shopping.

River View Hotel ▮
382 Havelock Road
Singapore 0316
Tel: 732 9922; Fax: 732 1034
Telex: RS 55454 RVHTEL
472 rooms and suites. Restaurants: coffee shop, Japanese, Szechuan, seafood and local fast-food; lounge bar; disco. Swimming pool. Tours arranged. Competitively priced hotel on Singapore River, convenient for city district and for sightseeing in Chinatown, though out of main business district in shabby surroundings.

Hotel Royal ▮
36 Newton Road
Singapore 1130
Tel: 253 4411; Fax: 253 8668
Telex: RS 21644
Cable: HOTELROYAL
331 rooms. Restaurants, Chinese, Japanese, Continental (cum disco) coffee shop. Bar and lounge. A little out of town.

Sea View Hotel ▮
26 Amber Close
Singapore 1543
Tel: 345 2222; Fax: 345 1741
Telex: RS 21555
Cable: SEAVIEW
435 rooms. Coffee shop.

Shangri-La Hotel ⦿⦿⦿
22 Orange Grove Road
Singapore 1025
Tel: 737 3644; Fax: 733 7220
Telex: RS 21505
Cable: SHANGRILA
750 rooms and 60 suites. Restaurants: Continental/French, Japanese, Cantonese, two coffee shops; disco; bar; cocktail lounge. Mini golf course. An agreeable high-rise oasis with impeccable service a couple of minutes' walk from Orchard Road.

Sheraton Towers ⦿⦿
Singapore Hotel
39 Scotts Road
Singapore 0922
Tel: 737 6888; Fax: 737 1072
420 Rooms. Restaurants, Italian, Cantonese, coffee shop.

Singapore Excelsior Hotel ⦿
5 Coleman Street
Singapore 0617
Tel: 338 7733; Fax: 339 3847
Telex: RS 20678 EXCELH
274 rooms and 7 suites. Restaurants: coffee shop, Chinese, Japanese, vegetarian; lounge. Function rooms; swimming pool.

Singapore Peninsula Hotel ⦿
3 Coleman Street
Singapore 0617
Tel: 337 2200; Fax: 336 3020
Telex: RS 21169 PENHOTE
306 rooms and 5 suites. Coffee house; lounge bar; disco; nightclub. Swimming pool. Hotel demands have moved on since the construction of the Excelsior and Peninsula, which is reflected in their prices, and you can have a reasonable no-frills stay very centrally in either hotel.

Strand Hotel ⦿
25 Bencoolen Street
Singapore 0718
Tel: 338 1866; Fax: 336 3149
Telex: RS 42036
130 rooms. Coffee shop.

The Westin Stamford and ⦿⦿⦿
Westin Plaza ⦿⦿⦿
2 Stamford Road
Singapore 0617
Tel: 338 8585; Fax: 338 2862
Telex: RS 22206 RCHTELS
Rooms: Westin Stamford, 1,253 including 80 suites; Westin Plaza, 796 including 47 suites. Restaurants: Continental, tea room, Cantonese, Japanese, Szechuan, coffee shop, cafe, Italian, Western, buffet; two bars; nightclub. Adjoining hotel

towers. The 70-storey Westin Stamford is currently the world's tallest hotel. The Compass Rose bar and restaurant on top storey give stunning views of Singapore. Have a high tea or evening cocktail in the bar at the very least. You can do this whether or not you are staying.

YMCA of Singapore ⦿
International House
1 Orchard House
Singapore 0923
Tel: 336 6000; Fax: 337 3140
111 rooms. Restaurants: McDonald's room service.

York Hotel ⦿⦿
21 Mount Elizabeth
Singapore
Tel: 235 0423; Fax: 732 1217
400 rooms. Restaurants: Thai-Chinese, coffee shop. Part of the Goodwood Park group of hotels.

Restaurants

There is a vast selection of food available, catering for all tastes. Restaurants in Singapore are notorious for changing, and many of the more popular air-conditioned restaurants do fill up, so take the precaution of reserving a table. Singaporeans tend to eat early: opening hours quoted below are those given by the restaurants, but it is wisest to arrive at most of these before 9 p.m. to be sure of unhurried and fairly courteous service.

Below is a brief selection of places to eat: try any of these, or follow a newspaper or a personal recommendation.

Chinese Food
Westlake Eating House
Block 4 #02-139 and #02-141
Queens Road
Singapore 1026
Tel: #02-139:474 7283;
    #02-141: 475 2982
Opening Hours: 11 a.m.–2.30 p.m. and 6–10 p.m. daily
Reliable favourite. Try the chilli crayfish, the pork with pau, the spring onion omelette. You won't be disappointed with any dish.

Beijing
Prima Tower Revolving Restaurant
210 Keppel Road
Singapore 0409
Tel: 272 8822
Opening Hours: 11 a.m.–2 p.m., 6.30–10 p.m.
Overlooking the city. A meal will last you a complete circle turn. Courteous service plus an extensive menu come at a very reasonable price. Lift does not go right to top. Strongly recommended.

Cantonese
Lei Garden Restaurant
Boulevard Hotel
200 Orchard Boulevard
Singapore 1024
Tel: 235 8122
Opening Hours: 11.30 a.m.–3 p.m. and 6.30–11 p.m.
Booking always necessary at this highly popular restaurant. Particular food promotions on sharksfin soup or steamed fish can be helpful when choosing from extensive menu.

Seafood
Choon Seng
892 Ponggol Road
11¼ M.s. Singapore 1954
Tel: 288 3472
Opening Hours: 12 p.m.–11 p.m.
Delicious seafood: try the pepper crabs or the chilli crab Popular so book in advance. If you find it full, try next door (see below). Due to relocate at the end of 1992.

Gold Coast Seafood Restaurant
UDMS Seafood Centre
East Coast Parkway
Singapore 1544
Tel: 448 2020
Opening Hours: 5 p.m.–12 midnight
All of the different restaurants in the UDMC Seafood Centre have their fans. This is one example. Freshly caught and cooked seafood.

Ng Tiong Choon, Sembawang Fishing Pond and Seafood Village
59 Lorong Chuntun
Off Lorong Gambas
Singapore 2775
Tel: 754 1991
Opening Hours: 11 a.m.–2 p.m., 5 p.m.–2 a.m.
Hidden north of Mandai Road, this restaurant is notoriously hard to

find, but worth the effort. Situated on a pontoon over the pond, you can borrow fishing rods and fish as you eat your lunch or dinner. Live shows and karaoke. You'll really need a good taxi or else a driver to find.

Ponggol Restaurant (Hock Lee)
896, Ponggol Point
Singapore 1954
Tel: 481 7958
Opening Hours: 8 a.m–11.45 p.m.
Another favoured haunt of seafood enthusiasts. A good place to try chilli crab, and also their peppered prawns and baby squid. Due to relocate at the end of 1992.

Szechuan

Dragon City Szechuan Restaurant
Novotel Orchid Inn
214 Dunearn Road
Singapore 1129
Tel: 254 7070
Opening Hours: 11.30 a.m –2.30 p.m., 6.30–10 p.m.
An enjoyable spread, and an opportunity to try some century-old eggs.

Golden Phoenix Szechuan Restaurant
Level 2, Hotel Equatorial
429 Bukit Timah Road
Singapore 1025
Tel: 732 0431
Opening Hours: 11.30 a.m.–2.15 p.m., 6.30–10.15 p.m.
An appetizing menu catering for all budgets, extremely popular with locals during the Chinese New Year. Quite small, so book at weekends. Try the Imperial Dinner.

Ming Jiang Szechuan Restaurant
1st Floor (Parkway Wing)
Goodwood Park Hotel
22 Scotts Road
Singapore 0922
Tel: 737 7411
Opening Hours: 12 p.m.–2.30 p.m., 6.30–10.30 p.m.
Small restaurant in the grounds of the Goodwood Park Hotel. The ambience and service can't be faulted.

Sze Chuan Court
3rd Floor, Westin Plaza Hotel
2 Stamford Road
Singapore 0617
Tel: 338 8585
Opening Hours: 10.30 a.m.–2.30 p.m., 6.30–10.30 p.m.
Pricey but excellent food in ambient surroundings.

Indian Food

South Indian
Annalakshmi Restaurant
Excelsior Hotel and Shopping Centre
#02-10, 5 Coleman Street
Singapore 0617
Tel: 339 9993
Opening Hours: 11.30 a.m.–3 p.m., 6.30–10 p.m. Mondays to Saturdays, 11.30 a.m.–3 p.m. Sundays
For a memorable South Indian vegetarian meal in air-conditioned comfort and great ambience, you cannot do better than here.

Banana Leaf Apolo
56–58 Race Course Road
Singapore 0821
Tel: 293 8682
Opening Hours: 10.30 a.m.–10 p.m.

Jubilee Cafe and Restaurant
771–773 North Bridge Road
Singapore 0719
Tel: 298 8714
Opening Hours: 10 a.m.–10 p.m.
The decor in this 1930s shophouse has not changed since it opened. The food is unpretentious and excellent—biryani, murtabak and the like—an ideal stop when visiting the Sultan Mosque and the Arab Street area.

Samy's Curry Restaurant
Tanglin Clubhouse
Block 25 Dempsey Road
Singapore 1024
Tel: 472 2080
Opening Hours: 12 noon–3 p.m., 6–10 p.m. (closed Thursday evenings)

North Indian
Delhi Restaurant
60 Race Course Road
Singapore 0821
Tel: 296 4585
Opening Hours: 11.30 a.m.–11.30 p.m.

Moghul Mahal
#01-11 Colombo Court
1 North Bridge Road
Singapore 0617
Tel: 338 7794
Opening Hours: 12.30 p.m.–3 p.m., 6.30 p.m.–11 pm
On ground floor of shopping centre near Empress Place and the Padang, the food is chilli hot, but well prepared and reasonably priced.

Moti Mahal Restaurant
18 Murray Street
Singapore 0207
Tel: 221 4338
Opening Hours: 11.30 a.m.–3 p.m., 6.30–10.30 p.m.
A massive menu of familiar and unusual north Indian dishes, with rave reviews quoted on the menu as "the best Indian Restaurant in South East Asia". Possibly a slight overstatement, but you won't go away disappointed.

Orchard Maharajah Restaurant
25 Cuppage Terrace
Cuppage Road
Singapore 0922
Tel: 732 6331
Opening Hours: 11.30 a.m.–3 p.m., 6.30–11 p.m.

Tandoor
Holiday Inn Park View
Cavenagh Road
Singapore 0922
Tel: 733 8333
Opening Hours: 12 noon–2.30 p.m., 7–10.30 p.m.
Very popular, it is worth booking a place even midweek, and you will not be disappointed with the food. Mouth-watering tandooris, as well as tasty butter chicken, rogan gosht.

Indonesian Food
Alkaff Mansion
10 Telok Blangah Green
Singapore 0410
Tel: 278 6979
Opening Hours: 12 noon–2.30 p.m., 7–10.30 p.m.
Try an Indonesian buffet here. To eat the Rijstaffel, you can either help yourself from the buffet downstairs, or have large dishes of the whole selection brought to your table. While it's an atmospheric setting, you may wait 30 minutes for an aperitif!

Rendezvous Restaurant
Raffles City Shopping Centre
#02-19
Stamford Road
Singapore 0923
Tel: 339 7508
Opening Hours: 11 a.m.–9 p.m.
Choose from a tasty buffet of beef rendang, assorted curries and vegetables. For dessert, try the chendol—one of Singapore's finest. Often crowded at lunch time, it is a congenial, busy and yet quite smart place to sample some of the tastiest Indonesian food.

Sanur Indonesian Restaurant
#04-17/18 Centrepoint
176 Orchard Road
Singapore 0923
Tel: 734 2192
Opening Hours:
11.30 a.m.–2.45 p.m., 5.45–
9.30 p.m.
No reservations possible at this popular eaterie on the top floor of Centrepoint, but just turn up and take your chance—it's worth it!

Tambuah Mas
#04-10 Tanglin Shopping Centre
19 Tanglin Road
Singapore 1024
Tel: 235 5455
Opening Hours: 10 a.m.–9.30 p.m.
A good selection of satay, rendang, various soups, and other favourites, including colourful desserts.

Japanese Food
Hill Top Japanese and Indonesian Restaurant
Jurong Hill
Singapore 2262
Tel: 265 1538
Opening Hours: 11.30 a.m.–
10 p.m.
Located just behind Jurong Bird-Park; this restaurant has a loyal local following.

Shima Restaurant
Goodwood Park Hotel
22 Scotts Road
Singapore 0923
Tel: 734 6281
Opening Hours: 12 noon–3 p.m., 6.30–11 p.m.
This restaurant comprises a downstairs sushi and sashimi bar and an upstairs teppanyaki restaurant, where fresh scallops, salmon and steak are chopped with dexterity and fried impeccably, with delicious results. Thoroughly recommended.

Korean Food
Seoul Garden Korean Restaurant
#02-56 Parkway Parade
80 Marine Parade Road
Singapore 1544
Tel: 345 1338/9
Opening Hours: 11 a.m.–3 p.m., 5.30 –10 p.m.
This chain offers a barbecue at your table: you select fish, meat and vegetables from a cold buffet and then watch them cook in a fondue-style contraption at your table, topping up with stock from time to time.

Malay Food
Aziza's Restaurant
36 Emerald Hill Road
Singapore 0922
Tel: 235 1130
Opening Hours: 11.30 a.m.–
3 p.m., 6.30–11 p.m.
A good and filling selection of Malay food, with the added benefit of serving hours up to 11 p.m. and friendly service too. Fish curries, beef rendang, udang sambal—the menu is explained in English.

Bintang Timur
#02-08-13 Far East Plaza
14 Scotts Road
Singapore 0922
Tel: 235 4539
Opening Hours: 11 a.m.–9.45 p.m.
The food here's good, though the place lacks atmosphere, situated on the second floor of the Far East Plaza amongst shops. Do not try to eat too late here—you will be hurried in your selection.

Nonya Food
Nonya and Baba
262 River Valley Road
Singapore
Tel: 734 1382
Opening Hours: 11.30 a.m.–
10.30 p.m.
Popular at lunch times, less so in the evenings, a range of nonya dishes awaits you here.

Peranakan Inn and Lounge
210 East Coast Road
Singapore 1545
Tel: 440 6195
Opening Hours: 11 a.m.–3 p.m., 6–11 p.m.
Although this is theoretically late opening, don't expect more than cursory service if you arrive later than 9 p.m. Very good food, despite the service.

Thai Food
Parkway Thai Restaurant
Parkway Parade #02-20
80 Marine Parade Road
Singapore 1544
also at
Centrepoint #01-59-62
Orchard Road
Singapore 0923
Tel: 348 0783 (Parkway Parade) and 737 8080
Opening Hours: 11.30 a.m.–
10 p.m., buffet lunch except
Sundays and public holidays

No reservations taken here, though usually tables on weekdays. Pleasant food, reasonably priced, though not the truly wonderful, and considerably more expensive, experience you will enjoy at the Thanying (see below).

Thanying Thai Restaurant
Amara Hotel
165 Tanjong Pagar Road,
#01-09/13
Singapore 0208
Tel: 224 4488
Opening Hours: 11 a.m.–3 p.m., 7–11 p.m.
For a thoroughly enjoyable meal, deferential and yet not over-humble service, and delightful food, I really recommend this restaurant. It is an oasis of calm, decorated in Thai style. The extensive menu and the helpful waiters advise you about the hotness of individual dishes. The air-conditioning is somewhat fierce: take a jacket or a long shirt.

Vietnamese Food
Saigon Restaurant
#04-03, Cairnhill Place
15 Cairnhill Road
Singapore 0922
Tel: 235 0626
Opening Hours: 11.45 a.m.–
2.45 p.m., 6–10.30 p.m.
Despite being in fourth storey of a car-park above Al Falah Mosque, the atmosphere is immediately congenial upon entering. The food is exquisite: try the prawns on sugar cane, the pan fried beef, crab claws, and steamed fish. Recommended.

Western Food
American/Tex/Mex
Chico's N Charlie's
#05-01 Liat Towers
541 Orchard Road
Singapore 0923
Tel: 734 1753
Opening Hours: 11 a.m.–10.30 p.m.
Very popular and busy restaurant; worth booking at weekends. Good margaritas, Mexican beers and some tasty starters and nibbles.

El Felipes
Lorong Mambong
Holland Village
Singapore 1027
Tel: 468 1520
Opening Hours: 11.30 a.m.–
9.45 p.m.
Another branch now at International

Plaza, Orchard Road. Well-cooked, brimming and sizzling plates of burritos, enchiladas and tacos, and interesting combination dishes, washed down with one or two iced margaritas. Recommended.

Hard Rock Café
Cuscaden Road
Singapore
Tel: 235 5232
Opening Hours: 11 a.m.–2 a.m.
(last food order 10.30 p.m.)
Singapore's branch of the international chain and remains a popular eating, drinking and music venue.

English
Upstairs English Restaurant
Tudor Court
145A Tanglin Road
Singapore 1024
Tel: 732 3922
Opening Hours: 9 a.m.–10 p.m. daily
Traditional English breakfast, brunch, lunches, coffees and teas and dinner, everything from steak and kidney pie to bread and butter pudding!

French/Continental
Alkaff Mansion
10 Telok Blangah Green
Singapore 0410
Tel: 278 6979
Opening Hours: 12 noon–2.30 p.m., 7–10.30 p.m.
It's a real taste of old colonialism. You can smoke here—they even have ashtrays. There are two eating options: the Indonesian buffet, or an inspired if fairly small selection of western (mainly French nouvelle cuisine) dishes, beautifully presented. Standard of service in this pricey restaurant variable.

Brasserie La Rotonde
Omni Marco Polo Hotel
247 Tanglin Road
Singapore 1024
Tel: 474 7141
Opening Hours: 12 noon–2.30 p.m., 7–10.30 p.m.
With Toulouse-Lautrec everywhere and gingham red and white table cloths, this brasserie is really trying to imitate a French bistro. The menu is pleasingly extensive and very tempting, with unusual dishes as well as the T-bone steaks and lobster thermidor. Booking advisable.

Compass Rose Restaurant
70th Floor
Westin Stamford Hotel
Stamford Road
Singapore 0617
Tel: 338 8585
Opening Hours: 12 noon–2.30 p.m., 7–11 p.m.
Spectacular views. French-style restaurant, reasonably priced by Western standards. Dress reasonably well and book in advance—earlier the same day should be fine. You are ushered to your table with rapid but unostentatious service.

Restaurant Latour
Shangri-La Hotel
Orange Grove Road
Singapore 1025
Tel: 737 3644
Opening Hours: 12 noon–2.30 p.m., 7–10.30 p.m.
Excellent French style cuisine, served immaculately in a pleasant setting; live pianist adds to the ambience. Expensive, but worth it.

Saxophone's
23 Cuppage Terrace
Orchard Road
Singapore 0923
Tel: 235 8385
Opening Hours: 12 noon–3 p.m., 7–11.15 p.m. (bar remains open until 2 a.m.)
An interesting and well-prepared French-style menu is worth exploring on a fine evening, when you can sit outside and listen to the live jazz. Imaginative use of locally fresh ingredients—sea bass, crab, tiger prawns—and also familiarity with and expertise in preparing beef, veal and other imported produce.

Italian
Pete's Place
Hyatt Regency Hotel
Scotts Road
Singapore 0922
Tel: 733 1188
Opening Hours: 11.30 a.m.–2.45 p.m., 6–11.15 p.m.
Delicious pizzas and pasta dishes as well as main course dishes. A selection of home-made breads is a speciality.

Hawker Centres
There are a number of hawker centres, where you can eat very reasonably, tasting a variety of dishes all cooked by different stalls. The etiquette for hawker centres is find an empty table and sit at it, regardless of which of the food and drink stalls you then patronize. Some centres have numbered tables, otherwise point out where you are sitting to the stall-holders as you order food. You pay when the dishes arrive, but double check the food prices before ordering, in case unscrupulous hawkers add something for trusting tourists.

Newton Circus Hawker Centre
Central and very popular with tourists and locals. Stays open till about 2 a.m. nightly and has a wide range of stalls.

Empress Place Hawker Centre
Has a number of good stalls, including an Indian style mee goreng stall and some excellent fish ball kway teow.

Taman Serasi Food Centre
On Cluny Road is almost exclusively Malay, with good satay as well as roti John and nasi padang.

Jalan Besar
Has good chicken rice and a variety of other, mainly Chinese, specialities—though try to take a table far from the hotter stalls, or you'll find the heat puts you off your food.

Marina Village Hawker Centre
Has numbered tables, a wide choice of foodstuffs, and like Newton Circus it is late opening. It also has numerous mosquitoes, so wear long trousers or take mosquito repellent.

Rasa Singapura Food Centre
Relocated from a central position on Orchard Road to the out-of-the-way Bukit Turf Club. Some excellent stalls.

The Satay Club
Connaught Drive
Remains popular, though it is scheduled for closure, and the hawkers are perhaps too aggressive.

Index

INDEX

INDEX